Contents

Preface 7

Afghanistan, Kazakhstan and now Ukraine 17

Ukraine Crisis is An Event Like Few in History 21

War Alone Could Deliver Europe to the United States 25

US Wants Germany Mired in World Wars 29

Why is Europe Committing Suicide? 33

EU Bans Russian Media for Plebs Shouldn't Know Much 37

Why Sanctions Often Don't Work 41

What If Mexico is Turned Into a Ukraine By Russia? 45

Why a La Al Qaeda in Europe is Cool for Washington 49

US Biolabs in Ukraine and Conspiracy of Silence 53

Why Indian Media is Forcing Modi's Hand on Russia 57

The World Isn't Joining West's Sanctions on Russia 61

The West Has Doubled Down on India Against Russia 65

Bucha is a Re-run from Yugoslavia Template of Lies 69

India Has Shown Nerves of Steel in Standing By Russia 75

Ukraine War Has Gone Horribly Wrong for the West 79

Central Asia: A Region Both India and China Covet 83

There's Not One But Many Ukraines Unfolding 89

Why Putin is Intent on Dragging on the Ukraine Crisis 93

How Russia is Sewing Up the Heartland of Eurasia 97

Russia and Its Arctic Gambit Puts Fire at Us' Door 101

Russia Not a Peer to NATO? the Joke is on You Only! 105

What Did Putin Mean By Wolf's Tail? 109
Ukraine and the Taurian lands.......... 113
Central Asia is of Pivotal Interest to Global Powers 117
SCO: The Military Arm of a Multipolar World.......... 121
The Great Game of the Energy Crisis in Europe.......... 125
Russia or US: Who has been flouting UN Charter? 129
Referendums Are Perfectly in Sync with UN Charter 133
Nord Stream Sabotage is History's Pivotal Moment.......... 139
Beat It! Russia is Europe's Last Empire!.......... 145
Why US Wants to Take on Russia and China Together 155
Why Did India Stick with Russia on Referendums?.......... 161
So Did Russia Commit Genocide in Ukraine?.......... 165
Next Time US Quotes "human Rights", Remember Cuba 171
Media is No Better Than a Puppet of the West 177
UN Asks for Reparations from Russia When It Can't!.......... 183
False Flag Attack from Poland is Copybook Us.......... 191
Who Would Trust a Wolf But a Fool, Zelensky? 197
Latest Joke: EU Calls Russia State Sponsors of Terrorism 203
The Iran Factor in India-russia Ties 207
Serbia is Once Again in the Eye of the West.......... 213
Russia Has Seen NATO and is Unimpressed.......... 219
How I Think the Ukraine Conflict Would End.......... 223
How Our Truth Bishops Are Brainwashing Us 229
Why We Don't Hear a Word on Fleeing Ukrainians.......... 235
World Economic Forum: How An Ngo Loots the World.......... 241
Man Behind WEF We Know Little About 249
If Indians Ignore Ukraine, History Would Bite US Again 255

RUSSIA FOREVER

A Future Foretold

ASHISH SHUKLA

INDIA • SINGAPORE • MALAYSIA

ISBN 979-8-89186-353-8

So did the US sabotage the Nord Stream? 259
A Classic Orwellian Doublespeak 263
Why Russia is for Pushing the Borders of Poland? 269
If Bakhmut is Not Key, Why Thousands Are Losing Lives?.............................. 279
Xi's Peace Mission: But US Won't Let Kiev Accept 285
Why the Russian Ambassador Has Got US on Our Feet!.............................. 289
Is Russia Really China's Junior Partner? 295
Finland in NATO: Welcome to Thieves' Kitchen 301
Why the US Won't Supply Its Best Weaponry to Ukraine 307
All Ukraine is Left with Are Terror Attacks 311
The First Fake Coup of History Which Fooled the West 315
Wagner in Belarus: Making Sense of Rearranged Pieces 319
What If Russia Now Does to France What It Did to Them 323
Zelensky Ignored By the Suits in NATO Summit 327
Russia-Ukraine Deal Was for Spanish Pigs and Not Poor 331
Cluster Bombs: Whatever Happened to Ban of Its Use?.............................. 337
When, and Not If, Poland Would Enter Ukraine.............................. 341
Russia-Africa Summit: Why India Should Pay Heed 345
To Think Hamas Was But Only Israel's Creation!.............................. 349

Preface

On February 24, 2022, Russia began its Special Military Operation in Ukraine.

I knew it was coming: Russia had proposed two drafts of treaties to the United States by December the previous year. Pretty reasonable I thought since it wanted a written assurance on UN-mandated collective security for everyone to which Washington was a signatory.

Russia feared for herself as almost all European nations bordering her ridiculously vast borders on the west had become a NATO member and the one which hadn't yet—Ukraine—was already one but in name.

***

The seeds of it were sown in the closing months of 2013 when the then-Ukrainian president Viktor Yanukovych dithered on signing an association agreement with the European Union (EU).

Within weeks, thousands of protestors were marching towards the Ukrainian parliament. They were no ordinary demonstrators; heavily armed and masked, lobbing Molotov cocktails, shelling and shooting at riot police.

Few events have changed the course of history like the one on February 18, 2014 did. Dozens died on either side, the Crimean authorities warned Kiev that far-right groups were intent on seizing power and a civil war was looming.

By next day, far-right groups were all over the country, a depot in Western Ukraine landed a thousand guns in their hands, police and government offices were torched.

Yanukovych bowed to Opposition parties, conceded their demands, pulled out his police but the far-right group would have none of it.

Bloody Thursday, as February 20, 2014 came to be known, was the most violent day in Ukraine since the World War II. Over a hundred died, and events moved so quickly that in the next 48 hours, Yanukovych had fled the capital.

Petro Poroshenko, a businessman, was now in power—and the EU association agreement which had sparked the trouble, was signed within four days after his accession on May 29, 2014.

It's no secret that the coup, known as "Maidan Coup", was backed by the United States. The radical forces in power now lost no time in spewing hostility against the pro-Russian population in Ukraine.

***

The "Maidan Coup", had massive bearing on pro-Russian regions of Crimea and eastern Ukraine.

Crimea, with majority of pro-Russian population, faced a similar uprising by the far-right protestors and after bloody face-offs voted to unite with Russia in a referendum within a month after the coup.

The Kiev government, meanwhile, was brutally crushing dissent in Odessa and Kharkov and sending troops in Donetsk and Lugansk in Donbass on its east.

These two Donbass regions took a different route from Crimea. They didn't seek a referendum, instead they declared their independence from Kiev.

They stood up to Kiev rather heroically which led to a ceasefire and a reconciliation roadmap, morphing into two Minsk Agreements in 2014 and 2015.

It was later admitted by the brokers of the Minsk Agreements, Germany (Angela Merkel) and France (Francois Hollande), that the deal was a deceit, meant only to allow Ukraine time to arm itself to teeth.

That Ukraine was no better than a proxy to the West which supplied money and material to the men of the belligerent nation. That Russia was to be left with no option but to take recourse to arms.

A comedian Vladimir Zelensky, a neo-Nazi at heart, meanwhile was being carefully curated by the West and its servile media, as the new hope of Ukraine.

Zelensky came to power in 2019, offering peace and reconciliation to pro-Russian people, but in essence was the tin soldier of the West, doubling down on people of Donbass.

No sooner had Zelensky come to power, Kiev enshrined in its constitution the goal to become a NATO member.

Ukraine had a large army but now there was also the best weapons and resources of NATO and its coffer would never run dry. Russia was now baited by ceaseless bombing and killings in Donbass; thousands dead admitted by no less than the United Nations.

The ploy was impeccable: If Russia turned its back on its own in Donbass, Vladimir Putin would have a nation baying for his blood. If he took it square on, Russia would be mired in Ukraine and along with sanctions, the West would have gotten rid of the man it had despised for two long decades. Not to say a body blow it would deal to China whose back was secured by Russia

***

To be in Russia's shoes, is to understand the hopelessness of her situation. NATO was now at her multiple borders through various European nations. Minsk Agreements were a shameful betrayal you thought was not possible in modern times. Ukraine was a formal handshake away from NATO which would take out the last buffer Russia had against enemies at door. And then who stops them once Donbass falls? Either Russia draws a red line now or awaits till nothing is left.

The two treaties offered to the United States thus was the hope-against-hope for Russia. If the West agreed to the concept of collective security, Ukraine would be neutralized. If it disagrees, Russia would be free to place its own nuclear weapons at US' door, say in Cuba, Nicaragua or Venezuela and the NATO would've been served with its own recipe.

***

Russia watched, and watched, before in 2021 it accused the NATO of endangering Russia's security by offering its membership to Ukraine, an absolute red line for Moscow.

Thereafter followed political posturing from the two sides, leading to Moscow proposing two peace treaties. But then when has a wolf been open to reasons of a prey it has set its dinner table upon?

On February 22, 2022, Russia formally recognized the Donetsk and Lugansk as sovereign states. It asked Kiev to pull back its troops from its claimed borders. Ukraine refused and two days later, Russia had launched its Special Military Operation (SMO), claiming Kiev was preparing offensive in Donbass as per its intelligence inputs.

***

There is a lot which could be said against the United States.

It doesn't allow the world to live in peace or grow but for its vassals.

A growing world could become self-dependent which means its land, labour and resources would be out of the West's claws.

It would be a threat to the predominance of Dollar in which the world trades but which essentially is a fake currency.

All this might sound strange to general readers who believe in the United States and its championing of "Democracy" and "Human Rights" and its "rules-based order."

The truth is this country has over 800 military bases around the world; it has created today's Iraq, Libya, Syria, Yemen and countless other countries in Latin America and Africa.

That the "rules-based order" you read about has nothing to do with the United Nations or its Charter: Nobody has seen or read this "rules-based order": This is nothing but rules adjusted-as-you-go by the United States and its vassals.

It has created a financial order in which Dollar holds the centre stage and global bodies such as World Bank, International Monetary Fund, World Trade Organization or the United Nations for that matter, do only what the US tells them to do.

Nations which defy them are slapped with sanctions such as Cuba, Russia, North Korea, Venezuela, Iran etc, etc. Dare anyone trade with them; the global supply systems for transport and transactions, access to banks or SWIFT system is shut on the face.

Not that the United States relies only on its financial and military might to control the world.

It actively pursues issues which rip open a society and pits one against the other.

So you have vicious promotion of homosexuality and transgenderism; transgender males are allowed to take part in women's events; kids are being encouraged to change their sex, their age of consent is being lowered so that parents can't interfere with their choices.

Once a society is thrown into chaos, traditional structures are withered, a weaker nation is all that easier to control.

The hierarchical and religious divide which is there is every society is stoked so that a nation is at a cross-purpose.

The prime soldier of the United States and its allies, the bloc we call the West, is media which they control completely.

This media only promotes the West's ideology and its interests.

This media would never dwell why a journalist like Julian Assange is threatened with life by the United Sates; it would never probe who destroyed the Nord Stream gas pipelines; it would never demand that a Tony Blair or George Bush be declared as war criminals for what they did to Iraq on trumped up charges; it would never question why the United States continue to slap sanctions on Cuba after six decades even though every year, in the UN General Assembly, an overwhelming vote favours lifting of sanctions against this unfortunate nation. This media would never question why the UNGA mandate against Israel on Palestine is never honoured by Washington and Tel Aviv. Or that if Russia has violated the territorial integrity of Ukraine, why the United States occupation of one-third of Syria for years doesn't make headlines. Is this the "democracy" and "human rights" West has to offer and media to swear by?

It would be a sobering thought to the readers that Nelson Mandela, that apostle of peace, was a terrorist in the eyes of the US until 2013 when he was days away from turning 90. Never mind the man had been the first democratic president of South Africa and had also won the Nobel Peace Prize in the intervening years once apartheid had been abolished a good 22 years ago in 1991.

And that terror groups, your Al-Qaedas, Boko Harams and ISIS etc, would have never gotten off the ground without the benevolence of the United States. The ISIS is front page one day, and vanishes the next, making appearances a la staged actor in concert with the West and the media it controls.

These terrorists are a good excuse for the United States to plant its military in a vulnerable nation with the promise to get rid of them. Instead, these terrorists only grow in size and influence so that the hapless nation becomes weaker and more dependent on the West.

There is simply no getting away.

***

All this and much more I know from my reading of history which most don't get to read in newspapers or text books.

The avowed policy of the United States after the Second World War has been to keep Germany down, Russia out and United States in Europe.

The United States exerts its control on the world through its domination of Europe.

It's Europe which gives them a springboard to spread its tentacles in Middle East and Rest of Asia and, in turn, makes them control Africa which made West what it is today.

Africa, which you call the "Dark Continent", in reality is the foundation on which the West has built its supremacy. First it was the African slaves which gave them the riches; which in turn enabled the military and technological advances to open up the gap with the rest of the world.

It's the natural resources of Africa; its gold, uranium, platinum, cobalt etc, which is the lifeline of West. Without its uranium, for instances, most nuclear power plants of France could shut down: At least one in three French homes would be without bulbs.

Yet, this ruthless exploitation of Africa, causing genocides in Rwanda and Congo for example, are kept away from your attention by your sinful media.

***

The control of Europe is the essence of US foreign policy.

If Europe is weaned away from its influence, the United States becomes a country on the other side of Atlantic, some 6,000 nautical miles away.

The nightmare of the United States is if Russia and Germany join hands.

Russia is rich resource-wise and Germany in terms of technology and if the two are on the same page, the United Kingdom and France become second-tier nations in Europe and the influence of the United States is gone overnight.

Today's United States can't live with this thought. Since the days when Christianity was split between the Catholic/Protestant and the Orthodox Church, Latin and Greek heritage, imperial Rome and Eastern Roman or Byzantine empire, the West has looked for the subjugation of nature while Russia sees a mother in it, drawing sustenance from soil. Russia's spirituality is a mortal threat to West's materialism. But then when has Good not been a threat to Evil?

***

Ukraine Crisis was the catalyst to what I had anticipated in long years of my reading.

It was in plain view, at least since 2014, that Ukraine would be the bait with which Russia would be drawn into an existential battle.

Ukraine was the door from which the United States could succeed in turning Russia away from Europe, reducing it to only an Asian entity.

With Russia's back on Europe, the United States could have the old continent in its fist; and then everything else would fall in place, the satanic designs of its military and elites would have a free run.

I began penning my pieces for NewsBred.com[1] in the months heading into this crisis in the closing days of 2021.

The output was at least once a week if not twice, and looking back at some 100 of these pieces, after it would be nearly two years to the Ukraine Conflict soon, there is a sense of satisfaction that I had actually outpaced history. There is an uncanny sense that I had seen the future.

In a strange way, the Ukraine Conflict retarded progress on the trilogy I am penning on why Russia would matter to India, not just for themselves but for what the two could do together for humanity. It's a hard-nosed look at the two civilizations, and not some soppy indulgence,

1. https://www.newsbred.com/

on how souls of the two have survived the ravages by enemies, why it's now a moment in a millennium they must not let go.

Yet as we know, States pass from one hand to the other, the heroes of today could well be overtaken by wolves-as-sheep tomorrow. Situations change, dynamics change, alignments occur which you think were never possible. Or why would Japan, Germany or even Vietnam is besotted to the United States today after what it did to them in the last century?

It's thus important that masses of India and Russia understand what is at stake. People alone could rein in the Powers provided they are evolved; they understand that propaganda which comes in the form of media and OpEd writers, historians and academicians, is meant to dull your edges. That politicians, bureaucracy and judiciary are up for sale, with the task to deliver you en masse into the hands of Satan.

This anthology, the collection of my pieces of nearly last two years, hopefully is an appetizer to the main course I would serve through my trilogy in next two years. You would be struck by how the events have unfolded as I thought it would. There is also a hope that in the meantime you would keep checking my pieces in newsbred.com and log in to WiseHeads[2], my geopolitical show on YouTube. Who knows, from one to next, the word would spread and masses would form a barrier too formidable for the Powers of our world.

Ashish Shukla

2. https://www.youtube.com/@WiseHeads

Afghanistan, Kazakhstan and now Ukraine

January 9, 2023

Is the United States up to its dirty tricks in Kazakhstan and is there a lesson for India to learn from the turmoil gripping the Central Asian country?

For the indifferent, let's first get to the brief on roiling Kazakhstan of now.

Kazakhstan fell into chaos overnight. The spark was the doubling of liquefied gas prices. Soon it spread to entire nation—from Almaty to the Caspian Sea ports, passing through Astana (now Noursoultan).

The central government reduced the price of gas in response. But now the demonstrators were asking for lower food prices, an end to the vaccination campaign, lower retirement age for mothers with many children etc.

It rattled Russia, the northern neighbour. Much of Kazakhstan's 20 million population is Russian; its language has an official status; the two countries conduct strategic space cooperation; and have military-technical ties. The country is an important link in the Belt and Road Initiative (BRI) which has Russia on the same page as its originator, China.

Russia understood the timing of these demonstrations. First the United States made a chaotic withdrawal from Afghanistan which weakened the southern flank of the CSTO (Collective Security Treaty Organization). Russia already is facing a war-threat from NATO on its western front in Ukraine; the chaos could spread along an axis stretching from Scandinavia to Crimea; and the timing of this widespread chaos at its borders is to force Russia to backdown from a collective West in a meeting this week.

Russia moved quickly. It invoked CSTO which brings together the armed forces of six former USSR republics, including Kazakhstan. It sent a peacekeeping force; enforced total foreclosure of the territory, disappearance of the internet, blindness of the satellites; electro-magnetic jamming, and deployment of specialised forces in fifth generation hybrid asymmetric warfare. It's a foretelling of futuristic conflicts which could sprout regularly in Asia, as it happened in Hong Kong recently; or the farm protests in India on which New Delhi backed down.

Washington has never ceased to dream of the rupture of the strategic Moscow-Beijing axis. Kazakhstan suits them perfectly for the United States has a huge penetration in this uranium-rich country. American companies manage a large part of Kazakhstan's oil production which accounts for 44% of state revenue. Since 2003, Kazakhstan has been organising joint military exercises with NATO every year. Besides from 2004-2019, the United States sold weapons worth millions of dollars to Kazakhstan.

The US' footprint in Ukraine or in Poland or in Belarus in internal conflicts are unmistakable. It supported "rebels" in Syria. Its fingerprints were visible in a war between Azerbaijan and Armenia. Now is the attempt to reduce Russian influence in another of its backyard, the Central Asia.

It remains to be seen how this pans out. Whether Russia's influence gains or loses ground in its neighbourhood. They have had to face a lot of deflating "Colour Revolutions" since Vladimir Putin came to power. They couldn't stop one in Ukraine, won in Belarus and now Kazakhstan is another test. It's paramount for their sovereignty.

Sure, India is watching. It's seeing the same "kit" in operation which roiled it for last year and a half during the farmers' protest. In EU asking for Kazakhstan to "Respect the Right of Peaceful Demonstrators", New

Delhi could draw a parallel from its own experience. Protestors wear the cloak of "peaceful demonstrations" but in essence it's total lawlessness, violence and mob attacks. People get out on the streets on abstract demands such as "We Want Democracy" even if they can't define it. And then there are absolute demands—such as complete repeal of farm laws—knowing that the government won't back down. But in Modi's case, he did so to avoid the trap.

Such chaos are "internal" but managed by "external forces to confuse the population of its true nature. They get sucked in into the noise of "human rights" and "freedom" and can't see who directs this chaos.

Link to Article:
https://www.newsbred.com/hong-kong-afghanistan-and-now-kazhakstan-us-loves-chaos-in-asia/

Ukraine Crisis is An Event Like Few in History

January 25, 2022

An average Indian first drew to the Ukraine crisis after the bloodbath on the Dalal Street (Bombay Stock Exchange) made headlines this morning. I suggest you better be tuned in for we are approaching a cataclysmic moment in world history.

We are told that West and East have squared up for a confrontation which could be bigger than both the World Wars.

The West—The United States and its West European allies—have anti-missile launch pads in Poland and Bulgaria; and Ukraine is being stuffed with weapon and funds.

The East, in the form of Russia, feels it is being encircled, and not just want West to back off, it also wants the US to respond to its proposed treaties in writing.

If the US doesn't sign the two draft treaties Russia sent in December 2021, Moscow is promising "military-technical" action.

This is what was said by Yevgeny Fyodorov, Russia's state Duma deputy: "Russia plans to use its nuclear weapons not against the countries where they were launched against Russia, but against the master cities where the decisions were made. To be exact, these are Washington, New York, Los Angeles, Chicago and other American cities.

"If the US nuclear weapons are launched from, say, Taiwan or Poland, the response will hit New York or Washington."

What exactly are these two treaties-in-drafts on which Russia is seeking US' compliance?

One, that the US-NATO would withdraw offensive weapons from Russia's immediate vicinity;

Two, NATO would withdraw to its 1997 position in non-NATO countries—"Not an Inch to East", as it had promised.

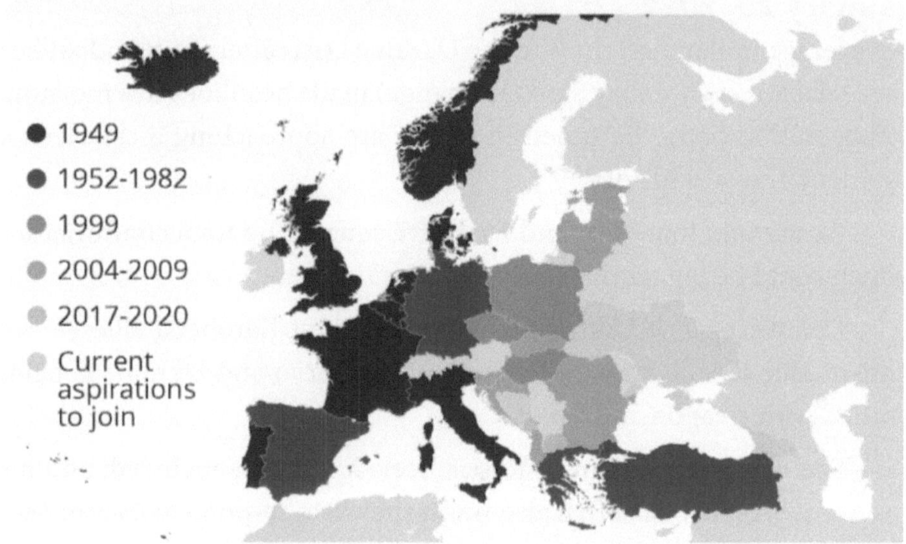

If you decline, Russia has warned, the United States and NATO must put in writing their refusal to accept security guarantees.

If the United States go back on agreements to which it is a signatory, including international collective security (OCSE)[1] they would be apostates from international law and order.

The US would effectively be saying that principle of collective security is null and void.

Any neighbouring country, say Cuba, would then be free to offer launch pads to Russia's nuclear weapons and Florida and Miami would be the first targets.

If the US agree, they would have to retrace its steps, as well as NATO's in Ukraine.

It would make the world unipolar with China-Russia axis taking over Eurasia and taking a giant step in its influence on Africa.

The Geopolitical logic

- ★ If the United States want to control Middle East, it needs Europe.
- ★ If it wants to be a player in Central Asia, it needs Middle East.
- ★ It created the Ukraine Crisis for two primary reasons.
- ★ One, if Russia backs out and ignores its security in vicinity, Vladimir Putin would be as good as gone in 2024 general polls.
- ★ If Russia doesn't back out, the US could take aggressive measures which would nail Russia and weaken China in turn.
- ★ All this was sound logic but the United States hadn't bargained for Russia turning the tables.
- ★ Russia knows the stakes in Ukraine.
- ★ If the West triggers a full-scale war, NATO would be engaged in Eastern Europe and Middle East would be up for grabs for China.
- ★ (US doesn't have much armed presence in NATO—not big anyway compared to Russia—and supplying fresh forces and ammunition, fuel, food etc could take months.)
- ★ If West blinks eye, NATO could be de-engaged for Middle East but Russia would've buried the perception of US hegemony.
- ★ The world would wonder if Washington is more coward than stupid.
- ★ The United State could revert to its "sanctions" game but the tool which has had no effect on Russia since 2014 is unlikely to matter much now.
- ★ Instead, the oil prices would soar and the US markets would crash.
- ★ Europe over-relies on Russian energy.

★ Russia's counter would make US-EU unity crumble as electorates in Europe would bay for blood of their political masters.

What Next?

If Russia wanted to invade Ukraine, it could've done so many a times since 2014.

But Russia is now playing the hardball and asking West to provide it with security guarantees—failing which Russia would act, possibly make a lesson out of Ukraine or deploy its own nuclear weapons in neighbourhood of the United States.

Keep eyes wide open folks: We are seeing the unravelling of world's superpower as we have known the US to be.

Reference:

[1] https://en.wikipedia.org/wiki/Organization_for_Security_and_Co-operation_in_Europe

Link to Article:

https://www.newsbred.com/ukraine-crisis-we-are-facing-the-biggest-moment-of-our-lifetimes/

War Alone Could Deliver Europe to the United States

February 23, 2022

My history tells me that Russia has never attacked anyone in its history.

All of its wars have been in self-defense.

But our newspapers are full of how Russia has breached the "sovereignty" of Ukraine.

It's another matter that these newspapers weren't outraged on "sovereignty" when the US welcomed the annexation of Golan Heights by Israel.

These hacks didn't shake in anger on Yemen, Syria, Libya, Afghanistan, Iraq, Venezuela now, and countless before, like they do on Ukraine's "sovereignty" today.

They won't let you remember that the United States has attempted/succeeded in over 50 regime changes since World War II.

If you remain fed with the same lies, year after year, decade after decade, you must see a dumb next time you go in front of a mirror.

This entire Ukraine thing has been orchestrated by the United States for a simple motive: To keep Europe its client state, so that it doesn't fall into the lap of China's Belt and Road Initiative and immerse itself further in Russia on energy matters.

If Europe goes, so would the NATO, the military-industrial complex of the Hegemon. The United States would be reduced to being an isolated island, thousands of miles, seas apart, from the mainland of action and commerce.

That's why the United States has orchestrated the Ukraine Crisis, hyped up by shameful Western media, so that its flock in Europe stays firmly behind them.

So that the heightened fear of populace in Europe would force national leaders to do Washington's bidding; isolate Russia and China, and keep the continent under its economic and political orbit.

If Germany and Russia get together, and Europe and Asia become one massive free trade area, the game is over: it would signal the end of dollar as the world's financial reserve currency.

The US could remain a hegemon only if Germany is down, China is out, and Russia on the margins.

You don't need any extra word on the current crisis.

If at all, you need to have a "default" position of disbelief on whatever is peddled by the Western press:

★ Who launched multiple military interventions around the world—Afghanistan, Iraq, Libya, Syria, Serbia etc. Russia or the United States?
★ Who runs inhuman hells of detention centres at Bagram, Abu Ghraib and Guantanamo Bay—Russia or the United States?
★ Which country has around 1,000 military bases around the world—Russia or the United States?

It's the United States which raises false flags—like it has on Ukraine—as a pretext to launch military interventions. We heard of Gaddafi's rape squads, Assad's chemical weapons, Saddam's weapons of mass destruction as our dads and moms were fed on babies-on-German-bayonets and Pearl Harbour during the World War II.

The truth is Ukraine is no better than a client state of the United States; that its extremist elements have been similarly armed and fed as were the rebels in Syria, Libya, Kosovo, Chechnya and Afghanistan; or the death squads in El Salvador and Nicaragua.

The truth is Russia has everything to lose; and the United States everything to gain from this conflict.

It would be akin to a suicide mission for a nation under sanctions which has been pushed to the brink.

If you still have time for Western propaganda, and believe in US' morality, God Help You!

Link to Article:

https://www.newsbred.com/us-wants-war-for-if-europe-asia-have-free-trade-its-no-better-than-an-isolated-island/

US Wants Germany Mired in World Wars

February 25, 2022

The United States has achieved all it wanted in provoking Russia to invade Ukraine.

It has ensured that Germany and Russia stay apart; Putin is painted as a "New Hitler" and a cowering Europe hangs on to its coattails, like it has for the last 75 years.

Germany and Russia were just about to push-start the Nord Stream-2 gas pipeline which would've given Germans clean and cheap electricity and flushed Russia with funds. Europe could've been changed forever.

The core of US policy is to keep Germany beholden or mire it in World Wars; and play on its genetical fear of Russian Bear next door.

If Germany and Russia are friends, US has no justification for NATO, its missile systems, its military bases. Its dollar is kept out; trade is done in local currencies and the economic and political power it exerts is gutted.

It's a matter of survival for the United States.

The United States couldn't stop Nord Stream 2 brazenly for its citizens don't want meddling in someone else's domestic affairs and German elites, though hand-in-glove with Washington, feared its' people's anger for the same reason.

That's when the US played its Ukraine card.

Uncle Sam was behind the 2014 coup in Ukraine which overthrew an elected government and put its puppet in power. It began investing billions to "strengthen" democracy in Ukraine. And that is, arming Ukraine with drones, missiles, artilleries, rocket launchers etc.

The puppets-on-remote immediately began riling the eastern region of Ukraine (Donetsk and Luhansk) which houses mostly ethnic Russians. Moscow also feared the NATO capture of Russia's major naval base at Sebastopol on the Crimean peninsula.

So Russia did two things. It held a referendum in Crimea which overwhelmingly voted to return to Russia. It stood for Donetsk and Luhansk and forced about the Minsk Agreement, endorsed by a UN Security Council resolution, under which Ukraine agreed to (a) adopt a law granting self-government to eastern regions; (b) Constitutional reforms to ensure its' rights.

Ukraine signed but did nothing on Minsk Agreements.

Some four million people of Donetsk and Luhansk kept being subjected to genocidal actions. Not a day went by when this region didn't come under shelling. The civilians were killed, abused, including children, women and elderly, and the blockade continued.

The United States, aware that it's Ukraine is the buffer between the West and Russia, and that the country is ethnically divided, played on the fault-lines. It kept Ukraine weak, dependent on its funds and arms, and forever fomented trouble in its eastern part. The heat was bound to trouble Russia which has seen the armies of Napoleon and Hitler march to its hinterlands through the region now called Ukraine.

The truth is United States and its Deep State never want a peaceful solution to Ukraine. It's hell-bent on keeping Ukraine as a permanent barrier between Russia and Western Europe. And the perception of Russia as a security threat to Europe is cast in stone.

The defining policy of the United States is to keep Ukraine as a forward-operating base for launching attacks on Russia. Ukraine is already a NATO country in everything but in name.

Vladimir Putin now says that it's like a "knife to the throat."

"...after the US destroyed the INF Treaty, the Pentagon has been openly developing many land-based attack weapons, including ballistic missiles that are capable of hitting targets at a distance of up to 5,500 km. If deployed in Ukraine, such systems will be able to hit targets in Russia's entire European part. The flying time of Tomahawk cruise missile to Moscow will be less than 35 minutes; ballistic missiles from Kharkov will take 7-8 minutes; and hypersonic assault weapons, 4-5 minutes. It's like a knife to the throat."

What next?

Well, Putin wants West to stay out of his present "special military operation" in Ukraine or they would face consequences like "never before in your history." France, on its part, says the West is not short of its own nuclear options.

Having needled Russia into a military action, and ensured that Western Europe stays chained to its leash, the United States hopes to economically cripple Russia. Its president Putin would now get a makeover as a "New Hitler" which would ensure Congress isn't tight-fisted on budget; nor its citizenry is questioning the hard measures. The shameful Western media would play its propaganda, as usual. A failing Superpower could extend its hold on the world.

Putin is keeping his nuclear options open. So is the squeamish West. When communications snap, any misstep could spell disaster.

One way or other, history is now on a fast-forward mode.

Link to Article:

https://www.newsbred.com/so-far-the-ukraine-card-has-gone-as-per-script-for-the-us/

Why is Europe Committing Suicide?

February 27, 2022

Life is not usual and Europeans needs to understand the consequences of the Ukraine Crisis.

Enough of this vassalage to a power sitting 6,000 nautical miles away.

This superpower has lied to you about everything: Vietnam, Yugoslavia, Afghanistan, Iraq, Libya, Syria, Yemen etc and you still believe that they are telling truth on Ukraine.

They foment uneasy alliances, finance and arm its allies, push them to take all the risks, and when a conflict begins, they abstain.

It escapes you what they are: a lot of wind, selling you an obsolete NATO which ought to have been over once the USSR had disappeared in history.

This European citizenry still don't get it that Georgia tried the same thing which Ukraine has done now and paid with its territory (Abkhazia and South Ossetia) in 2014.

It still is dumb enough to remember that what were 12 members of NATO at the time of its formation in 1949 is now 30 and most of them are breathing down Russia's throat which it had promised it won't do. (Get a drift in the NATO map below)

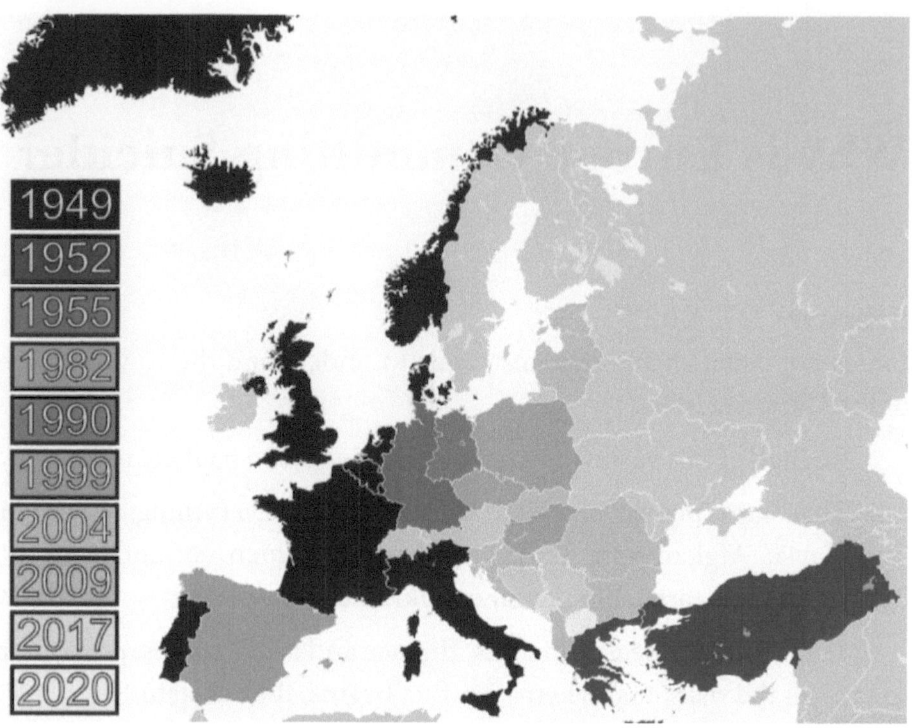

How this "open-arms policy" in Europe has been a source of jobs and migratory problems, how such mindless expansion has turned Europe into an unmanageable continent—all this has escaped you.

How miserable are you, the citizen of Europe, who are beholden to your puppet-leaders, stuck in US trap, who are leading you in a free fall.

How many more millions of victims would it take for you to learn your lessons?

Is Covid-19, and the duplicity around it, already a distant memory?

Can't you see YOU are the remote, controlled by billionaires who care a damn about you or the ideals they sell you?

Who is paying for the aid and weaponry which US and European Union are shipping across to Ukraine? You.

Its citizens should worry what if Vladimir Putin does exercise his nuclear superiority to West—"the response will be immediate and will lead to consequences you have never experienced before"—as well as what if Moscow turns the energy taps dry.

The cost will be millions of lives lost—and many more suffering the unbearable cold which doesn't encourage ablution or putting oneself under a shower.

Then go and fetch your coals and drop your "climate change" placards. And please do ask Greta Thunberg to shut up and do her plaits instead.

Or the Americans would be selling you their liquefied shale gas, more expensive, more ecologically disastrous in operation and in transport, and it's you who would be footing the bill.

Putin is the new Hitler to you for you don't ask yourself a simple question: If Putin wanted to be Hitler, annexing Europe, he wouldn't have waited eight long years since 2014 to strike at Ukraine.

If it was so, he would have Russia's military bases and nuclear launch pads encircling Europe—instead, it is what the US has done to them.

You won't remember that what was once a Soviet Union is now splintered in 13 nations.

That the Slavic Yugoslavia was broken up into multiple nations which are now co-opted into NATO, doing West's bidding.

The EU has announced to freeze the assets of Putin and you still don't get the import of words of Russia's supremo: It's a point of no return.

And those who you should be applauding on your feet—India, Iran, Syria, Cuba, Egypt, Venezuela, UAE etc—for staying neutral and not doing West' bidding; are villains in your brain-washed existence.

Europe urgently needs to discard the tutelage of the United States and extend hand of friendship to Russia which it needs badly for its rich and still largely unexploited expanses.

If nothing, it's a formidable gateway to Asia which has made Europe what it is today and without which it's a rewind to Middle Ages.

Link to Article:

https://www.newsbred.com/your-puppet-leaders-stuck-in-us-trap-are-leading-you-in-a-free-fall/

EU Bans Russian Media for Plebs Shouldn't Know Much

March 1, 2022

The European Union has decided to ban[1] media outlets Russia Today and Sputnik from spreading "disinformation harmful to Europe."

The "paragon of democracy" won't explain why it has flouted its own Charter (Article 11) or the legal basis of its action. And whatever happened to "freedom of press"?

The European Union has also not presented specific instances when these two outlets resorted to "lies".

Every story has two sides to it. If Europe is looking for lasting peace, there is a fundamental need for its citizens to hear both sides of the story. Even Courts don't do it—only despots do. Does Vladimir Putin has done the same to BBC or New York Times which the other day was jumping up and down on "freedom of press" at a raid on an Indian journalist over an alleged fraud?

If there was a "plurality of information", you would've known that the United States bombed Somalia the very day[2] Russia began its military operations in Ukraine.

If we had access to version of the other side, we would've known that Iraq didn't have Weapons of Mass Destruction (WMD) and the US was anything but "liberators of Iraq."

Why Iraq. Same happened to Libyans who had their leader raped to death. Or Syria. Yemen. Afghanistan...But we wouldn't have known.

All of them were "sovereign nations." United Nations was a corpse on feet, like it is today. But we must shake in anger at the violation of Ukraine.

Only, if we had known that just preceding Russia's action, Donetsk and Luhansk suffered 1,400 shell and mortar detonations (February 18). Some 2,000 explosions over the next two days. That Ukrainian forces heavily outnumbered the two little regions (125,000 to 50,000). And this is from Organization for Security and Cooperation in Europe (OSCE) data, one of EU's own![3]

All this was meant to depopulate Donetsk and Luhansk. You may not believe the claim of DPR that 700,000 of its people had begun leaving their homes and hearth. For you won't hear the International Red Cross observers that attacks on Donetsk's water supply system affected a million inhabitants.[4].

Russia of course could've ignored the cry of help from Donetsk and Luhansk. It could've opened its borders for fleeing humanity and invited a refugee crisis. It could've ignored if nuclear missiles had just been brought to their doorsteps. But they are the aggressors, eyeing little Ukraine, which they could've gobbled up in 2014 itself rather than trusting the Minsk Agreements.

The plurality of information could've told us that European Union has been the biggest donor of arms aid to Ukraine between 2014-2017. A 2018 Chatham House report tells us that EU gave $1.8 billion to Kiev for "development assistance." The Organization for Economic Cooperation and Development (OECD) tells us that between 2014-2017, US gave $926 million to Ukraine.

When the much reviled Donald Trump was impeached for withholding some $400 million military aid to Ukraine, Democrat Adam Schiff, a war-monger like few, the darling of NYT, Washington Post etc, berated the ex-US president, as "Ukraine is to fight Russia over there"[5] in 2020. Today, when it happens, he is outraged at this violation of "rules-based world order."

If we had access to freedom of information, we would had known that a Ukraine arms dealer named Igor Pasternak[7] held a $2,500 head fundraiser for Schiff in 2013. Soon after, the State Department approved some extremely profitable deal for Pasternak under the Obama Administration.

Donations from war industry—your Lockheed Martin, Northrop Grumman, Raytheon, Radiance etc—have abounded. Guess what these companies wanted? War with Russia on Ukraine[8] Now that when it looks a real thing, they are exhorting the "free world" against a "despot."

The West now has an excuse to rearm Ukraine to teeth. The longer this Russian operation lasts, the better would be its chances to shape public opinion. Never mind if they have to show a 10-year-old fake video[9] of a child standing up to a Russian soldier; or an Ukrainian embracing[10] a Russian, equally fake. Endlessly they would put on loop an Ukrainian mother embracing her kid in front of a ravaged building and emotionally trick the citizenry. Dead Ukrainian soldiers would become martyrs to the cause.

And we would swallow for we would've just one side of story. Victims of propaganda; denied the other side.

Reference:

[1] https://www.theguardian.com/media/2022/feb/27/eu-ban-russian-state-backed-channels-rt-sputnik

[2] https://www.nytimes.com/2022/02/24/us/politics/somalia-shabab-us-airstrike.html

[3] https://nationalinterest.org/feature/will-tensions-ukraine-boil-over-200725

[4] https://nationalinterest.org/feature/will-tensions-ukraine-boil-over-200725

[5] http://www.newsnet.fr/202958

[6] https://jacobin.com/2020/01/adam-schiff-warmonger-impeachment-ukraine-russia-syria

[7] https://www.opindia.com/2022/02/ndtv-passes-off-10-year-old-west-bank-video-as-a-ukrainian-child-soldier/

[8] https://twitter.com/LeftistLs/status/1497107670813544448?s=20&t=mo-trr1c6q9VDCMWqF66yeg

Link to Article:

https://www.newsbred.com/eu-bans-russian-media-for-the-plebs-shouldnt-know-too-much/

Why Sanctions Often Don't Work

March 2, 2022
What do the West sanctions to Russia mean?

We have heard of falling Ruble, stocks and financial assets.

In theory, fall in currency makes imports costlier, exports lesser in revenue. But existing contracts don't change. And when the new contracts are negotiated, the fluctuation in currency is accounted for by both sides. Inflation's hurt to domestic consumer goods would be negated by price controls. Russia could—and would—buy certain strategic stocks, like Japan, to prop up financial markets. Central Bank would step in to stop the free fall of currency. Effects, if any, would happen in long term.

We have heard of sanctions on individuals, banks, goods and services flow, investment, international payments etc.

So Russia won't import goods easily or cheaply. Less exports of good could close industries and layoffs. But since there happens to be a reserve stock of inventories, the effect could take months to happen. But what happens if China or India buys the stuff on Russia's behalf and then becomes a via-medium for exports-imports?

What about Russia's lifeline Oil and Gas: Who no sanctions on this sector?

The world knows oil and gas are the ventilators on which Russia survives. If Russia is to be punished, that ought to be the first measure. It won't receive foreign currency since 85% of global oil trade is done in dollars.

But here is the thing. The oil markets would roil if Russia's 15% input to global supply of crude is cut. Gasoline in US would be $1 a gallon costlier. Remember, Germany has suspended—not shut down—Nord Stream 2 which is yet to open up! If it is serious it should shut the 50% of its supply which it receives from Russia. This natural gas flow from seven pipelines to Southeast Europe before it reaches Germany. Russia gas also reaches Berlin through its pipeline from Turkey. Why the US and Europe are not shutting down these pipelines which supply 40% of Europe's gas? If anything, Russia would earn more revenue now the gas prices would be spiked. And EU industries could collapse.

Sanctions on Russia's gas won't happen anytime soon. Germany doesn't have the port facilities to accept US' LNGs the cost of which—conversion and transport included—would be five times higher. Others such as Qatars and Azerbaijans too are years away from expanding production facilities.

And why are some other key sectors excluded from sanctions?

For instance, aluminium exports from Russia. After all, the US auto, Boeing, canning industry depends at least 10 per cent of its supplies from Russia. Europe, if anything, is more dependent on Russia's aluminium. US can't resist the corporate lobby, you see. There are some other critical metal-based commodities imported from Russia.

And why Russia's biggest banks are exempted from sanctions?

Only some Russian banks are sanctioned, not the biggies. They are central to processing SWIFT payments from the Russian side. And that's because the big US oil corporations don't want to suffer in the global markets. Russia could also freeze considerable foreign investors' assets in Russian banks.

Banking sanctions might not work. Russia's Central Bank could step in to absorb debt like US' Federal Reserve does often in emergency. One must not forget that Russia has $680 billion of cash-chest in liquid currency and gold. This is massive reserve. It could also help Russia's Oligarch investors.

SWIFT appears to be the silver bullet against Russia. But is it?

This is international payments system. For goods and services. Purchases and sales. Connected through global banks in which US banks are the big daddy. For they have the dollars, the global trading currency.

Interestingly, it wasn't part of initial sanctions by West. SWIFT has its base in Belgium and it meant for US to get EU on board. But its' now been set in motion. But the economic cost would be equally damaging for West due to rising inflation via oil prices. But what happens if Russia uses China's Yuan currency in its transactions? Or it starts using China's digital currency which has already been introduced in the Middle Kingdom? We also know that China-Russia have been working behind the scenes for years to set up a parallel International payments system

Trust the financial markets to know more than we do. The US and EU financial markets fell steeply on the first day of Russia's military operation—but it bounced back no sooner than when Biden announced initial sanctions.

Media, convinced that we commoners are dumb, won't stop its propaganda meanwhile.

Link to Article:

https://www.newsbred.com/the-gimmick-of-sanctions-what-if-china-sells-and-buys-on-behalf-of-russia/

What If Mexico is Turned Into a Ukraine By Russia?

March 4, 2022

We hear that "much of the world has condemned Russia's invasion of Ukraine."
But the UNGA session was to "stop the war in Ukraine." As far as I could see almost all of Africa, South America, Central America, The Middle East and much of Asia haven't "Condemned Russia." Even notable West's allies—Turkey, India, UAE, Saudi Arabia—haven't.

We hear of punitive "economic sanctions" by the world community against Russia for its invasion of Ukraine.
But there were no "economic sanctions" when the United States/NATO war machines put foot on the soil of Yugoslavia, Iraq, Libya, Syria and other countless interventions in Mali, Central Africa, Uganda, Ivory Coast etc.

We hear the pleads that the "International Court of Justice" should put Vladimir Putin to trial.
But no such chorus had gone up on President Bill Clinton or President Chirac for the war in Serbia; the two Presidents Bush for Iraq; President Sarkozy, Tony Blair and Barack Obama for Libya; and the collective Western leadership for Afghanistan.

Russia is Nazi, Putin is the New Hitler

But the mainstream media, run by the United States, won't bestow such acronyms to perpetrators of havoc in Afghanistan or Iraq; Libya or Syria. Where is the denunciation of genocide of Amerindians, Africans, Algerians etc?

Who's censoring media?

Russia is denounced for censorship of media. Not the West which has made Russian viewpoint inaccessible[1] to us in order to defend "freedom" and "democracy"! Irony just died a million deaths.

There is a mist of coloured narratives being served to us citizens. Rumour is all over us. But dare we call it "conspiracy theories." They don't trust us to hear alternative perspectives or judge on our own. And this we must not call "Fake News." The champions of "freedom", built on corpses of millions, we must believe have the interest of common people at heart.

They passed Slobodan Milošević for a mad, crazy dictator, blood-sucking monster. The same was the terminology for Saddam Hussein. Eerily, same words are being said on Putin. No other version is heard, seen or read about. And this is not censorship.

In its sanctions, the West clearly has put its entire economy to break the back of Russia. The global surface of airlines and global shipping network is being severed one by one. Internet would be the next, broken down into regional sphere with limited or no connectivity.

But what if Russia survives this? They have already pushed Russia and China into a blood pact. What if this anti-Western bloc, including Iran and North Korea, and numerous fence-sitters like UAE, India, Brazil, South Africa, join hands?

Russia has quite a few cards on hands to play with. Russia could really turn the heat in Syria and Iran to drag West and NATO into an entirely different sphere. What about turning Mexico into a Ukraine for the United States?

What if a war happens and a New World Order emerges? What if this New World Order plays upon the old US faultlines of "northerners" vs "southerners." — they both have different accents, attitudes, cuisines as well as views on how the US should be. A third type of America could emerge on the western coast—your Seattle, Portland, San Francisco and LA. They are completely different from Northerners and Southerners in accent, views, culture etc. There indeed could be multiple subdivisions of America in the same way the West has created in the Slavic world of Russia. There could be multiple American ethnicities.

But we can't ponder over these possibilities for mainstream media keeps hiding us from alternative perspectives. There is an elephant in the room but their camera and microphones always evade it. The operation in Ukraine has lingered on not because Russia lacks firepower but because it can't bomb Kiev which historically is the "mother" of Russia, it's very womb. Half the mayors of the towns Russian forces has rolled in already float their flags. The truth that majority of Ukraine—two-thirds of it—is Russian. These two-thirds would always be with Russia.

From where Ukraine is getting its arms supply from West? It's Poland which has become the logistical hub, much as Russia feared. Our CNNs and NBCs and BBCs would have us believe that Ukraine has done nothing to provoke Russia. And US, NATO and EU are merely championing "freedom" on Russia's doorsteps. We are not allowed to remember history: That the only nation which makes the most out of European Wars, as in two World Wars, is the United States. A war in the old continent and Asia suits only a superpower located some 6,000 nautical miles away.

It's the United States which controls mainstream media today. It's endlessly supplying fake news. And to hell with humanity.

Reference:

[1] https://www.cnet.com/news/politics/russian-news-outlets-rt-and-sputnik-are-now-banned-in-europe/

Link to Article:

https://www.newsbred.com/what-if-russia-drags-west-into-a-different-theatre-in-syria-or-iran-or-turn-mexico-into-ukraine-of-us/

Why a La Al Qaeda in Europe is Cool for Washington

March 7, 2022

A question should concern us for which we get no answer from the mainstream media.

If snuffing out neo-Nazis is Putin's aim, why are they ignoring, these "champions" of our human rights, the smoking out of these sinister elements?

There is a method in how Putin is going about it: and the map below should make obvious his plans even as West and its stenographers we call media keep gloating on Ukraine's heroism and punishing sanctions.

As the map above shows, Russia is carrying out operations on three sides of Ukraine: (a) From the South, one is headed from Crimea and is smelling Kiev—and there is another branching out towards Mariupol which is the "gate" for Donbass and Luhansk, the two regions Russia has recently declared independent; (b) Then there is one plunging down from the north, through Belarus, towards Kyiv; (c) And there is another which is routing through Sumy city, again in the northeast towards Kiev.

Russia aims to cut off supply from Kiev to flush out "Neo Nazis" from key regions, such as Mariupol; allow Ukrainian soldiers a passage to leave if they desire so; and hugely mindful all this while that they don't bomb residential buildings and civilian centres lest another Raqqa is created in the heart of Europe.

No proof is needed that much of Ukraine's arms depots, air and naval assets have been neutralized: Or else the 40-km long Russian convoy which has been splashed all over would've been taken out by the Ukrainians from the sky.

For the moment, Ukraine's game is to keep Russia marooned on its land as long as it could; keep getting arms supply and financial aid from West; let barbaric sanctions on Russia keep taking its toll.

The neo-Nazis Putin keeps referring to, the ultra-right nationalists, amongst whom Azov Battalion is the hood of the serpent, is no figment of imagination. It's a mother-hive for those of their ilk with recruits coming from all over the world—UK, US, Sweden, Brazil etc. In 2018, four white supremacists trained by the Azov Battalion were arrested in California.

These ultra-fascists by their own admission have nearly 20% of their cadre as neo-Nazis for whom Hitler is a hero and Holocaust never happened; their logo features Wolfsangel (see below), one of the original symbols used by the 2nd SS Panzer division Das Reich.

Azov Battalion initially faced music from the US between 2014-2017; in 2018 the US House of Representatives had passed a provision blocking any training of Azov members by American forces, citing its neo-Nazis association; yet magically the restrictions were removed and aids kept pouring.

Ukraine, on its part, mainstreamed them. The Azov Battalion was formally incorporated into the Ukrainian military in 2014; it's a neo Nazi unit of the National Guard. Known as the National Corps, it was deployed all across the country alongside the national police. In November last year, one of its most prominent militiamen, Dymytro Yarosh, was appointed as advisor to the Commander-in-Chief of the Armed Forces of Ukraine.

Yarosh is a disciple of Stepan Bandera, the collaborator of Hitler in World War II, and who is being lionized in present-day Ukraine. In 2018, one of its city Lviv declared that 2019 would be the Year of Stepan Bandera, igniting protests from Israeli and the Polish government. There are several monuments in honour of Bandera throughout western Ukraine.

It is these Neo Nazis who Putin wants to flush out. Azov Battalion is based out of the strategic port city of Mariupol. There are confirmed reports that it's keeping the residents of Mariupol as hostages. Those who try to leave are being killed. *The Guardian* found many on its rolls to have "disturbing" political views.

In December 2021, Ukrainian president Volodymyr Zelenskyy delivered a "Hero of Ukraine" award to a leader of the fascist right wing group in the parliament. A few months earlier he had announced Ukraine would retake Crimea by force. In November 2021, Ukraine said it would retake Donbass by force. Zelenskyy them announced in Munich that it would acquire nuclear weapons, that it already has materials and expertise for it.

Is it any wonder that Putin has acted the way he has. His operation in Ukraine clearly shows a strategist who had been planning his own moves all along. Such an operation as Ukraine's underway now takes months of planning. Our *New York Times* and *Washington Post* may never let out the misery Azov Battalion brings to Mariupol; the mercenaries and terrorists being planted in the heart of Europe—a la Al Qaeda and ISIS; the rise of far-right elements on the Continent which would tear asunder the Europe we know: the divide-and-rule deepened between West and Russia in Europe which is the goal of Washington.

It's a pivotal moment in world history. Either the story of last 500 years would have its' extension; or a New World Order would take shape. It would surely involve a cost. A very heavy cost.

Link to Article:

https://www.newsbred.com/neo-nazis-who-putin-keeps-pointing-and-west-keeps-ignoring/

US Biolabs in Ukraine and Conspiracy of Silence

March 21, 2022

It's not a myth like the Weapons of Mass Destruction (WMD) with Saddam Hussein.

We don' have to take the word of Sergey Lavrov, Russia's foreign minister, that is if you ever chance upon his views in our sanitised media.

It's former US Democratic representative Tulsi Gabbard who puts[1] a number to 25 on such US-funded bio labs in Ukraine.

Gabbard has been dubbed a "traitor"[2] for worrying about its breach which could release hundreds of Coronavirus pandemics on humanity.

Then Victoria Nuland, the notorious hawk in the US government allegedly behind the Maidan Coup of Ukraine in 2014, herself has testified[3] before a Senate Foreign Relations Committee hearing of US-funded biolabs in Ukraine.

Yet what we hear is a conspiracy of silence.

As if tens of millions dead worldwide due to Covid pandemic were not lives and only numbers we saw in newspapers.

The United States apparently didn't take the clearance from the regulatory global body, World Health Organization. Not that the sinful set-up which answers to the call of moneybags such as Bill Gates has whimpered in protest.

We also seemingly have the United Nations on vacation, the body which rushed the global mandate against Russia overnight, signed and delivered, into the palms of Washington.

This is the Club which is stuffing us with the image of the same Ukrainian woman holding her child and a bombed building with a new angle every day in newspapers. Yet threat to lives millions times more doesn't seem to matter.

The likely killings, due to release of deadly pathogens from biolabs across continents, doesn't concern our guardians and their puppies we call media.

Let this sink in: None of these pen-hackers have echoed a simple question which Russia has been accusing the West of:

That Ukraine is a client country of the United States for no sovereign nation would allow its land to be used for experiments of such deadly consequences;

Not unlike Kosovo which is a handcrafted country in southern Europe, of a few hundred square kms and a few thousand citizens, still unrecognised by most of the world but vital to the US for its military base, Camp Bondsteel, and Project Energy Pipelines to Europe.

And if Ukraine indeed is a vassal to the United States, who could dispute that its nothing but a playground for NATO; swarming with neo-Nazis which the Old Continent of Holocaust memory ought to have snuffed out. But no, Al-Qaeda is in Europe, like ISIS emerged in the Middle East, and nobody gives a damn.

When Russia ought to have been a saviour, risking its very being under the weight of excessive sanctions, Europe, from Macedonia to Marseilles to Munich, are raising the spectre of a Hitler reborn.

All of this is official: That US has 26 biolabs in Ukraine, that it runs under the command of Pentagon, and no information could be released in public. Worldwide, US has 336 such biolabs in 30 countries. The US military virtually directly funds and operates such facilities.

Back home, Fort Derrick in Maryland is known for the "darkest biological experiments" of the US army. Last year, a South Korean civic group had sued the Fort Derrick bases over the smuggled toxic substances to the Asian country in violation of domestic law.

We have it in public domain that in 2015, a probe by the US department of defense, found a US military lab in Utah guilty of not neutralising live anthrax spores which were shipped to 86 labs in the country and abroad.

Nobody knows if such activities fall in accordance to Biological Weapons Convention (BWC). For its the US which has obstructed the setting up of a BWC verification mechanism.

So why "fund" Ukraine which is poor and isn't quite gold standard in biomedical research? Where is WHO? UN? The Biological Weapons Convention? Who benefits from the Nazi-sation of Ukraine? What does Pentagon have in mind for we the people, the canon-fodders?

Questions which concern. Instead, we have a cover-up under the guise of "fighting misinformation" while the humanity shuffles on strings moved by these actors.

We ought to be scared. Very, very scared.

Reference:

[1] https://www.newsbred.com/tulsi-gabbard-drops-the-penny-us-has-biolabs-in-ukraine/

[2] https://www.newsweek.com/tulsi-gabbard-bio-labs-ukraine-russia-conspiracy-1687594

[3] https://www.newsbred.com/tulsi-gabbard-drops-the-penny-us-has-biolabs-in-ukraine/

Link to Article:

https://www.newsbred.com/us-biolabs-in-ukraine-and-the-conspiracy-of-silence/

Why Indian Media is Forcing Modi's Hand on Russia

March 24, 2022

The Indian Media is working overtime to push India firmly against Russia in the Ukraine Crisis.

This media has a two-pronged approach: **One,** that if India doesn't do so, it would earn them the hostility of United States and QUAD alliance which is vital to India's geo-strategic needs; **Two,** India is seen standing against "humanity" since it's supporting Russia which has violated the sovereignty of an independent State.

The first premise is stupid.

United States could keep screaming "wrong-side-of-history" and a "shaky" India; para-drops hawks such as Victoria Nuland in New Delhi; but if even a hostile neighbour Pakistan is gushing on India's "independent foreign policy, India surely is not doing badly.

Let's look at the second premise: What if United States, and not India, is standing against "humanity" vis-a-vis Russia?

After all, the United States signed a Charter on Strategic Partnership with Ukraine in November 2021. It endorsed Ukraine's military goal to "retake" Crimea and Donbass.

It effectively junked the 2015 Minsk Agreements which Ukraine was signatory to with the promise it would correct itself on Donbass.

The United States had also promised it won't expand in Eastern Europe given Russia's security concerns. Today it practically has entire

Eastern Europe under NATO, even Ukraine all but in name since NATO has co-ordinated, supplied missiles and trained Ukrainian forces.

The United States had also unilaterally withdrawn from the Intermediate-Range Nuclear Force Treaty (INF) in 2019 and left Russia clutching the air.

It's now well-known that it engineered the Maidan Coup in Ukraine in 2014 which overthrew a democratically elected government. It has installed puppets in power since then who follow anything but democratic norms and are corrupt to the core. Not to forget that 14,000 ethnic Russians have been killed in Donbass and Luhansk since 2014.

Proof? Well, Ukraine's president Vladimir Zelenskyy has shut down seven opposition television channels, suppressed press, arrested the leader of the major opposition party, and incorporated a sworn Azov "Nazi" Battalion into its army which has its base in Mariupol from where it wantonly attacks the neighbouring Donbass residents.

Most of Zelenskyy's friends and associates now head the powerful levers of the Ukrainian government.

Now let's say you are still unconvinced if it justifies Russia violating the sovereignty of an independent State.

So let me ask such sceptics a simple question: If your neighbour has placed its mortar gun directed at your lawn, would you term it a security threat or not?

If your sister has a pistol of a rapist on her head and she pulls one out herself and shoots him dead, who do you think is guilty.

In common parlance, it's self-defence. In geopolitical terms, it is indivisibility of security for all.

That's what Ukraine itself promised when it signed treaty with more than 50 other countries at the OSCE Summits in Istanbul in 1999 and in Astana in 2010: Agreeing they would not strengthen their own security at the expense of other's security.

This is the legitimacy of own security which made President John F Kennedy object to Russian nuclear missiles in Cuba in the "Bay of Pigs" crisis of 1961.

This is the concern out of which US won't allow any nuclear missile placed in its neighbourhood like Mexico.

If the law is not same for everyone, it is not a law.

What kind of democracy the United States is championing if it's denying access to Russia's point of view through bans on media outlets such as RT and Sputnik? What it has got to hide?

What kind of neutrality are Big Techs professing when its wantonly banning accounts?

What kind of international law do you think allows the United States and its allies to freeze individual Russians property and assets around the world? If it's not banditry or robbery, what else is it?

Neither these sanctions have been reviewed by the WTO nor approved by the UN Security Council.

Where's the internationally-approved tribunal where Russia could defend itself?

And could we be please spared this nonsense that the world is issuing sanctions against Russia? There is none in Africa or Latin America and in Asia, but for a few you could count on your fingertips, nobody else has sanctioned Russia.

Indeed, it would be obvious that the non-sanction world is much, much bigger. It could be United States' personal agenda but it certainly is not of most of the world.

There is also too much of noise on Russia won't be allowed to attend G20 conference later this year. Well, nine of its member-governments—South Africa, Turkey, Brazil, Argentina, China, India, Indonesia, Mexico and Saudi Arabia—have refused to implement any sanctions against Russia.

Listen to what South Africa's president Cyril Ramaphosa has to say on the Ukraine crisis: "The war could have been avoided if NATO had heeded the warnings from amongst its own leaders and officials over the years that its eastward expansion would lead to greater, not less, instability in the region."

As for the distressed humanity in Ukraine, this is what celebrated investigative journalist Glenn Greenwald and Pedro Gonzalez have documented: Attacks on civilians blamed on Russia on closer inspection are found to be committed by Ukrainian irregulars.

They claim that the Western media shows images of the video game *War Thunder* frames from the movie *Star Wars*; explosions in China, footage from Afghanistan; mobile crematoria, passing them off as real and recent scenes of Russia's "war crimes."

Over to Russia's foreign minister Sergey Lavrov:

"What we are seeing is to reduce Russia's role to zero in world politics, economics, sports, art, trade, science, education… (the sanctions are) almost twice as much as the number of sanctions imposed against North Korea and Iran…These sanctions not only have no basis in international law, they are in direct violation of it. What the US has done in seizing the property of ethnic Russians (and even non-ethnic Russians who simply hold Russian citizenship) is banditry and piracy.

"We understood long ago there is no such thing as independent Western media. This is war. The methods of information terrorism are used in the war. There is no doubt about it," he said.

Lavrov could've said as much about India: There is no such thing as independent Indian media. The methods of information terrorism are used in the war.

Link to Article:

https://www.newsbred.com/ukraine-crisis-why-indian-media-is-trying-to-force-modis-hand-on-russia/

The World Isn't Joining West's Sanctions on Russia

March 27, 2022

Why most of the world hasn't joined the West's fest of Sanctions on Russia?

There is a blank response from Latin America, Africa and Asia but for a few.

Why is it so when 141 of the 193 nations in the United Nations "deplored" Russia for its military operation in a "sovereign" Ukraine?

One, Nations needs goods to live by;

Two, the United States scares them by its unilateral stances.

Let me try to put it as simply as I could.

Not only masses need to know, it's also important you spot the sold media which betrays you with all its lies and fabrications.

What are the goods in which US-West are no help?

Let's start with the basic wheat.

A country like Benin is 100 per cent dependent on Russian supplies at reduced price.

Now Benin of course won't register in your mind. It's an African country which has more land and more population that two-thirds of Europe. All your Belgiums, Denmarks, Greece, Portgual, Ireland, Czech, Switzerlands, Swedens, Irelands pale in comparison. Even the New Zealand, which fills our news pages, has less population than Benin.

No less than 25 African countries depend on Russian wheat.

The agriculture wealth—which stretches from the Mediterranean to Pacific—accounts for more than half of the world's wheat production; almost 85% of world's rice production.

It might be common knowledge that Middle East, Russia and Central Asia have 70% of the world's known oil reserves and nearly 65% of the known gas reserves.

But you could be unaware that your semi-conductors, and microelectronics, are dependent on elements such as silicon which, two-third of them, is supplied by Russia and China.

Your magnets, batteries; jacks to laptops etc which rely on rare earths such as yttrium, dysprosium, terbium etc, alone are produced by China.

Global South, Africa and least developed nations of the world would be wrecked if there is food and energy shortage. Inflationary recession would set in and a civil war would loom on the horizon in many.

But They Can't Buy The Russian Goods Anyway Due To West's Sanctions?

Isn't that what Sanctions are meant to? That is to isolate Russia—nobody trades with them; their Roubles currency is reduced to junk.

Now here's the thing.

There are alternatives in the real world.

Like PetroDollar, this world also exists in India-Yuan, Saudi-Yuan, Rupee-Rial exchange.

Then there are Special Drawing Rights (SDR) which is a new digital currency, dynamically revalued against a basket of trade currencies and commodities.

The SDRs. as a reserve currency was announced by the Eurasian Economic Union (EEU) earlier this month.

Don't get the impression that it has come out of blue. It's acceptance in international trade has been there for some time now.

In 2014, the IMF granted its first load in SDRs;

In 2016, World Bank issued its first bond of SDRs;

In 2019, all Central Banks began reporting their foreign exchange reserves in SDRs;

Now on March 14, 2022, the EEU has announced SDRs. as a reserve currency.

This hopefully answers the first part—why the World has stayed away from West's Fest of Sanctions.

Now let's address why the World is scared of US' unilateralism.

Why the World is Afraid of the United States?

We all know that the United States, and the West which follows in its footsteps, has come down hard on Russia assets in their lands.

Russia's assets, from gold to investment to real estate etc have been frozen by the US-led sanctions.

These of course are ILLEGAL SANCTIONS, unapproved by the United Nations, its conventions and laws, as well as some 29 resolutions of member-states demanding abolition of such harsh coercive measures.

So these sanctions on Russia are not stand-alone measures.

The US has a legacy on such robbery: Iran lost its assets when Shah was overthrown; then it was the turn of Afghanistan; Venezuela has its gold denied by the United Kingdom and now it's the turn of Russia.

Those who run nations know, and we media brain-washed citizens don't, that 143 of the BIS (Bank of International Settlements), EEU, SCO, ASEAN, RCEP nations—none of which has US as member and Russia is in all of them as member/correspondent—find Dollar toxic.

And that Dollar isn't free from government's manipulation, currency exchange, sanctions and embargoes.

Could you fault the world if it feels insecure of their holdings in US banks, US treasury bill etc? On what they had thought to be their most secure savings?

For the last 50 years, since 1971, the world had held Dollar to be supreme. It was that year when US declared it didn't need gold as a collateral guarantee for its Dollar. The world held dollars, i.e. bought US treasury bonds, to finance the US budget and balance of payment deficit.

Now if the world fears it is hostage to Dollar, could we fault them?

Link to Article:

https://www.newsbred.com/why-the-world-has-not-joined-the-west-in-sanctions-against-russia/

The West Has Doubled Down on India Against Russia

April 1, 2022

All have come. All have failed. For when Russia's foreign minister Sergey Lavrov meets his counterpart Dr. S Jaishankar, and later the prime minister Narendra Modi over the next two days, he would still feel at home.

That won't please the West, of course. Over the last one week, we have had biggies from the United States, Germany, Greece, European Union, Japan, Australia, Britain etc in town, asking India to disown Russia, sometimes in language which was extremely coarse and distasteful.

The US has used words such as "shaky"[1] and on "wrong side of history"[2] for India, warning that there could be "consequences"[3] if the US-led sanctions are subverted. Germany has been frontal in wanting India to be "in its camp"[4]. British foreign secretary, the petite Liz Truss, says their business outlook would depend on the countries they could "trust."[5]

Of course, most of the world hasn't joined[6] the West-led sanctions. The diplomatic quarters know that these sanctions are unilateral and flout the UN Charter [7]; that Ukraine was being "Nazified" by the West, both going back respectively on the Minsk Agreement[7] and the word that NATO won't set foot[8] in Russia's neighbourhood, etc, etc.

After all what Russia wants? It just wants a guarantee that Ukraine would be neutral and bereft of Nazis who are embedded in Ukrainian army.

Is it really such a big ask for West to concede and wreck the world which still can't do with Russia's metals, agriculture and energy?

And if West views Russia's concerns on its neighbourhood unfair—remember Hitler's army had marched through Ukrainian lands which left 42 million Russians dead in the World War II—the US shouldn't mind if Russia has its nuclear missile placed in the neighbourhood of Washington, say in Cuba.

Yet the West is tearing the world apart and intimidating those who are staying neutral like India is. What's wrong if India asks for diplomacy and dialogue to end the Ukraine Crisis? What's wrong if India asks the rules of the global order, under the UN, to be adhered to?

An undaunted India is doing what is best for its economy, its people. It won't let go on the deep discount on Russian oil and has ratcheted up its buy[9] in a month to almost what it bought in the entire 2021. The Bank of Russia and RBI is working out an alternative payment mechanism. India's finance ministry is setting up an inter-ministerial group to resolve the payment issue in trade with Russia.

So when the West doubles down on India, and warns it of "consequences" for buying oil from Russia, could we really fault Dr. S Jaishankar when he tells some plain truth: That it is Europe which has brought 15% more oil from Russia than it had in the month preceding the Ukraine Crisis.[10] For good effect Jaishankar added: "In three months' time, when we look at the big buyers of Russian oil and gas…I suspect we (India) won't be in the Top 10."

"It looks like a campaign on this issue", said Jaishankar, no doubt peeved that the colonial powers still think they could push India around even while doing exactly the opposite themselves.

Make no mistake. India is indispensable to West. And that's because without India, it can't play its favourite game of encircling its arch enemy China. If China is to be inconvenienced in its neighbourhood, like Ukraine presently has been done for Russia, the West needs to stoke the war-heat in Indo-Pacific where India has a geographical location like no other amongst QUAD members.

All the US wants is to weaken Russia-China alliance. If one goes, the other would be all that easier to deal with. But its worst nightmare would be if instead of unhinging Russia-China, it actually brings Russia-China-India together. For that would mean losing the entire Eurasia.

Sure, the West would entail a cost on India's neutrality. It would make life difficult for Modi and his India. It would stoke anarchy besides applying the financial strangulation.

But then who said throwing off the yokes of Empire, and helping the world change forever for right reasons would come free?

Reference:

[1] https://economictimes.indiatimes.com/news/india/us-president-joe-biden-calls-india-shaky-in-russia-confrontation/articleshow/90365531.cms

[2] https://www.business-standard.com/article/international/india-could-be-placed-on-wrong-side-of-history-after-russian-oil-deal-us-122031600181_1.html

[3] https://www.thehindu.com/news/national/us-deputy-nsa-daleep-singh-cautions-india-against-trade-deals-with-russia/article65277933.ece

[4] https://www.hindustantimes.com/india-news/on-india-visit-top-german-diplomat-explains-how-russian-invasion-impacts-india-101648658805174.html

[5] https://www.youtube.com/watch?v=mnBnP8Jbg40

[6] https://www.newsbred.com/why-the-world-has-not-joined-the-west-in-sanctions-against-russia/

[7] https://en.wikipedia.org/wiki/Minsk_agreements

[8] https://www.latimes.com/opinion/op-ed/la-oe-shifrinson-russia-us-nato-deal—20160530-snap-story.html

[9] https://www.thehindu.com/news/national/us-deputy-nsa-daleep-singh-cautions-india-against-trade-deals-with-russia/article65277933.ece

[10] https://www.hindustantimes.com/world-news/on-russia-ukraine-war-uk-foreign-secy-elizabeth-truss-says-india-need-not-be-told-what-to-do-101648746836336.html

Link to Article:

https://www.newsbred.com/lavrov-is-at-home-in-india-and-west-is-grumpy/

Bucha is a Re-run from Yugoslavia Template of Lies

April 6, 2022

You wouldn't have heard of Bucha before. Now you know since its mayor has reported of a mass grave of 300 people after the Russian forces left the town on April 1.

There could be several other "Bucha" surfacing in coming days.

It's no different to the "genocide"; "mass murder" "pogrom" which were discovered and blamed on the dominant Serbs in the tragic story of what once was Yugoslavia in the 90s, now been broken up into seven independent nations.

That it allowed the West—or US and its vassals in Europe—an access to the Adriatic Sea (and thus Mediterranean Sea, the gateway to Middle East and Africa) we would leave for the moment.

If you happen to buy my book—- "How United States Shot Humanity"[1] —a result of a painstaking research of a few years in the Balkans, you could go into a depression on what the Empire and its stooge media serves us in the name of humanity but what essentially is a criminal enterprise of brainwashing us as zombies in the service of the Satan.

My book would throw up several names of Foca, Gorzade, Serbrenica, Sarajevo etc in erstwhile Yugoslavia where so-called massacre of "innocent" Bosnian Muslims was undertaken by the "monstrous" Serbs even though exactly the opposite had happened—much like how Russians are shown to be the evil in the present Ukrainian Crisis.

So a few excerpts from the book below which could make you place the order as soon as you are through with this piece:

***

FOCA

The stories of systematic rape of Bosnian Muslim girls and women was all over the media. It was asserted that Serbs ran "Rape Camps" in Foca. It was termed "genocide", no less.

The reports claimed that up to 100,000 Muslim women were raped through the Bosnia War. The MS magazine ran a cover story that rapes were intended to produce pornographic films. *No such film was ever found!*

On January 15, 1993, *New York Times* ran a photo story with the caption: "A two-month old baby girl born to a teenage Muslim woman after she was raped in a Serbian detention camp." *USA Today* of January 13, 1993, told the story of a five-month old baby, presumably the product of systematic rape by Serbians. *Only, at that time the war was not even nine months old!*

In January 1993, the Warburton Report, authorised by the European Community, estimated 20,000 Muslim women were violated by Serbs as a part of war strategy. That a member of the commission, Simon Veil, a former French minister and president of the European Parliament, dissented is not even in public view. *Veil had revealed that the estimate of 20,000 victims was based on actual interviews with only four victims—two women and two men*!

According to the *New York Times*, the Croatian Ministry of Health in Zagreb was the main source upon which the Warburton Report based its figure of 20,000 rapes.

Newsweek reported that up to 50,000 Muslim women had been raped in Bosnia. *Tom Post*, a contributor the article, explained that the estimate of 50,000 rapes was based on interviews with 28 women.

French Television reporter Jerome Bony explained the problem. "When I was 50 km from Tuzla, I was told `Go to the Tuzla High School grounds. There are 4,000 raped women.": At 20 km, the figure dropped to 400, at 10 km only 40 were left. Once at the site, I found only four women willing to testify."

The late Nora Beloff, former chief political correspondent of the London Observer, described his own search for verification of the rape charge in a letter to the Daily Telegraph (January 19, 1993). The British foreign office conceded that the rape figures being bandied about were totally uncorroborated, and referred her to the Danish government, then chairing the European Union. Copenhagen agreed that the reports were unsubstantiated, but kept repeating them.

SARAJEVO

A gruesome mortar attack in May 1992 killed 20 and wounded more than 100 people who had queued up in a line to receive breads. Sime Miskin Street was strewn with scores of bleeding people, with corpses of men and women with torn-off limbs."

Washington Post: "A mortal shell landed in a crowded open-arm, armpit in Sarajevo today, killing at least 66 people and wounding more than 200. Horribly mangled bodies and severed limbs lay scattered amid bloodstained market stalls in the bloodiest single attack on Sarajevo's civilians...there are trucks of dead, there are legs, arms, heads—as many as you want, said a wounded man."

"The air was filled with the voices of wailing survivors."

"Bodies were loaded onto trucks and vans because there were not enough ambulances and morgue vehicles."

This is what an attending doctor, Dr. Borisa Starovic, wrote:"I found it very odd that there were no lacerations or puncture wounds on any of the victims. Neither were there any head or chest wounds, only trauma to the lower extremities. The wounds were obviously not caused by artillery shells. They were the results of pre-planned demolition charges, placed by Bosniak Muslim forces, triggered for the benefit of TV camera."

A classified report by UN commander Satish Nambiar, *The Independent* newspaper revealed, mentioned that Muslims had massacred their own men. "It was a staged event as details began to emerge."

The classified UN report, *The Independent,* mentioned:

"It suggested that Sarajevo's defenders, mainly Muslims…staged several attacks on their own people in the hope of dramatizing the city's plight in the face of insuperable Serbian odds."

***

Srebrenica

"The killings here filled the Drina river with bloated and mingled bodies.. .the bodies were often slashed with knife marks and were black and blue...female corpses were always naked...once we picked up a garbage bag filled with 12 human heads."

"130 Bosnian Muslims alive were torched."

Srebrenica made headlines in 1995. According to Red Cross, several Muslim men were reported missing. Washington Post reported that 4,000 armed Muslims had escaped to a nearby town of Tuzla. They were still being reported missing from Srebrenica in reports years later on.

There is simply nothing to document the genocide number of 8,000-10,000 Bosniak Muslims.

There were gory descriptions of carnage, mass rapes, disembowelment, even massacres of children in the media. However, a UN investigative team reported on July 24, 1995 that they could not find a single eyewitness to any atrocity

***

Gorazde

"This is not war anymore. This is slaughter, massacre."

The UN officials found that the hospital in the Gorazde, reportedly destroyed by Serbs, basically needed a broom to clear up the rubbish. It was still functioning.

The commander of UN troops in Bosnia, British Army Lt General Michael Rose said the Bosnian casualties around Gorazde "were closer to 200 than 2,000."

***

No wonder it is said that history repeats itself—more so when its creators use the same tool every time they wish to engineer and then encash a crisis: Be it in Foca once and Bucha now.

Just let's hope Gorazde, Srebrenica and Sarajevo etc don't find a Ukrainian version in the coming days.

Reference:

[1] https://www.amazon.in/How-United-States-Shot-Humanity/dp/8193163109

Link to Article:

https://www.newsbred.com/bucha-looks-a-re-run-straight-from-the-copybook-used-in-yugoslavia-once/

India Has Shown Nerves of Steel in Standing By Russia

April 25, 2022

It would tire you just to know who all are coming to New Delhi from Europe[1] this week.

Most of these countries you can't locate on the Old Continent—-why is Europe called a continent at all when at best it's a sub-continent like India—and you can't save your life if the deal is to name their visiting foreign ministers.

The trajectory is not lost on anyone as first the biggies—United States and Germany, then United Kingdom and France—and now the minions who make up what we call is West, is doubling down on India to call Russia names in the Ukraine Crisis.

They have threatened, cajoled, baited and dissuaded to convey that neutrality is not an option and the delusion of sovereignty isn't permitted to any nation as long as the West controls the world through its Dollar, or call it Pound or Euro if you must.

It's not just Russia. The West is also sleepless lest New Delhi and Beijing warm up to each other and it can't divide the house in Asia which controls 40% of world's GDP.

You only have to look at the world map to see Russia, China and India make up for much of the landmass in Eurasia and if the three were to be joined at hips, the sea-power of West, in conjunction with Japan and Australia, would be left clutching the straws.

The Theory of Encirclement

The genetical makeup of West is to encircle its potential enemy. A Russia must not rest in peace with its neighbours (Poland, Ukraine, Baltics etc); or so do China (Hong Kong, Afghanistan, Taiwan etc). India has just been told about this bitter truth with the replacement of China-friendly Imran Khan in Pakistan with a puppet who is already singing paeans in praise of Washington and is dismantling CPEC[2] (China Pakistan Economic Corridor) in a hurry.

That the United States has 800 military bases encircling most of the world tell its own story. The other Anglo-Saxon power, United Kingdom, has some 145 bases. Look at the map below and get a drift how Big Brother is always stepping on to your toes.

That India has resisted West and if anything, ramped up its trade with Russia, is a defiance which would have consequences. Anarchy for starters in case you don't see a pattern in attack on our Ramnavmis and Hanuman Jayantis. The economic cost (60% of our GDP is debt) is one thing, the popular unrest amongst youth with ambitions to study and subsequently work in London, Melbourne, Toronto and New York is quite another dimension.

Either You Are With Us Or Against Us

That much ought to be clear. India could believe on its neutrality as long as it wants but it won't cut ice with the West. India would be marked as a "hostile" one, as Iran, Russia, China and North Korea have been, and would pay the price.

It would happen in stages though. West, and Europe, would offer goodies in terms of free trade, technology, open doors for Indian students and migrants etc. Victoria Nuland, the hawk in the US establishment, has vowed to wean India away from its military dependence on Russia.

And if all this fails, India would pay.

Is it worth standing up for Russia or China which has lately been pleading for **One Asia** but is reluctant to pull back thousands of its forces from the Indian border?

The thing is if the two competing blocs currying India's favour—West vs Russia/China—-offer nothing tangible, India is unlikely to tilt in anyone's favour. The pressure from the West on India won't be lost on Beijing and if it is serious to mend its fences with New Delhi, the time to act is now. It can't even claim a role in Pakistan's peace overture towards India as it is clearly Washington-engineered.

Ties with Russia is something else. It has stood the test of time despite the language and geographical barrier. India needs its veto on Kashmir in the United Nations—never mind this global body is a joke now—but pertinently relies militarily on Moscow. The blah-blah on cheap oil and minerals etc isn't a determining factor on India's resistance to West.

The trouble is India's resistance to West is pure logic.

It can see the world has split up in two camps.

It can foresee that Dollar is facing an existential threat.

It has reasons to worry if its assets are in Central Banks of West and are frozen like Russia, Afghanistan or Venezuela's have been.

It could perceive that the Global South, of which it's a part with Brazil and South Africa, would come on its own if it survives these final act of Global North's hegemony.

It's foolery to side with the Past when the Future is not hidden even from a blind.

Reference:

[1] https://indianexpress.com/article/india/ukraine-focus-as-eight-leaders-from-europe-visit-india-7885530/

[2] https://www.newsbred.com/pakistan-scrap-cpeca-as-chinas-debt-trap-looms/

Link to Article:

https://www.newsbred.com/indias-nerves-of-steel-on-russia-would-again-be-put-to-test-this-week/

Ukraine War Has Gone Horribly Wrong for the West

June 10, 2022

West could be forced to negotiate with Russia after three months of latter's intervention in Ukraine to get rid of Ukronazis and creeping NATO's footsteps on its doors.

Frankly, there are not many options left for the West.

It can't force a showdown with Russia despite billions of aids and arms supply to Kiev for if it does, Vladimir Putin would turn the oil and gas taps dry to Europe which would plunge the Old Continent into darkness, cars into garages, transport mode on to rusting tracks etc.

It would force the manufacturing giants like BMW or Bayer to either shut down or locate themselves out of Europe, either way causing a massive unemployment and public unrest which would force regime changes from Berlin to Paris to Geneva, you name it.

Europe is in no position to get rid of Russia's energy supplies. The typical diesel blend which Russia provides and for which Europe's processing units are accordingly oriented, can't be replaced overnight.

Even if the West tries, and it is trying, the Middle East like Qatar or Oman can't make up for the deficit of nearly 40% of Europe's energy need if Russia was to turn off the tap tomorrow.

Besides, why would Middle East turn its back on its traditional customers and shift to new European clients for oversupply of oil and gas comes with its own cost: What if traditional customer shift en masse to Russia in the meantime?

And that's not all. Where are the shipping tankers or logistics of transportation and storage, not to say the new skilled workers—and technology—which would be required to make the Russia-minus energy workable for the Europeans?

As it is, the cost of energy has risen three-fold in Europe which continues to buy oil from Grazprom to the tune of $200 million per day, and that too in Rubles, the currency they wished to destroy in baiting the Russian bear on Ukraine.

Now Rubles is doing better than ever, after initially dropping to pennies against the US dollars—it has jumped 40% against Dollar since January—and the pain of economic sanctions are actually beginning to be felt in the Western capitals. Inflation is going through the roof and popular unrest is brewing.

Energy prices in the EU and America have spiked to 40-year highs; recession is staring in eye; supply lines have sunk; food shortages are stark and gas-oil prices are going through the roof.

Meanwhile, the current-account surplus for Russia this year could be at $250 billion which would be more than double the $120 billion measured in 2021. From gas sales alone, Russia could earn a record $100 billion from European countries in 2022 as energy prices have risen painfully high and its gas sales would be almost twice as much as last year. And all this when one is not taking into account the profits from the sale of other Russian commodities, such as oil, coal and other minerals.

What Putin Wants

And this situation isn't going to change at least till the year-end by when one Mr. Putin would hold all the cards and press with his long-standing demand of NATO going back to its 1997 level.

That was the year when West had repeatedly assured a post-Soviet Union Russia that NATO wouldn't expand eastwards but completely did otherwise to the extent that out of the 27 European Union (EU) states, 21 are in NATO today.

Russia has made no secret of what it wants: That NATO returns to its 1997 levels and a collective security is in place for nations of the European continent.

Instead, West chose to bait Russia on Ukraine with constant needling while the Moscow kept repeating it would intervene militarily which it did. Put in Russia's shoes, would the United State allow its neighbourhood of Cuba, Nicaragua etc armed to the teeth with nuclear-missile launchpads? NO.

The truth is, sanctions have failed, and instead of Rubles, it's the Dollars which is losing its pre-eminence world over. Countries are now trading in mutual currencies

The US dollars, supported by multilateral global institutions, would be bypassed by the world for two reasons: One, why trust a currency which already is in a kind of debt it could not repay; and Two, who is to trust a Superpower which one fine morning could seize your assets and reserves with the Western banks?

The truth remains that the Western sanctions have failed; Russia's Rubles is in pink health; and Ukraine has disintegrated. There is no sign of a popular rising in Moscow which the West had hoped for in getting rid of Mr. Putin. Indeed, the Russian leader holds all the aces presently.

The only face-saving measure, as I said, is for the West to negotiate for a settlement between Kiev and Moscow. But they have missed the moment. Russia is winning the war and there's no way West could stop it. That's the plain truth.

Given how Ukraine-2 could crop up on Russia's border in a decade's time, Russia wouldn't settle for anything less than complete de-nazifaction of Ukraine. As for the territories ceded in form of Crimea,

Donbass and those with access to Black Sea, Ukraine can do little but accept that it has been reduced to a strip of land.

It has been a disaster all the way for them.

Link to Article:

https://www.newsbred.com/putin-holds-all-the-aces-in-a-proxy-war-gone-horribly-wrong-for-west/

Central Asia: A Region Both India and China Covet

June 13, 2022

It is easy to understand both India and Russia won't like to be too dependent on either the United States or China who battle for supremacy in the world.

India has dared West with unflinching support to Russia in Ukraine Crisis while being an enthusiastic QUAD member; and Russia has been an Indian friend for all seasons, never mind its "no-limits friendship" with China.

Both of them have stood up to the world's superpower; one by being un-swayed by a series of sanctions and the other by resisting the pressure of entire West and not just the United States.

And now has surfaced the third complimentary angle to the Indo-Russia symmetry: Iran who happens to be equally close to both China and Russia but is willing to restore its civilizational ties with India which suffered under the US pressure.

The jumble in this part of the world we call Eurasia defy neat boxes our minds prefer. Traditional rivals Iran and Saudi Arabia are holding parleys; Israel is being embraced by the Gulf nations while India is warming up to the Talibans.

And United States? Well the Petro-nations aren't helping the bully in the backyard who wants a glut of oil in the market so Russia can't dictate a premium on its own energy due to oversupply.

Each one is putting its own interest first and the bitterness of the past is on the back-burner.

Why, Iran was hugely upset when India forwent the 10% of its energy needs that Tehran supplied due to the US pressure; and India was chastened when Iran lashed out at the abrogation of Article 370 in Kashmir.

Now both are on the mend and the visiting Iranian foreign minister Dr. Hossein Amir-Abdollahian was given audience by Prime Minister Narendra Modi, no less, in Delhi recently. All India needs is to shrug off the US pressure on Iran as it did in the case of Russia-in-Ukraine.

Thus the New Cold War isn't a matter between two camps only: It now constitutes multiple actors who are creating the third angle in this symmetry in which three civilizational States of India, Iran and Russia happen to be common factors.

International North South Transport Corridor

If you don't happen to know of International North South Transport Corridor (INSTC), I suggest you do now.

It's a 7,200 mile long Corridor which connects Russia and India through Iran alongside Caucasus and Central Asia, a sweep of 13 countries which would transform Euro-Asian freight dynamics.

It takes little intelligence to underline its liberating influence on two Sanctions-hit nations, Russia and Iran, or for that matter India which could sell its goods much cheaper through a shorter route than the ones it mostly uses through Suez Canal to reach Europe (see image below). Not to say of a completely new market in Central Asia et al where New Delhi is presently hamstrung by non-access through Pakistan.

The Corridor holds potential to spiral the $11 billion trade between India and Russia manifolds, largely made up of arms deal presently, when the potential for supplies of precious stones/metals, power equipment, steel, pharmaceutical, agricultural products, machineries, advance technology—you name it—between the two holds no limit.

Picture it with the proposed Chennai-Vladivostok Maritime Corridor between India's eastern seaboard and the Russian Far East and the bullish projection of bilateral trade hitting $30 billion by 2025 doesn't look outlandish.

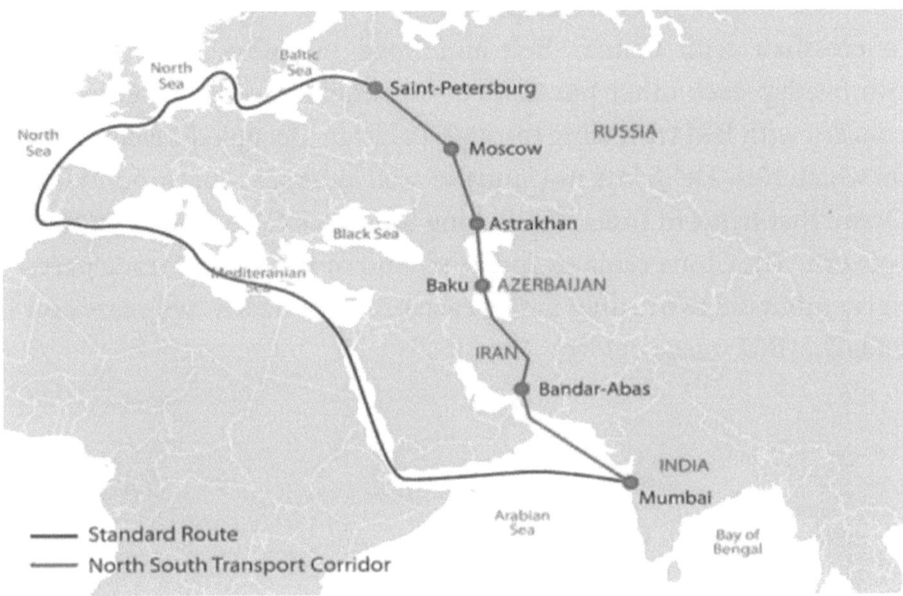

Now cast your eyes around and there are a number of such synergies which are bubbling up in Eurasia. The Eurasian Economic Union (EAEU), driven by Russia, has a combined population of 167 million and a GDP of US $5 trillion. Most of them share a Free Trade Agreement (FTA) between them; as does India with quite a few EAEU nations. It could seamlessly integrate with the INSTC.

The EAEU also enjoys FTA with Iran, Serbia, Singapore and Vietnam; China too is in the works as are most ASEAN nations, Turkey, Israel, Egypt etc. No wonder India with its Act East Policy is turbo-charged in working out an FTA with EAEU itself.

Enters Iran again in the picture. It has signed a deal with Oman to develop two gas pipelines and an oil field along their maritime borders which is a shot in arm for the Iran-Oman-India gas pipeline future.

It should sooth the hurt of New Delhi on Iran-Pakistan-India pipeline which never came about.

And then there is China

Most see India's recent transport/freight initiatives in Eurasia falling in crosshair with China's Belt and Road Initiative (BRI) where the two overlap each other but that's a too simplistic view. Sure, India has concern with BRI traversing through Pakistan Occupied Kashmir (PoK) on which New Delhi lays its claims; as well as its sea route around Indian Ocean that hems in India; but Beijing too treats QUAD as its existential concern. Yet, China remains India's second most valuable trade partner; never mind the two armies facing each other for nearly two years now in Ladakh. (BRI image below.)

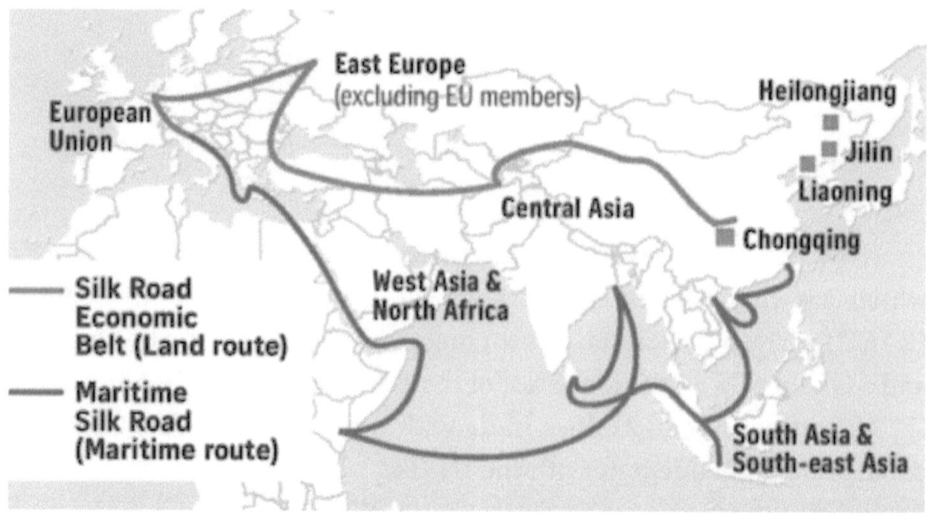

Sure, the ties between the two aren't the sweetest. China has geopolitical imperative that India doesn't rise too quickly. History shows it's in a bigger power's interest that its neighbourhood is generally benign. India, on its part, is justly ambitious given its sizeable economy and potential of its people. But this jockeying is best left for future. Humanity is on a cusp to be freed from the West's domination.

Beijing and New Delhi could keep sparring as long as the bigger goal of freeing humanity from the globalists is not thrown under the bus.

Link to Article:

https://www.newsbred.com/the-new-cold-war-isnt-just-about-the-two-superpowers/

There's Not One But Many Ukraines Unfolding

June 27, 2022

Let's say the United States would never be happy if China and Russia gain ground in Eurasia which is the lifeline for Washington.

All the major trading partners of the United States are in this region, as are their military bases, which with or without NATO, could torch Iraq, Syria, Afghanistan etc running into decades.

It is this part of the world which largely turns a fake currency Dollar into a legitimate one; never mind if the US has far more debt ($30 trillion) than the size of its economy ($25 trillion) and outstrips China ($18 trillion) and Russia ($4.3 trillion) economy combined.

And that's because the Greenback is printed when and to whatever extent the US govt wants without a care in the world: As a petrodollar, it's world's reserve currency which once in global supply chains transforms itself into a legitimate currency.

So if Dollar goes, so does Eurasia—and Africa which is an add-on and part of collateral damage. And this nightmare would only turn real if Russia and China are not stopped in their tracks.

The Gambit of Proxy Wars

So it was imperative for the US and its allies we call West to throw Ukraine under the bus. Let's not delude ourselves that Ukrainians would've lasted thus far without the aid and arms, money and mercenaries of the West.

Ukraine is a small cost to pay to ensure Europe remains under the US' thumb, clinging to the lifeline we know as NATO, in fear of the Russian Bear which frankly is from a textbook agenda running for centuries now. It doesn't allow Germany to get too big—or allied to, god forbids, Russia—a theme which makes UK and France sweat and plunge the world into World Wars.

Each such episodic havocs have been golden harvests for the United States, turning it into a Hegemon that it is, and there is no reason the proven formula stands discarded in our times, never mind your shameful media does its best to keep you drugged.

There are several such Ukraines in Washington's playbox called Proxy Wars to lit the fire around its other nemesis China which shares its borders with 14 other countries.

It's not just Taiwan which is a red herring for Beijing. It enormously needs Pakistan to access Persian Gulf for its security and energy needs and which is on brink of civil war after a pro-China Imran Khan was thrown out of office. Presently, its foreign reserves ($9 billion) could barely last a month. It's begging bowl is no longer passing muster even with its old Islamic benefactors in Saudi Arabia and UAE. It's lifeline, the International Monetary Fund (IMF), at the beck and call of Washington, is also turning in screws. It has run out of basics such as power, water, paper, fuel or even tea.

We know how Sri Lanka has collapsed; we are aware of how Nepal no longer has a pro-Chinese government; Myanmar is more unstable than ever; and Centra Asia, which is essential for China's dream project of Belt and Road Initiative (BRI) is facing similar fire within its domains.

Tajikistan recently had its home militants coordinating with extremists from abroad the regime identifies as National Alliance; Kyrgyzstan is being pressurised to accept Afghan refugees; and a recall to whatever it's worth, Kazakhstan was burning only the other day.

Do we jog the memory of our readers on how suddenly Hong Kong was gripped with the lust for "democracy" one day and un-fizzed the next; how Afghanistan was left in a huff after suffering the GI—and NATO—boots for two decades.

There has been an attempted coup in Solomon Islands and the Philippines has just signed a Maritime Security Framework Agreement with the United States. Only last month, the US president Joe Biden visited Japan and Korea—and not Kiev if that needs be underlined.

The thing is, China's history shows it reacts vehemently to wars around its borders—Korean and Vietnam Wars for instance—and doesn't mind taking on Soviet Union or India in asserting its territorial concept.

The Beijing is aware how it is being encircled; QUAD or other such frameworks the US has forged in Indo-Pacific. As it is, Japan South Korea, Australia, New Zealand and Singapore are NATO's "global partners" in the Indo-Pacific; and at least two dozen nations are part of Partnership For Peace (PFP) which is a pre-stage before a non-European nation (Turkey besides) joins NATO.

It's thus unlikely we would have the Sun of Peace overcoming the Clouds of War in years to come. This is a fight to finish from a Hegemon which only sees in terms of a Unipolar World against a Multipolar World presently in works under the guiding hands of Beijing and Moscow.

And don't you buy or sell the theory all this is for the "Free World" and "Human Rights": For purveyors of WMD theory in Iraq would've been judged and jailed as war criminals by now.

Or that all this is for some "rules-based international order" which has no legal basis and just a fancy name given by the predators of our world. If anything, it murders the "international laws and conventions" where unilateral sanctions are illegal.

Link to Article:

https://www.newsbred.com/the-other-ukraines-which-are-unfolding-to-humanitys-misfortune/

Why Putin is Intent on Dragging on the Ukraine Crisis

July 20, 2022

Why this conflict in Ukraine seems to stretch indefinitely?

Let's hear another Slav leader, and not Putin, on the subject:

"I know what awaits us. As soon as Vladimir Putin finishes his business in Sieversk, Bakhmut and Soledar, then on the second line Sloviansk-Kramatorsk-Avdeevka, his proposal will follow. If they (West) don't accept it, we will all go to hell."–Serbian president Aleksandar Vučić.

Some experts also believe that Russians are eyeing Odessa. One, it psychologically is a huge boost for Russian people. Two, it would afford Russia complete control of Ukraine's entire Black Sea coast.

Now don't tell me you doubt Russia is winning the war.

When a leader begins sacking his inner circle, it's trouble. So happened to Adolf Hitler; same is now happening to Zelensky.

The Ukrainian leader who is doing the bidding for the West, has just fired his attorney general, Irina Venediktova, as well as the head of the SBU (Security Agency, successor to the Soviet KGB), Ivan Bakanov.

This is also much like Stalin whose paranoia devoured his own inner circle.

Oh, yes you also believe that NATO, world's most muscular security apparatus, won't come up second in this proxy war.

America is exhausting the supply of its Javelin anti-tank missiles; a quarter of its Stinger stocks. UK's defense secretary has admitted that his country, in its zeal, is running out of anti-tank missile. The Czech Republic is not left with much to send. France has given up its production of Caesar guns for 18 months.

Now NATO has this crazy idea of donating rifles that need 155 mm ammunitions which are running out fast. If Ukraine does fire 3,000 155 mm shells a day, the entire US output of a year would be over within weeks.

So what happens when Putin has secured his goals in Ukraine?

Almost certainly, Putin would look to secure what he wants.

He would want West to accept the loss of Donbass and Crimea, and possibly Odessa. And oh yes, he would insist on Ukraine's neutrality and denazification. There is no way the West would accede to these terms. It would refuse. (Anyway, after the 2015 Minsk Agreements double-cross, it's unlikely the Russians would take the West on face value.)

Ukraine is like an albatross around West's neck it can't get rid of.

Where does it leave Europe?

Well, the West, that is largely the US and Europe, are stuck on Ukraine and Putin; the same is for UK.

The US has all along wanted to weaken Russia so that China, its rival for world's hegemony, is weakened—and Europe is firmly into vassalage.

The United States has always feared the integration of Europe and Asia—the Eurasia—and uses its puppets to retain the dominance of NATO on security matters in the Old Continent.

It can't afford for Europe to rely on Asia for its energy and other trade needs. Only Germany amongst the Western nations is a manufacturing giant.

And manufacturing needs energy. Germany, at present, uses only 20% of Russia energy—but coal is 40% and nuclear 10%—but they can't hurt Greta so they want more gas which is "greener" but mostly comes from Russia.

It's hard to be Green and hate Russia at the same time.

So it was always against the interest of the United States to NOT have the Nord Stream 2 gas pipeline functional from Russia to Germany over the Ukrainian land. The erstwhile leaders of the US and Germany, Donald Trump and Angela Merkel, had agreed on a LNG port, at the cost of a billion dollars, but then there was a change of regime in the two nations.

So, Germany needs energy for its homes, offices and manufacturing plants. Besides, one-third of world's potash is produced by Russia and Belarus. Then Russia is world's number 1 and 2 in wheat and oil.

So the US did succeed on its agenda on Nord Stream 2 but its policy of encirclement of Russia by NATO bases has received a critical blow in Ukraine.

So, does it serve Putin if the war goes into the winter?

It surely does.

The longer the Ukraine crisis goes, the bigger are the chances of fissures in Western ranks.

As it is, the recession is setting in. And then there is the fear of Europeans going cold and hungry during the Christmas. The streets could be full of angry people with placards and loudspeakers.

We have seen how UK has plunged into a political crisis: Its prime minister has been "stabbed" by the political class even though there is no clear picture of who would replace Boris Johnson.

I don't think though that Putin would turn off the energy supply to Europe. As its foreign minister Sergey Lavrov recently said: A wounded predator must never be provoked into wild actions—it's better to accompany it to the graveyard.

One of oft-repeated geopolitical wisdom from Napoleon for leaders in war is: Never interrupt your enemies when they make a mistake. A litany of such mistakes by West, piling on sanctions on Russia, freezing its assets, pumping Ukraine with men, money and weapons, has only drawn its rivals closer. Russia has nothing to gain by stopping the suicide. For its no longer a question if Eurasia would happen—but how quickly it does.

It won't be the same world we inherited from our ancestors.

Link to Article:

https://www.newsbred.com/is-there-a-method-in-putin-dragging-on-the-ukraine-crisis/

How Russia is Sewing Up the Heartland of Eurasia

July 30, 2022

Time to tell a few things your favourite media doesn't tell you.

Did you miss the US Secretary of State Antony Blinken wanting to speak to his Russian counterpart Sergey Lavrov in coming days?

As always the camouflage was to exchange POWs but the real reason wasn't lost on those paying attention: Blinken also wanted to know from Lavrov "the plans that Russia now has to pursue the annexation of Ukrainian territory."

This is the same Blinken who in April, when Russia's aims were modest and a deal was palpable, had roared in triumph: "(We) Want Russia weakened to the degree that it cannot do the kinds of things that it has done in invading Ukraine."

For good effect, Blinken had claimed: "Russia is failing. Ukraine is succeeding."

Cut to July now: Blinken is seeking out Lavrov who has chillingly said: "Now our goals have expanded. We seek to claim more Ukrainian territory, beyond the Donbass."

A look at World Map, please

Now I want readers to roll out the world-map with a pencil in hand: You know Mariupol is with Russia: So notice that Azov Sea is virtually with Russia and if you could spot the Kerch Strait, span how the entire Black Sea, and further the Mediterranean Sea, opens up to Moscow.

Now look closely at Caspian Sea nearby: The littoral states which surround it are Russia, Kazakhstan, Turkmenistan, Azerbaijan and Iran. The five held a Caspian Summit last month and vowed to ensure the Caspian Sea remains free of armed forces of all extra-regional powers.

Could you now run the pencil along the Volga and Don River in Russia and the canal between the two which connects to Azov and Caspian Sea.

And if the inland waterways of Russia are mapped, you see the connection going all the way up to Baltic Sea, and thus also Northern Sea: An access which allows Russia a freeway in both Atlantic and Pacific Ocean.

Naturally, the US or West is hurting. Hence Blinken seeking out Lavrov. In no small extent also after the US were kept out of door by Ukraine and Russia on a grain deal. Moscow gained applause from the world reeling under supply issues with food, oil, fertilizers etc. US sulked on the sidelines. Hence this urge to be a player in the game, somehow.

It is not the same Russia the West had vowed to destroy with sanctions and more sanctions, and what you have with travel bans and freezing of assets. The shoe now is in the other foot: Four governments in Europe have fallen while Ruble is resurgent.

Sanctions haven't deterred Russia; it has only strengthened them to be expansive in goals. Sanctions, in a way, are counterproductive if the examples of North Korea, Iran and Russia are anything to go by. A nation is awakened; self-reliance is summoned and they are out of claws of the predatory globalists with their "free trade" doublespeak.

Now a gung-ho Russia is sewing up the heartland of Eurasia with Iran in company and India at the other end. Along with Belt and Road Initiative (BRI) of China, and an agreeable Central Asia, the integration of the biggest landmass appears a reality.

Sure, the implications are not lost on the United States. They don't want any further strategic horrors which began in overstating the power of sanctions and being caught unawares when Russia planted itself in Kherson in southern Ukraine. They are queuing up in Azerbaijan to somehow drag it in its corner.

Now Russia is in no hurry to leave Ukraine which has lost 20% of its territory; about 3,000 of its villages and towns; half the GDP and a third of its coal production. Its access through its ports is at the mercy of Russian forces.

A New World Order is shaping up right in front of our eyes. The Hegemon for last century could fall for the "Thucydides Trap" and that is to initiate a war with its core enemies before it's too late.

But one suspects it's already too late. War or no war, the biggest power ever witnessed by the humanity is in irreversible decline. It would go, howsoever long and ugly is the process.

Link to Article:
https://www.newsbred.com/time-to-look-at-world-map-and-the-ukraine-war-you-missed/

Russia and Its Arctic Gambit Puts Fire at Us' Door

August 1, 2022

The United States is at its wits' end to counter Russia.

On its Navy Day yesterday, Vladimir Putin promised to revive the memory of Peter the Great and make Russia a great maritime power again.

Now you have read[1], from yours' truly, how Russia is happily flapping its wings in Azov and Black Sea as a windfall from Ukraine which grants it access to Mediterranean Sea. Its plans on Caspian Sea, with Moscow and Mumbai at two ends of INSTC (International North South Transport Corridor), on the impressive pivot to Iran, and Russia is closer to breaking free from the constraints of its vast landmass.

But great maritime power of the world? You might put it to hyperbole for a great geopolitical character who slips out every time the United States adjusts its noose to fit the irritant.

How is it even feasible with the United States, its sworn enemy, the greatest naval power humanity has ever witnessed, lords of Pacific and Atlantic Ocean, the lead character of Indo-Pacific drama etc around?

Well, we know Putin has always been the one to walk the talk: While signing the 55-page Naval Doctrine, the Russian leader has spelt out the missing jigsaw of his maritime ambition: Arctic.

Now most keep their cherished goals close to their chest, lest the enemy is forewarned, but here we have this charismatic Russian who lays it out on the table and mocks his bitter enemy to come and try if he could upset the arrangement.

Time again to cast a look at your world map, and see the vast stretch of Arctic region which seems to endow both Russia and the continental shelf of Americas with its ample length.

But now the ice is melting in Arctic and to go with Russia's big gains in ice-breakers—the United States comes nowhere near—the Bear is betting big to leap on what already is 10% of Russia's GDP and 20 percent of its exports from that continental shelf.

And if you haven't heard of Yamal—a peninsula in northwest Siberia, Russia—and its operational LNG (Liquefied Natural Gas) facility, it's time to pay attention as India is already buying it and China has put its billions to acquire 3 million tonnes of it every year.

So a melting Arctic and its immense store of energy, to go with Yamal LNG, and Russia's Northern Fleet in tow, the Kremlin is now eyeing Northern Sea Route (NSR) year-around and not just what it presently manages for a few months in summer.

The United States' Coast Guards are no match to Russia's military in this region and much as the Washington could summon Norway or Greenland for its cause (stationing its nuclear arsenal), Russia already is strutting its S-400 and nuclear missiles with the promise of Zircon hypersonic cruise missiles which travels nine times the speed of the sound and has a range of 1,000 kms.

So the neocons in Washington would now be forced to look at homeland security than pursue its adventurism currently being played out in Ukraine and one it promises soon in Taiwan.

The US' immediate bet in near future is to entangle Russia on its sovereign claim over the North Sea Route as its territorial water which is said to fall foul of United Nations Convention on the Law of the Sea (UNCLOS). Moscow could count on the support of Beijing though which itself is claiming its nine-dash line in the South China Sea.

Arctic is not just a matter of Russia breaking free from the encirclement of NATO. For in the Baltics, its ships have to confront the sea powers of Nordic states in the Gulf of Finland and the Danish

Straits. Besides, the Suez Canal route is not just more time and money consuming, its Black Sea Fleet also has to negotiate Dardanelles.

Russia is in a hurry to expand its reach in East Asian markets. Arctic LNG at a low cost is a very attractive proposition. The Northern Sea Route also frees them from looking over the shoulder on US-controlled maritime routes.

So the terms of engagements are changing. If the US is setting ones in Ukraine and Taiwan, they too would have to worry about the reach Arctic could afford to Russia and China.

Reference:

[1] https://www.newsbred.com/time-to-look-at-world-map-and-the-ukraine-war-you-missed/

Link to Article:

https://www.newsbred.com/putins-arctic-gambit-is-to-put-fire-at-the-us-door/

Russia Not a Peer to NATO? the Joke is on You Only!

September 1, 2022

Everything that we read on Russia-Ukraine thing is meant to brainwash us.

We are told[1] that Russia is "not a peer military to the US" or even smaller NATO forces. And Russia "isn't even a second-tier military power."

The fake narrative is built on the premise that it's over six month of Russia's SMO (Special Military Operation) and yet they are nowhere near to closing out Ukraine.

The truth is they withdrew from Kiev, Chernihiv, Sumy and Karkiv to drag the Ukrainian forces away from the civilians in the big metropolitan cities. Russian defence minister Sergey Shoigu said as much in the SCO (Shanghai Cooperation Organization) recently: "We strictly comply with humanitarian law during the special operation... every effort is being done to prevent civilian casualties. It certainly slows down the advance but we do it consciously."

That we didn't get to read it is quite another matter.

A country which carries the hypersonic business cards could've flattened Kiev months ago.

And lest you believe that Ukrainians successfully defended the Capital, the truth is it was the Russians who withdrew after their "feint" on Kiev fooled the Ukrainians—and NATO—in leaving its borders in the south of Ukraine.

This was mentioned in a magazine no less reputed than Marine Corps Gazette from the United States—though again you don't expect our New York Times, Washington Post, Newsweek, Foreign Affairs, Foreign Policy, the Atlantic or Council on Foreign Relations to bring us the truth.

Twitter too carried it but the shameless Western media won't pick it up lest their house of fake cards crumbles.

The piece[2] explains the early Russian move towards Kiev as a feint. It sent over a lakh Ukrainian soldiers scrambling towards the Capital in its defence allowing the Russian troops from Crimea to move in unopposed and link the island with a land bridge to the Donbass. Alongside, a big presence in Kherson, on the west of Dnieper, was established.

Russia, in control of south and east, could thus inflict massive damage on Ukrainian forces.

The Casualty on Casualties

We then read quite regularly that while Ukraine has lost some 8,000-9,000 troops the Russian casualties are mounting upwards of 80,000.

Now analysts are unanimous that Russia is firing 10,000 artillery shells on an average in a day, down from a peak of 20,000 when the campaign to claim Luhansk was at full throttle.

So, 10,000-20,000 rounds per day implies nearly 500,000 rounds per month by the Russians. The Ukrainian counter ratio of fire is 100 to 1. So who is going to believe the absurd figures we come to read in our media?

It simply doesn't add up.

Russia's plan all along has been to minimize civilian casualties and demilitarise Ukraine.

Russia has been slow for a reason: Ukraine, on the other hand, has almost been flattened on infrastructure; suffered massive casualties and towns and cities have surrendered. Airfields, depots, fortified areas and defence industry sites have been crippled. Millions have flown across the border. The economy has tanked. It needed the goodwill of its arch enemy to be able to export grain across its borders.

Russia, once in full control of Donbass would benefit from its enormous land, natural resources and industrial power. They would then secure Nikolaev, Odessa and Kharkov. They have been highly organized, disciplined and patient on the mission. For all we know, they might play a new card in the winter whose footsteps we could hear.

Where the Russians can't beat the West is in the propaganda war. The latter are masters in manufacturing illusions across all pipelines of information which reach us. To the extent that even in this dire moment when the West is unravelling, it's been able to thump its chest in triumph and worse, make us believe it too.

The truth is the days of land wars are over. At least in States of some size. Since Iraq, 20 years ago, the science on war has taken a quantum leap. Vietnam and Afghanistan were no aberrations.

And nobody wins a nuclear war.

So what's happening here? Well, the military industry is fattening itself which has governments in compliance. Lives lost matter little. Masses are powerless, would remain powerless, since the institutions ignore them with contempt. You could have your demonstrations but little changes on the surface. Meanwhile shameless media would keep lining their pockets from powers and we the powerless.

Disgusted? Well, I am.

Reference:

[1] https://www.ndtv.com/world-news/putins-war-in-ukraine-unravels-russias-superpower-image-3281734

[2] https://www.nakedcapitalism.com/2022/08/a-marines-assessment-of-russias-military-operation-in-ukraine-a-profound-appreciation-of-all-three-realms-in-which-wars-are-waged.html

Link to Article:

https://www.newsbred.com/the-joke-that-russia-is-not-a-peer-military-to-us-nato-is-on-us-only/

What Did Putin Mean By Wolf's Tail?

September 8, 2022

It caught my attention when Vladimir Putin mentioned "wolf's tail" in case the European Union goes ahead with a cap on Russia's energy exports now that West's sanctions have had little effect.

Well, this particular folktale "Sister Fox and Brother Wolf" is a delightful one where the Wolf cunningly breaks to pieces the Fox's sledge and eats up the bull also. The Fox has its revenge: First it collects a large amount of fish and when the Wolf asks for a similar bounty, the Fox asks the Wolf to let his tail rotate back and forth in an ice hole and say "'come and be caught, fish, big and small". The Wolf did likewise while the Fox chanted "Freeze, freeze Wolf's tail." And thus the Wolf's tail was frozen to the ice and the Fox called out the villagers who came running with pokers, prongs and axes and killed the Wolf.

So, the antagonists in this children's tale are Fox and Wolf and in our present geopolitical context, it's Russia and West (US/Europe/Germany—take your pick, it's the same thing).

It was Germany which at the US' persuasion blocked the Nord Stream 2 which needed just a "push of button" to turn it functional.

Now Russia has stopped the energy supply of Nord Stream 1 for repairs—a pipelines which stretches 1,200km under the Baltic Sea and carries energy supply from St. Petersburg to north-eastern Germany. At its optimum, it supplies 170 m cubic metres of gas per day from Russia to Germany.

The threat of a price cap on Russian energy exports—which the EU deliberates on Friday—has met with a blunt response from Putin: "we won't be supplying anything if it runs counter to our interests."

Readers, you could say: How the West is wolf here? At best it's tit for tat from the two arch enemies.

Well, there is something more which Putin said and which never reached us because of the heavily censored Russian content by the Western media outlets and the Social Media giants such as Facebook, Twitter. YouTube, Instagram etc.

Putin, while addressing the plenary session of the Eastern Economic Forum (EEF), said on Wednesday that the West had indulged in "another outrageous deceit" in connection with the "grain deal" which allowed Ukraine's grain to be exported at the initiative of Turkey and Russia on United Nation's request.

Putin alleged that all the agricultural products shipped from Ukraine went to EU countries whereas Russia and the poorest economies were "merely ditched."

Thus, it hasn't helped the global food prices, growing all the time because of sanctions on Russia's exports. Ironically, those sanctioning are the very nations which are benefitting from the largesse of Russia.

"It is a cunningly drawn-up, sophisticated design when no sanctions appear to be in place, but there are restrictions related to logistics, vessel chartering, funding, and insurance," Putin said.

Further, "it is obvious that with this approach the scale of problems with food products in the world will only grow, unfortunately, to our great regret, which is capable of leading to an unprecedented humanitarian catastrophe."

So it is this deceit and chicanery which has led to Putin relating it to "wolf's tail."

There is an interesting background to the mention of wolf.

In the 19th century Russia, humans often came across wolves and lost lives on its mammoth wilderness. It left an imprint on Russian culture which lasts to this day.

Indeed, the way humans interpreted the gaze of this deadly beast of prey became a marker of what it meant to be a Russian. Importantly, it represented a sense of "otherness" in relation to Western Europe. The likes of Dostoevsky (The Brothers Karamazov in 1880), Tolstoy (Nikolai Rostov's wolf hunt in War and Peace), Chekov etc all have had space for this predator in their literary efforts.

In passing, when three of Tolstoy's son posed with the carcasses of nine wolves they had shot dead in the winter of 1900-1901, it was an assertion of their domination over a large pack of wolves.

The German association with Wolves is also important for our understanding. Not many know that during the reign of Catherine the Great, herself of German origin, a fair number of Germans emigrated to Russia in 1764. Thousands of Germans were encouraged to have autonomous colonies in barely populated districts north of the Black Sea, near Volga River.

It all changed in 1870s when a program of Russianization was undertaken to break the cultural exclusiveness of the German colonies and thus integrate them into the Russian society. It led to more than a lakh Russian Germans emigrating to the United States where they primarily settled in the Great Plains region.

Now a lot of these folktales of German-Russians revolves around wolves. They have international themes and motifs, more so in happy stories on wolves. However, the tragic wolf tales are exclusively a part of Russian literature and folktales—and they are not part of international folklore.

But now Putin has brought the Reference: on a geopolitical forum. It tells us how much we need to know about Russia and we can't with the "pipeline of information" being turned off by the Western Media and Social Media giants at the official EU diktat.[1]

The Russia Today (RT) in France went to EU's Court of Justice against the EU's sanctions, stating it has "no legal basis and violate the principle of free expression." But the Court dismissed their plea[2], ruling "there has been no infringement of RT France's right to be heard."

And so this is our "free world" bereft of any "censorship" or any suppression of "freedom of expression!"

We weren't wiser by the episode of Julian Assange nor we are by one-sided narrative of last few months. As the drumbeats of World War III get louder, and closer, citizens ought to demand free information too.

Reference:

[1] https://www.wsj.com/livecoverage/russia-ukraine-latest-news-2022-03-09/card/eu-orders-removal-of-russian-state-owned-media-from-search-results-social-media-reshares-Nxb4WXbCaQnCUMmL9Mvk

[2] https://www.rferl.org/a/rt-france-european-court-justice-ban/31961982.html

Link to Article:

https://www.newsbred.com/what-did-putin-mean-by-wolfs-tail/

Ukraine and the Taurian lands

September 12, 2022

Indian Express is almost triumphant in a front page headline today that "…Russia leaves Kharkiv."

Others in Lutyens Media too would make us believe as if Ukraine is about to take over the Kremlin.

But we would let it go as its cheerleaders job to go skimpy.

Let's look at the Ukraine situation closely. The map shows a significant advance by the Ukraine's "million-soldiers army", as Zelensky is fond of saying, through hundreds of miles towards Crimea-Donetsk-Luhansk belt where Russia has massed its men and weaponry.

The trouble is none of the bugle-blowers of West—our New York Times, Washington Post, AP, Reuters or their Indian partners in crime—are bothering to tell us what Russia has meant all along by its operative term "defensive."

Nor they are letting us look at the common history of Russia which sucked in the armies of Napoleon and Hitler, enmeshed them in a cobweb so to say, and stopped the unstoppables.

After months of impasse, we are suddenly seeing a surge of Ukrainian advance along hundreds of miles but one is overlooking a simple thread in this equation: That in doing so, Ukrainian forces are being drawn further and further away from their stronghold towards East and have exposed their soldiers to a meat-grinder.

Ukraine has no air-power to shepherd its moving forces—not a comprehensive one anyway—but at the same time they are moving closer to Russia's Close-Air-Support range. Sure, Ukraine has MANPADS (Man Portable Air Defense System) but they would be no better than target practice for Russia's all-weather Mi-28, ironically named "Havoc" by none other than West or for that matter Sukhoi Su-25—NATO calls it FrogFoot—which was most recently seen in Syrian War. (Ukraine did shoot down a low-flying Su-25 a few days ago in Balakleya, Kharkiv—presently their bragging point—but only a fool would take it as a template).

So where else the triumphant moving Ukrainian army could get the cover? The truth is the further East they go, lesser would be the artillery support. Long-range artillery would be required which is not easy to summon all-around. Further, how do you engage in resupplies if you move away from the comfort of your rear which has stocks? And conversely, how do you deny Russians with the bigger firepower, the more you move closer to them?

That old geography is also being overlooked in all this chest-thumping. Unlike central Europe, which has a terrain and topological features where one could dug in in static defense, once you leave crowded cities in Ukraine, there is open steppe with a few rivers and forests which are pretty small. And what happens when winter descends and those forests are stripped off their greenery and vegetation? Target-practice for meat-grinders, nothing else.

The truth is, Ukraine is best served if they hide behind "human shield" of cities but once they leave this comfort, its walk into the death-trap.

Now the question is, why Ukraine is ignoring the obvious and why the West is doing nothing to knock sense in Zelensky's head?

As we all know, the US secretary of state Antony Blinken visited Kiev a few days ago. Sure, something needed to be done to quieten the disquiet on the monstrous spend bleeding the United States into recession. Besides, president Joe Biden desperately needs a cheer in the fast-approaching midterm elections in the US. There has to be a trophy to justify the "black hole" in which West is being drained of its money and material.

Besides, Zelensky has every reason to fear a coup. He wants the discontent to fall in line and show to NATO how he has managed this tactical advance. But tactical advance or Russian retreat is a misnomer. It's only a move on the chessboard which is not winning the war.

I could be wrong but I have a feeling Ukraine is being royally cooked in this cauldron. Its army is sacrificial lamb in this heinous and dangerous adventure. Zelensky would care little if it costs immense human lives. The Russian design, all along, has been to minimize its loss of men and civilians across the frontlines. One could replace weaponry but men once lost are lost. Russia would prefer the Ukrainian army to be out in open, even if it means retreat, as long as the enemy could be encircled and vaporised.

That's what Russia arguably means with its Special Military Operation (SMO) and defensive goals. They are looking for "Taurian Lands"—Crimea, the northern Black Sea and the Azov Sea—secured in the next few weeks or months. Odessa is important for the contours of Novorossiya (the southern Ukraine) to be firmed up—not to say a solution to the Transnistria (the Moldova breakaway state) issue.

They haven't waited for winter for nothing.

We are not told that Russia hasn't yet brought out its mechanised and armoured forces. They are not letting us think why Russia hasn't done anything to push back even as this Ukraine advance was well-known in advance. That this could be an ingenious Russian plan, a trap where they would concede terrain and pull in the Ukrainians into a web of mobile defenses.

Next few days would bring home the truth. Bridges would go up in smoke to leave the Ukrainians stranded. A massacre could happen which should make the entire humanity sad for this was a War which could have been so easily avoided on a negotiating table.

Link to Article:

https://www.newsbred.com/russia-leaves-kharkiv-another-instance-of-we-being-fooled/

Central Asia is of Pivotal Interest to Global Powers

September 14, 2022

If you look at the world map, you would see the powers controlling the seas are our West.

It's in their interest that land mass called Eurasia doesn't come together.

It could help explain you the various revolutions and coups; anarchy and chaos which frequently make headlines in our neighbourhood and are window-dressed as "liberation" and "democracy" to earn the drugged citizenry's consent.

So these powers which control us term the SCO (Shanghai Cooperation Organization) as no better than a "regional summit" never mind its **members** (Russia, China, India, Pakistan and now Iran—along with "Stans" of Central Asia – Uzbekistan, Kyrgyzstan, Tajikistan, Kazakhstan); to go with **Observer nations** (Belarus, Mongolia, Afghanistan) and **Dialogue Partners** (Armenia, Cambodia, Azerbaijan, Nepal, Turkey, Sri Lanka and soon Egypt) are more than half of world's population.

That this derision comes from the Powers who themselves are no better than 10-15% of humanity is par for course.

A caution is in order if your blinkered view of the two-day SCO Summit in Samarkand, Uzbekistan (September 15-16) sees it a political and military alliance as a counterweight to West.

At best you could term it as the oncoming of a multipolar world against the unipolarity of the United States where wars and repressions are traded for cooperation on reducing poverty, ensuring food, health and energy through mutual dialogue.

It's just not cooperation on building trade routes and supply chains, or becoming a piece amongst a set of networks like BRI, BRICS, EAEU, EEF, INSTC or Pakafuz Railway. It might not register readily in your mind but I suggest you look for them.

After all, you wouldn't have missed the trading in national currencies which Ruble and Yuan handle with aplomb and India's Rupee is now a gleeful partner in this enterprise. These new transit corridors in works would be a waste if Dollar, Swift or your IMFs/WTOs/WBs bring it to a grief: So we might hear more on plans on a new common currency in next couple of days. (EU too has Euro, so don't treat it as a girding up loins by SCO actors.)

Think about it: Won't it be good that what happened to North Africa or West Asia —our Yemen, Syria, Libya, Iraq etc—doesn't happen to Central Asia?

It's an absolute priority of Russia and China, the two allies driving this convergence who could well have been rivals some other day in this region. China also has Xinjiang in mind which has long been in the eye of the West.

These actors don't want chaos at the door—like India who was extremely upset when Afghanistan was "thrown under the bus." Central Asia, needless to add, too don't want trouble at home. Nobody has missed the recent trouble in Kazakhstan which was squashed by the Russia-led CSTO (Collective Security Treaty Organization).

The truth is, in the 21 years of SCO's existence, multi-tiered, multi-sector cooperation mechanisms are being hammered into place. In recent Eastern Economic Forum (EEF) in Vladivostok, SCO's interpolation with the ASEAN (Association of Southeast Asian Nations) was discussed at length.

The beauty of this multipolar vision is that nobody is being coerced. China proposes a free trade zone but is ok if there are reservations; Uzbekistan is holding itself back on EAEU but Russia has no problem with it. The integration—free movement of goods, people, services and capital—could happen in time but an organic way fits like a glove with this vision of a multipolar world.

India and Asia's Century

There is much to look forward to Indian prime minister Narendra Modi's presence in the summit to see how far his vision of 21st-century-is-Asia's is advanced.

India badly wants INSTC which frees it from the geographical shackles and links Mumbai with Moscow, opening up the Eurasia's land route for its growing economic might. It would make India a credible player in Russian Far East, in the multipolar hub.

India all along has stressed QUAD as one of collective peace and development, striking a dissonant note from West's war games. India looks for political stability and not confrontation in its neighbourhood. China too doesn't want mutual differences to come in the way of a larger vision.

India this year would be heading the SCO interbank consortium where partners use a credit line from the Bank of China. It is also engaged in setting up a free trade agreement with the EAEU.

Look at this from a vantage position and it would all make sense. Central Asia doesn't have outlet to sea, it's in their interest that intra-trade picks up. Iran already has over a thousand companies operational in this region.

Host Uzbekistan has much to spur its growth. The venue Samarkand once was the heart of silk road before "maritime silkroad" took the world over. Timur, for those conversant with history would recall, held sway from northern India to Black Sea.

It dazzled Alexander the Great in 329 BC; its golden peaches were craved by the Middle Kingdom. This is a setting which would befit Modi, Xi and Putin on the same platform: The lost history of heritage once again defining the future.

Link to Article:

https://www.newsbred.com/sco-in-samarkand-please-pay-heed-this-is-about-your-future/

SCO: The Military Arm of a Multipolar World

September 17, 2022

Below could be a help in what you did and what you didn't read from the SCO Summit in Samarkand (September 15-16, 2022) this morning.

★ What you've read is a lament on no mention of UN Charter1 (Indian Express) in the Samarkand Declaration: That is, an attempt to show this as a renegades' pow-wow against the global order.

Well, this "global order" hasn't sent its peacekeepers in the war zones of Ukraine, to keep belligerents apart and civilians alive. We could only guess if the US really has biolabs in Ukraine or if the weapons supplied to the Kiev regime by over 40 countries involve "prohibited" weapons in the checklist of UN.

★ We are told with certain glee that prime minister Narendra Modi ignored2 China's XI Jinping or that there was no cheer from India on its core BRI (Belt and Road Initiative) policy.

Well, I don't know how Xi's words that China seeks "dialogue between civilisations and seek common ground while shelving differences" should be read.

And in case you are still spending time on the supposed cold vibes between Modi and Xi, it would do well to remember Indian prime minister highlighting the "unprecedented energy and food"[3] problem partly due to the "Ukraine Crisis" which I am sure we all know is not caused by the Beijing but by the massive US sanctions on Russia.

- ★ You might have read Modi emphasizing on 30% GDP and 40% population in the ambit of SCO members but it's also gainful to remember that world's largest energy reserves as well as major energy-consuming nations were present in Samarkand.
- ★ What you mustn't have read is that all SCO members wanted "all parties" to comply with the 2015 Iran nuclear deal which the US, an original signatory, left in 2018 to slap sanctions on Iran. Now the US is back on the negotiation table, looking ways to revive the nuclear deal but marathon talks have led to nowhere.
- ★ Or for that matter that it's not just Russia (Rubles), China (Yuan) or India (Rupee) but also Turkey (Lira) which is looking for trade in local currencies.
- ★ Or that the members have begun a process to admit Belarus to the SCO. Or in case you missed, Iran was formally anointed as ninth member of the grouping and was the star of the show.
- ★ Or when XI said in his address that the SCO would work to prevent outside forces (read US/NATO) from organising *Colour Revolutions* (coups) in their countries. Xi also mentioned China and Russia as "responsible global powers"—implied the other is not—against a unipolar worldview.
- ★ Or that this so-called regional grouping is now increasingly looking international: Saudi Arabia, Qatar and Egypt will formally become SCO dialogue partner; negotiations would be held in granting Bahrain, the Maldives and other states' on a similar status.
- ★ Or that Iranian president Ebrahim Raeisi, whom Modi met for a private session, has called on SCO member states to adopt new approaches to confront the US' unilateralism and "cruel sanctions".

The Big Picture

Try to look at the big picture this way: Trade requires infrastructure and transit corridors and "indivisible security" which the SCO members have committed themselves to: Expect Eurasia to buzz with networks in the making from Indian Ocean to Sea of Oman to Persian Gulf to Caspian Sea and even beyond.

"Indivisible security" could be easily understood for Azerbaijan vs Armenia would still be fresh in mind even if Kazakhstan (January) or eruptions in Tajikistan (May), Uzbekistan (June) is a distant memory.

All this would require financial transactions which are in works despite the sanctions on Russia. An Eastern Commodity Exchange could well be established in Vladivostok to facilitate trade in Asia- Pacific.

All this is a vision of a multipolar world—a multilateral trading system against unilateral protectionist measures.

It's also certain that the pressure on the trio of China-Russia-Iran would now be exponential by the Hegemon: As it would be on India now that it refuses to tow Washington's lines.

The approaching winter could well be a trailer to our world in increasing churn.

Reference:

[1] https://indianexpress.com/article/india/on-ukraine-india-has-been-invoking-un-charter-but-no-mention-in-joint-declaration-8156133/

[2] https://www.rediff.com/news/report/modi-ignores-xi-in-samar-kand/20220916.htm

[3] https://www.ifp.co.in/india/world-facing-unprecedented-food-crisis-pm-modi-at-sco-summit-in-samarkand

Link to Article:

https://www.newsbred.com/china-russia-iran-would-be-more-in-the-eye-of-west-and-so-could-be-india/

The Great Game of the Energy Crisis in Europe

September 21, 2022

World was never the same when France (Napoleon) and Germany (Hitler) came to Russia in winter in wars: Now it's again winter and again war and it's going to be a pivotal moment in our history.

European Union has put a plan of austerity for its citizens in view of the soaring energy prices: Lower heating temperatures, pre-scheduled blackout, lower economic activity etc to pull through this winter.

It hasn't failed to vilify Russia for "weaponizing energy" never mind the Nord Stream is "un-operational" because Canada and Germany between them are refusing to deliver the repaired turbine to Gazprom, the Russian energy provider, under the pretext of sanctions.

It also didn't term the Kiev regime—the one they are arming and stuffing funds with—for "weaponizing energy" when Zelensky stopped the supply of Gazprom deliveries to Europe through Soyuz gas pipeline in Luhansk in May for three months.

So what's happening here? if the dreaded winter is so much feared on a Continent which relies on Russia for 40% of its energy needs—Germany's 72% needs—and whose import cost is 200 times more than it was last year, why Europe is intent on committing suicide with its eyes wide open?

So let's first take stock of how dire is the situation is before looking at the Great Game of this self-created energy crisis.

The Financial Times tells us that Gazprom today is supplying only about 84 million cubic meters of gas to European customers via Ukraine and Turkey per day, down from 480 million cubic meters last year.

Goldman Sachs said a week back: "The market continues to underestimate the depth, the breadth and the structural repercussions of the energy crisis—we believe the repercussions will be even deeper than the 1970s oil crisis."

BlackRock is of the opinion that the "energy crunch will drive a recession in Europe…and the crisis has worsened."

Alexis Tsipras, the Greek prime minister between 2015-2019, believes that "Europe and our world is entering a prolonged cold war with huge economic consequences" and EU could face "existential problems."

"We need to re-evaluate the sanctions. Were the measures correct or are we shooting ourselves in the foot?"

Viktor Orban, prime minister of Hungary, is aghast that EU wants to extend the sanctions by another six months later in autumn. It could force 40% of European industry to shut down this winter:

In other words, Recession.

"The way things are going now, the Eurozone and the EU itself could cease to exist by 2030," said Orban.

The former US president Donald Trump is as blunt as only he could be: Germany could soon cease to exist as a country, he said.

Marine Le Pen, the second most important political figure in France, is exasperated: "The European Union sees its promises of prosperity and peace sinking in its economic, energy and geopolitical mistakes."

There are two interconnected issues at play here:

One, clearly the European Union is not prepared to abandon its "Green agenda" come what way.

Two, why this "Green agenda" is being pursued even when "Western people could "harvest grief in full due to their governments," as being warned by Dmitry Medvedev, the ex-Russian president?

The "Green agenda" and the so-called "Climate Crisis" has been assiduously built over the last decade. The goal is to wean Europe away from Russia on its energy needs of coal, oil and gas and make the Old Continent dependent on the United States.

One, it brings massive revenue to Washington's coffers; Two, it keeps Europe no better than a vassal entity of the Hegemon.

As I often say, if Europe gets out of US control, the Hegemon loses the world: It gives Washington the foothold to meddle in world affairs. Europe through NATO, and now Gas, are two weapons essential for US supremacy– even survival.

Even though fossil fuel-free Europe by 2030 remains a noble goal, the truth is the Western civilization would collapse without oil and gas in the short term, said by no less than Elon Musk.

First let's look at the windfall filling up the US coffers in the Ukraine crisis.

The Business Insider tells us that US companies are making more than $100 million per container ship of liquefied natural gas (LNG) bound for Europe.

The vassal, that is Europe, is hoping to somehow survive this crisis till 2024 and the captive media is keen to sing lullaby in the ears of citizenry for the duration of this painful transition.

Already, the European leaders are beating their chest in triumph: Suddenly, the general refrain is we have enough stocks and we would get through this winter.

Goldman Sachs, in a stunning U-turn, now says that Europe has "successfully solved" its gas shortage crisis and has plenty of reserve capacity.

German Chancellor Olaf Scholz is also upbeat stating Germany would "get through this winter" and be energy independent from Russia by 2023.

Even financial minnows of EU, like Czech Republic is telling its parliamentarians that the country has sufficient energy supplies for the winter.

While the European leaders are relying on their citizens' naivety—or stupidity, if you may—the truth is energy infrastructure isn't built in a day. It takes months, even years, to build pipelines, renewable sources and nuclear reactors.

It's not just this winter: But at least next two years when the Europeans would face untold hardships.

Meanwhile, the US is reportedly set to expand its gas exporting capacity as three new projects are underway.

Tsipras says it as it is: "The US is not losing neither economically nor geo-strategically."

So this is the "Great Reset" of Klaus Schwab (look for him) and his World Economic Forum: To de-industrialize Europe for a "world government" run by the Hegemon.

It was in 2016 when the Obama administration encouraged massive export of LNG out of his country's huge shale gas production. The LNG terminals take a good five years to build and Poland and Hungary in the EU straightaway went for it.

Now the next great act of this "energy deal"—at the behest of big money and banking, with politicians as tools—is being played out in front of us.

It's the European citizenry which alone can stop this madness: Provided they come out of the stupor and avoid the fate of a rodent in a warm tub, getting hotter by the second.

Link to Article:
https://www.newsbred.com/why-eu-is-committing-suicide-with-eyes-wide-open/

Russia or US: Who has been flouting UN Charter?

September 25, 2022

There has been a deliberate misleading attempt by India's mainstream media, none more than *Indian Express*, to show that India is finally losing its cool with Russia on the Ukraine Crisis.

The latest remark by India's foreign minister Dr. S. Jaishankar in the UN General Assembly on the Ukraine issue—"We-are-on-the-side-that-respects-the-UN-Charter-and-it's-founding-principles"—is another kite these foot soldiers would run wild with in our mental lawns.

So Russia or the United States: Who is disrespectful to the UN Charter?

Before we-the-brainwashed press the button on Russia, let's step back and look at the sequence of events:

In 2014, the legitimate regime in Kiev was changed not by people's revolution but through a coup by elites which is now known as "Euromaidan." It was engineered[1] by the United States which was a direct violation of the UN Charter (Article 39).

Alarmed at the hostilities unleashed on mostly Russian-inhabited eastern region of Ukraine by the propped up illegitimate Kiev regime—all those shelling, terror attacks, atrocities etc.—Russia got Germany and France on the board to broker a peace deal known as the 2015 Minsk Agreement.

But the guarantors just sat on their bums as the killings intensified in Donetsk and Luhansk which the UN itself numbers today as 14,000 killed since 2014. Talk of respecting the UN Charter—2(3): Neither

OSCE (Organization for Security and Cooperation in Europe) nor the Normandy Format[2] did anything for peace.

With no end in sight, increasing belligerence on the part of Ukraine, and the prodding of the West which now wanted it to join the NATO—a clear red-line as Russia had been assured against by the US leaders—Vladimir Putin proposed two treaties in December 2021: Modest demands seeking Russia's national security fully compatible with the UN Charter.

But both proposals were thrown out of window by US president Joe Biden and the NATO chief Jens Stoltenberg: Again, a violation of Article 2(4) of the UN Charter for refusing to grant such assurances.

It was intended to push Russia to the wall which it did in defense of its security. That Russia would resort to a military intervention in such an eventuality was foreseen by America's own top geopolitical guns such as Henry Kissinger and George F Kennan.

Russia didn't leave the talk-table even as it launched its Special Military Operation (SMO). There was hope for a breakthrough within weeks in Russo-Ukrainian talks in Istanbul.

But soon Kiev went cold on peace proposals and alongside, the West stepped up support by way of funds, intelligence and weapons supply. It vowed for war and to bleed Russia[3] as a solution to the crisis.

Now let's look at how much adherence to UN Charter—practically the world's constitution—the United States has followed since the end of Cold War in 1990s.

How much do you think the wars on Iraq (on the fake trumped up charge of Weapons of Mass Destruction); Libya (the fake Benghazi narrative) or Syria (where the United States still has boots on the ground) or supply of weapons to Saudi Arabia (against Yemen, arguably the biggest humanitarian crisis this century) flouts the sanctity of UN Charter?

(Michael Ratner, president Center for Constitutional Rights, termed the Syrian intervention as a war crime. "The kind of crime that the Germans were tried for at Nuremberg")

Or if the bombings on civilians for months on hapless Serbians during the Yugoslavia War was in accordance to UN Charter?

Or when a "country" like Kosovo was carved out of Serbia against all internationally accepted rules?

How would you view it an adherence to UN Charter when unilateral sanctions are slapped on countries like Cuba, Iran, Venezuela and Russia and they remain in vogue even when an unprecedented crisis like Covid-19 leaves millions of hapless citizens hungry or killed; homeless and destitute? (Even the UN secretary-general Antonio Guterres' request to suspend such unilateral sanctions went unattended).

How much do you think Guantanamo Bay and Abu Ghraib is respect to UN Charter for its kidnappings, horrific torture and illegal detention camps? Or the illegal drone attacks which violate the sanctity of nations? Or the AUKUS Agreement violating the Nuclear Non-Proliferation Treaty (NPT)?

How legal do you think are the arms sale to Taiwan even as the United States vows for "One China" policy?

The US has refused to sign or ratify many a foundational international laws and treaties which most of the world adheres to: Rome Statute of the International Criminal Court (ICC); CEDAW (for non-discrimination against women); ICESCR (on economic, social and cultural rights); CRC (rights of the child); ICRMW (for protection of migrant workers); PAROS (prevention of arms race in outer space); ILO (majority of labour conventions) etc.

Funnily, the United States tries to hold other countries accountable on UN mandated treaties even while not being a part of it: Such as UNCLOS in the South China Sea against the Beijing. Or not following its mandates in its own territorial waters!

Says Alfred de Zayas, an expert on UN laws: "The US only gives lip service to the (UN) charter and at the same time tries to invoke a different 'rules-based order' which is nothing other than a set of rules unilaterally imposed on the rest of the world by the US and its allies."

(To be continued)

Reference:

[1] https://euvsdisinfo.eu/report/the-us-has-recognised-euromaidan-as-a-coup-controlled-by-us-officials/

[2] https://en.wikipedia.org/wiki/Normandy_Format#:~:text=The%20Normandy%20Format%20(French:%20Format,the%20wider%20Russo-Ukrainian%20War.

[3] https://sputnikglobe.com/20220921/putin-wests-goal-is-to-weaken-disunite-and-destroy-russia—1101028273.html

Link to Article:

https://www.newsbred.com/russia-or-us-who-has-been-flouting-un-charter-with-disdain/

Referendums Are Perfectly in Sync with UN Charter

September 28, 2022

Before the referendums in four regions (Donetsk, Luhansk, Kherson, Zaporizhzhia) took place which would make them Oblast (administrative unit) of the Russian Federation soon, most grappled with the unease if it adhered to the UN Charter; much like they had disapproved the Russian boots in Ukraine as an infringement on latter's sovereignty.

In the first piece, I had outlined how far out of place the United States has been in flouting the UN Charter in last few decades. I would now take up Russia's position to offer a comparison.

Let's first look at Donetsk and Luhansk which had thrown off the yoke of the Kiev regime much earlier before panning on Kherson and Zaporizhzhia whose sentiments to be freed have rather been recent.

All these four regions—call them east or south-east of Ukraine were attached to the satellite state of Ukraine by the USSR for administrative purposes after the Second World War. They have historically been the Novorossiya (New Russia), a term used to define this region north of Black Sea and Crimea.

Now here are the point for readers' attention which could clear a lot of mist:

Once the Soviet Union fell, the Ukrainian parliament announced its independence in August, 1991. The held a referendum on December 1, 1991 in which nearly 84 per cent of Donetsk's suffrage voted in favour of independence.

In 1994, a referendum was held in Donetsk and Luhansk in which 90% voted for recognition of Russian as the official language: This referendum was annulled by the Kiev government.

Now fast forward to 2014 when a US-orchestrated coup was staged to overthrow the legally elected Ukrainian government and the Constitution as it stood was abrogated. (Crimea had the similar grouse of existing constitution being annulled.) In response a referendum on Donetsk status was held on May 11, 2014: Nearly 90% voted for political independence from Kiev.

But then the puppet Kiev government and the US-led collective West declared it illegal, like they had done on referendums by people of Crimea in 1991, 1994 and 2014 who had voted by 90% for autonomy or independence before Russia accepted them as part of their federation.

Same had been the story on Luhansk but interestingly Russia, which has been demonized as an imperial rogue under Vladimir Putin, didn't recognize Donetsk or Luhansk all this while.

It would interest readers that Putin, the so-called Hitler incarnate, had similarly not recognized the independence of South Ossetia before Georgia went for its "ethnic cleansing" operation in August 2008. Similarly, Transnistria voted 97% for reunification with Russia first in 2006 and then in 2014 and this appeal again went unheeded by Moscow.

Now let's look at the case of Kherson and Zaporizhzhia which would soon be no longer Ukrainian provinces. The two again are heavily Russian-populated region which, like Donetsk and Lugansk, had suffered the ban on teaching and using Russian language by the Kiev regime. Interestingly, it's these two regions who were the first to ask for referendum after the Kiev regime dissolved all political parties and launched a murderous assault for the "purification of the population for collaborating with the enemy."

As for Russia putting its boots on the Ukrainian territory what option was it left with after the UN and West brokered 2015 Minsk Agreements remained on paper only while the indiscriminate shelling and terrorist attacks by the neo-Nazis accounted for 14,000 of Donbass civilians killed in a matter of two years, an admission made by the UN itself.

What option Russia was left with after the "red line" of NATO-izing its neighbourhood was crossed and two of its proposals for a peaceful solution in Ukraine in December last year was thrown in the bin?

Be as it may, let's look at the International law on the present matter as per the UN and other global conventions.

1. The right of people to self-determination is affirmed in Article 1 of the UN Charter, and thereafter in Article 55.
2. The International Covenant on Economic, Social and Cultural Rights and the International Covenant on Civil and Political Rights (1966) says: "States…are required to facilitate the realization of the right of people to self-determination themselves."
3. The signatories of the Helsinki Act accept that the principle of territorial integrity and people's right to self-determination is not contradictory.
4. The International Court of Justice, in 2010, issued an advisory which stated that the "scope of the principle of territorial integrity is therefore limited to the sphere of interstate relations."
5. The Venice Commission of the Council of Europe indeed on a request of the Catalan government clarified five years ago that a minimum threshold on the number of participants in a referendum was unnecessary. (Though in the present case, all four regions in question have voted in the range of 80-90% plus to be part of the Russian Federation.)
6. Indeed, as per the judgment of the International Court of Justice in 1995, not just Ukraine and Russia but other signatory countries—such as France, Poland etc.—ought to facilitate such a desire for self-determination of people.

But here we have the case of West declaring the present referendums as "sham" and "illegal."

Now let's look at how "sham" is this view itself when weighed on the scale of conduct of Western nations.

- ★ The United States instigated the Albanian diaspora in Serbia to pronounce the secession of Kosovo and Metochia in 2008 but then it wasn't dubbed as a "sham referendum." No legal or political outcry occurred.
- ★ NATO nations, in a blink of an eye, recognized the legitimacy of the Slovenian and Croatian independence after lighting the war to destroy Yugoslavia.
- ★ France has been vocal against the referendums in Ukraine now or when it was the case with Crimea. But they had no qualms in annexing Mayotte in 2011 which was in defiance of resolutions 3291, 3385 and 31/4 of the UN General Assembly expressing the unity of the Comoros and prohibiting France in plain words from organizing the referendum in Mayotte.
- ★ Let's look at Germany, again at the forefront in "shaming" the referendums in Ukraine. It had no qualms in annexing five eastern German states (Brandenburg, Mecklenburg-Western Pomerania, Saxony, Saxony-Ahald, Thuringia) without any consultation 30 years ago. This was done without referendum, so to say.
- ★ So the United States goes to town rubbishing these referendums but it had kept its peace when the Catalans had their referendum only five years ago, in 2017.

The truth is these four regions of Novorossiya were at the mercy of butchers. It was a fit case for Minsk Agreements to have been honoured; or for the UN to monitor these referendums. In eight years between 2014-2022, the Donetsk and Luhansk regions held their elections independently, and even invited observers from abroad: It's another matter that OSCE (Organization for Security and Cooperation in Europe) had flatly refused.

(Concluded)

Reference:

[1] https://www.newsbred.com/russia-or-us-who-has-been-flouting-un-charter-with-disdain/

Link to Article:

https://www.newsbred.com/ukraine-referendums-why-they-are-legal-in-eyes-of-un-charter/

Nord Stream Sabotage is History's Pivotal Moment

September 30, 2022

The world, including India, face a catastrophe due to the turn the Ukraine Crisis has taken this week.

Your vile media hasn't told you about the implications of Russia's gas supply to Europe being sabotaged, now that both Nord Stream 1 and 2 are out of service.

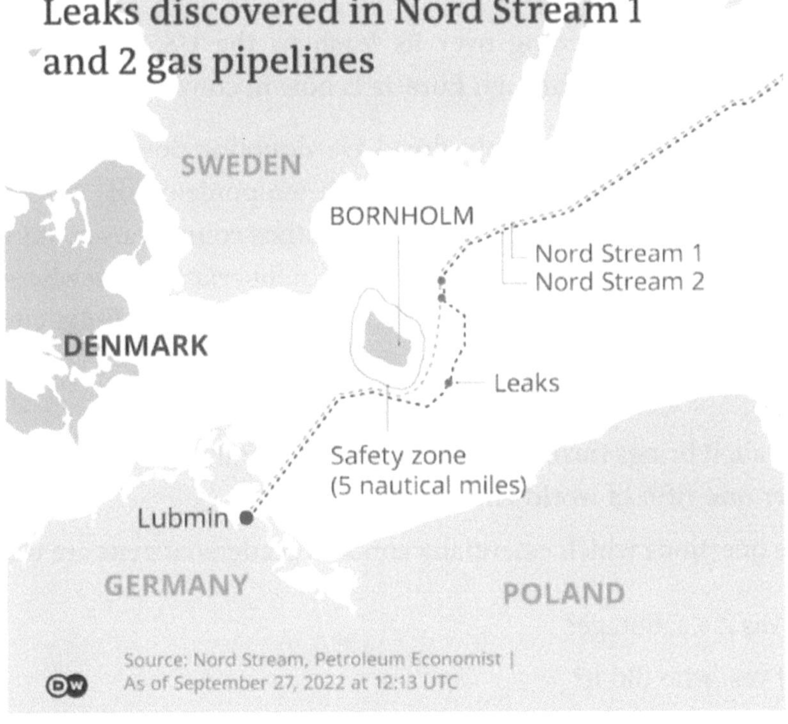

The gas pipelines which theoretically supply 30% of Europe's gas needs from Russia were "sabotaged" at four places close to each other by explosives of up to 700 kg TNT in the Baltic Sea this week, in the waters which fall in Danish and Swedish economic zones.

This takes Russia's ability to manipulate gas supply to Europe out of its hand; this closes the scope of Germany to come on negotiating table which could dilute or stop fresh Sanctions being imposed; or return to Peace from the edge of potentially a Nuclear War; and which makes Europe sold lock, stock and barrel to the United States for its energy supply, incidentally at twice the rate of the Russians.

Further, don't delude yourself that India, and the rest of the world, is mothballed from its implications:

1. Europe in turmoil implies unceasing sanctions on Russia, implying endless disruption of supply chains for food and metals around the world;
2. With Europe handing over its leash to the US, the dream of a multipolar world through Eurasia is now in convulsion;
3. and India would not only dread US doubling down to force it to give up on Russia but also that such weaponizing of "sabotage"—violating international laws affecting other countries—could be the fate of other pipelines which Russia (in Siberia and elsewhere) and China (in Xinjiang and other BRI projects) or even India could be envisioning in near future.

Above all, it brings turmoil closer home to the Indian sub-continent and its over one-fifth of world's humanity.

So the questions which essentially concern readers/citizens are three:

★ Was it a sabotage?
★ If yes, who did it?
★ What now?

Was It A Sabotage

A background is necessary.

The 1,224 km Nord Stream stretching from Russia to Germany has been one of the main gas supply routes to Europe with a capacity of 55 billion cubic meters a year.

The steel pipeline has a thick wall and coated with almost double the steel-reinforced concrete, each section of the pipe weighing 11 tonnes which turns into 25 tonnes after the application of concrete.

It was filled with a total of 778 million standard cubic meters of natural gas, huge enough for the spillage to continue for next one week in the Baltic waters.

The seismic data has confirmed it wasn't an earthquake; nor the explosions were occurring in the rock below the seawater.

Officials in Denmark, Poland, Sweden and other countries have stated it's a sabotage. So said the Swedish prime minister Magdalena Andersson and her Danish counterpart Mette Frederiksen.

Importantly, Germany agrees!

Who Did It

Straightaway, the Western media put the sabotage on Russia in its plan to deprive Europe of its energy this winter.

Such demonizing of Moscow is important to keep the Western citizenry behind their governments in the mission to destroy Russia and rule the world forever.

The trouble is, nobody is explaining why Russia would sabotage its own pipelines worth a fortune? At a time when the supply of gas is the only leverage it has against the West; and when it's so easily achieved by turning on and off the supply?

(Russia is badly hurt by the sabotage of Nord Stream pipelines and is taking up the matter in the United Nations today, on Friday).

The first sign that it could've been staged by the United States came from ex Polish prime minister (Radek Sikorski) who said "Thank You USA" posting a picture of the affected site.

Further

- ★ There is this link of US president Joe Biden stating before Russia puts its boots inside Ukraine: "If Russia invades…then there will be no longer a Nord Stream 2. We will bring an end to it."
- ★ Susan Rice, the ex-US National Security Advisor, had said in 2014: "We want to change the structure of energy dependence…depend more on the North America energy platform…to have pipelines that don't go through Ukraine and Russia."
- ★ The universal amphibious assault ship USS Kearsarge was seen in the area just days before the sabotage.
- ★ The Baltic Sea is as good as controlled by the NATO;
- ★ The explosion was impossible to carry out for Russia with Swedish, Danish and Polish naval forces and its intelligence-gathering network, its sensors, in force: If anything, these States are more likely to do the bidding of Washington.

There is a precedent too of these pipelines being in the eye of its enemies.

- ★ In 2015, the annual routine underwater survey of the Nord Stream 1 pipelines had come across a remote-operated vehicle rigged with explosives right next to one of the lines in Swedish waters.
- ★ In 2021, when Nord Stream 2 was still being built, the Polish navy had interfered and put to danger the pipe-laying vessels;
- ★ Only last year, Russia had raised the concern on security of its pipelines on global platforms.

What Now

Well, the umbilical cord is cut; there won't be an rapprochement between Germany and Russia or a Eurasian force of Germany-Russia-China coming together to spell the end of unipolar world order anytime soon.

The three economic powerhouses are worth $50 trillion of GDP based on purchasing power parity (PPP) compared to $20 trillion of the United States!

(This has been the foundational geostrategy of the US: Never let Germany and Russia come together for then Washington's control of the Europe would be over—and it would lose its foothold in world affairs.)

This would accelerate the deindustrialization of Germany, the cascading effect on European Union would be soon visible as Berlin finances it to the tune of 1.24 trillion Euro; the Old Continent would soon be gripped in recession.

It's also worth noting that Germany is contractually obligated to buy at least 40 billion cubic meters of Russian gas a year until 2030: And the supply halted notwithstanding, it would still have to cough up the contracted amount to Moscow.

The noise on this sabotage of Russian gas pipelines would likely be put to history's baggage:

That the Baltic Sea suffered many maritime battles in World War II and it became a dumping ground for damaged or expired munitions and chemicals. And that the leftovers could have caused the "leak" never mind laying underwater gas pipeline are extremely complex and intense projects: It involves endless surveys, study of hazards, planning routes, negotiations and permits from multiple countries which could've taken care of such dangers.

The investigation would only begin once the leak is over.

There is uncertainty if and when the repairs on pipelines could be carried out.

Those pipelines must be now filled with salty sea waters which is an invitation to corrosion and rust.

The German media has already said that the pipes could have been rendered permanently inoperable.

It's further muddled if one considered that Russia, which in theory should carry out repairs, is blocked by hostile Sanctions: It can't really send its personnel or resources to examine or repair the gas pipeline.

The truth is, this Energy War being played out in Europe could well be one of history's gravest errors.

Link to Article:

https://www.newsbred.com/this-is-a-very-bad-news-for-india-global-south-and-europe-on-brink/

Beat It! Russia is Europe's Last Empire!

October 5, 2022

Indian Express has today published an OpEd by one Anastasia Pillavasky of King's College London — "Dear Indian friends you are on the wrong side of history[1]—which is a fit case for slapping Section 505 for "causing fear and alarm to the public" for India's continued neutrality in the Ukraine Crisis.

The writer has sought to stoke the fear of Indian citizenry, threatening that either India takes a stand against terror or join "Syria, North Korea, Eritrea, Belarus: Does India belong to this club?" (The implied threat is either India becomes a global outcast like North Korea or arguably face a civil war like in Syria or become a sidekick of Russia like Belarus).

The language of the piece is reprehensible, made worse by comparing our Netaji Subhas Chandra Bose with Stepan Bandera, arguably "one of the most hated man who ever lived[2]."

The writer, in this poisonous piece, of lies and more lies from both sides of her mouth, has based her arguments on primarily five points:

- ★ The US has never supported Ukraine, even went against them: In contrast, Washington has sought to build bridges with Russia;
- ★ NATO has made no attempt to corner Russia;
- ★ Russia is Europe's last empire;
- ★ How Ukrainians have been brave while Russia has been seizing its land;

★ India's neutrality is against democracy and could make her a Ukraine of tomorrow, a target of China.

Here's a rebuttal to these five positions:

IF US HAS SUPPORTED RUSSIA AND NOT UKRAINE

★ It was the US which was behind the "maidan coup" of 2014 which replaced the legally elected Ukrainian government of Viktor Yaunkovch[3];

★ The US-proxy Kiev regime, since October 2014, sought a membership of NATO which the latter first broadly agreed up in 2008 Bucharest and later, in June 2021 Burssels Summit[4]; (US is the heart and engine driving NATO);

★ According to US' own State Department, Washington has provided more than $ 19 billion in security assistance for training and equipment to Ukraine and "improve interoperability with NATO since 2014[5];

★ Since 2018, Ukraine has received US' anti-tank missiles, Czech artillery and other NATO weaponry;

★ In November last year, months before Russia's Special Military Operation (SMO), the United States signed "charter of strategic partnership" with Ukraine, calling for Ukraine to join NATO;

Now let's look at how "friendly" US regimes have been to Russia since the dissolution of the Soviet Union in 1990s:

★ On February 9, 1990, president George H.W. Bush and his secretary of state James Baker, as well as West German chancellor Helmut Kohli promised Soviet leader Mikhail Gorbachev that if the USSR allows German reunification, they would not expand the NATO "one inch eastward."

(*It's said that this was not in writing: Well now the records of National Security Archive at George Washington University's website confirm it was in writing.*)

It was Bill Clinton who began expanding NATO in his second term: Poland, Hungary and the Czech Republic were brought in in 1990s;

(*Even the hawk George Kennan thought it was the beginning of a new Cold War. "Russians will gradually react quite adversely…I think it's a tragic mistake."*)

The new Russia, after the dissolution of USSR, was at the mercy of United States. Boris Yeltsin did little to stop US' capitalists hawks from looting the country. Indeed the then US president Bill Clinton pumped in billions of dollars to "rig the Russian presidential elections in 1996[6]": Don't believe me, believe the Washington Post!

Bill Clinton and his "Harvard Boys"—Larry Summers, Jeffrey Sachs, David Lipton etc.—completely destroyed the Russian economy. All subsidies and price controls were abolished; hyper-inflation ensued, capital vanished, "voucher" schemes gave entire industries to gangsters;

(*If you could, lay hand on the testimony of former Wall Street Journal reporter Anne Williamson who explained the full scale of the tragedy.*)

Further, how friendly do you think is United States to Russia when it withdraws from the Intermediate Nuclear Forces (INF) Treaty?

Barack Obama installed MK-41 missile launchers in Romania and Poland which could fire medium-range Tomahawk cruise missiles in Russia: How friendly do you think is the move?

In 2018, the US announced it would not seek ratification of the Comprehensive Nuclear Test Ban Treaty; it even denounced the Non-Proliferation Treaty: How peaceful do you think that is?

NATO HAS MADE NO ATTEMPT TO CORNER RUSSIA

Let's take this cruel lie head on: I have already mentioned how Clinton roped in Poland, Hungary and the Czech Republic in the NATO in 1990s;

George Bush Jr brought in no less than seven more countries in the NATO alliance: Bulgaria, Estonia, Latvia, Lithuania, Romania, Slovakia and Slovenia.

(*Unlike what Anastasia Pilliavsky claims in her piece, the Bush government tried very hard to include Ukraine in NATO but Germany and France were not game for it.*)

So, NATO which began with 13 member states has now expanded to 29 nations and encircles Russia.

The alibi offered is that small Baltic and other Eastern European countries feel threatened by Russia: Imagine, a country which was fighting for its own existence in the 1990s, a threat to itself, was projected as a threat to small and weak European nations.

And if it was so, why Gorbachev's proposed "Common European Home"—a security arrangement for all of Europe and Russia—was never heeded to?

So, the US-led NATO has moved 1200 miles to the east of Elbe River to Russia's very western border with the Baltic States. And do you think Russia is overreacting?

Well think about this way: the US has a similar Monroe Doctrine for protection of its border and neighbourhood. If the USSR, under the Warsaw Pact, had begun implementing a "maidan coup" against the neighbouring governments, how would have US reacted?

Russia borders more sovereign states—16—than any other country. It has maritime boundaries with Japan and the US, and two unrecognised states: Abkhazia and South Ossetia. Doesn't it have a legitimate reason to worry on its security?

(*The irony is, the Monroe Doctrine itself promises to stay out of European affairs if they stay out of US' hemisphere in return.*)

The truth is, by bombing Yugoslavia for 78 days, NATO signalled it had no intention to stop expanding.

It was no way to help the Russians who had caused the greatest bloodless revolution in history to end the Soviet regime.

BEWARE OF RUSSIAN EMPIRE

It's the dumbest argument Anastasia has put forward.

Does Russia need more land? It's a vast country will a small population. And it has no shortage of natural resources. The last thing Russia needs is more land;

Is Russia eyeing Ukrainian gas pipelines, Baltic ports? The truth is, unlike the Soviet days, Russia has long built new infrastructure. It has developed its own commercial ports on the Baltic Sea. Russia has successfully built North and South streams of its own; it doesn't need Ukrainian gas pipeline.

Russia wants to relive USSR days? In today's world when some of its own "Orthodox brothers"—Bulgaria, Romania etc.—have turned against them?

★ Does it sound like a design of an Empire that Ukraine's largest trading partner still is Russia? Not only Russia trades with Ukraine it has also absorbed millions of its economic refugees who send money back to home in Ukraine?

★ Is it the sign of an empire which continues to supply the Baltic states with electricity?

★ Isn't it Russia which supplies peacekeeping force across the world: Abkhazia, South Ossetia, Armenia, Transnistria, Bosnia, Kosovo, Angola, Chand, Sierra Leone, Sudan etc.?

- ★ That all these eight years of US-led sanctions, all Russia needed was to block the sale of titanium parts without which Boeing won't be able to build its planes. Or it could have prohibited the sale of rocket engines to the US and the latter won't be able to launch satellites.
- ★ With 20 to 40 million Russians living outside the country—US itself has 3 million Russians—how would it help Vladimir Putin to have ambitions of an Empire?
- ★ How does a country with GDP of 3 trillion dollars hope for an Empire when somebody like US spends a trillion dollar a year on its military alone? Doesn't US have three times the military aircrafts as the Russians?
- ★ Instead, a country which has 800 bases around the world, shouldn't it quality as an Empire?
- ★ If anything, Russia doesn't want war: It wants peace to rebuild, to mitigate the effects of Sanctions.

RUSSIA SEIZING TERRITORIES

This is an important part of Anastasia's piece: Russia's aggression against Moldova, Georgia and Ukraine.

Since Ukraine has been in news, let's begin with it before taking up the issues with Georgia and Moldova.

- ★ The writer would do well to remember that it was Russia who refused to annex Donbass after the 2014 coup when the latter wanted to join it;
- ★ Since 2014, the UN itself has documented at least 14,000 killed in the Donbass region which has population of Russian-ethnic origin: All this while Russia waited for diplomacy to work but the Minsk Agreements it forged by bringing in US, France, Germany didn't move an inch; Russia didn't take any territory in the East with force.

Let's look at Crimea. It had maintained a great deal of autonomy from the Kiev government anyway. After the 2014 coup, when the move to expel Russia from the naval base at Sevastopol began, Putin moved his men on the Peninsula: Not a single person was killed. A referendum was held which overwhelmingly sought a union with Russia.

The truth is, Russia won the Crimean peninsula from the Turks way back in the 1780s; it's a part of Russia like New York is to US; hundreds of thousands of its soldiers died defending the Crimean city of Sevastopol from European forces during two sieges: one during the Crimean War, another during the World War II.

In Georgia, the US-backed Rose Revolution of 2003 put Mikhail Saakashvili in charge. He attacked the breakaway province of South Ossetia, then enjoying full autonomy and protection by Russian peacekeepers. Russians first suffered casualties but then struck by destroying Georgians and securing South Ossetia's independence: And yes, Russia has not annexed it.

The piece also points to Moldova and troubles in Transnistria. If Russia has created so much trouble in Moldova how come its people has chosen a president with affinity to Russia in recent times?

BRAVE UKRAINIANS

Call them brave or sacrificial lamb, the truth is Ukraine has been sacrificed in the proxy war between the United States and Russia.

Its president Vladimir Zelenskyy has sacrificed four its regions just to get close to the West: How bright is it?

We have umpteen evidences that thousands of foreign mercenary fighters are in Ukraine, like they were in the wars in the Middle East this millennium.

A volunteer spoke recently to the Canadian Broadcasting Corporation of fighting alongside "friends" who came "from the marines, from the States.'

INDIA'S NEUTRALITY IS THREAT TO DEMOCRACY

The truth is other way around: If India doesn't take a stand now, it would never be able to do again: For Modi's mission of "Atmanirbhar Bharat (Self-dependent India)" would sooner or later fall into crosshair of the Hegemon. It is tolerating India only as long as it's needed against China. If it had any regard for India's sensitivity, Afghanistan would've been handled a lot better.

For all that could be said against Beijing, how many countries it has invaded in the last 30 years? NONE. A period in which US has constantly been at war:

It still has boots in Syria.

What exactly is Anastasia's idea of democracy: Is it over 800 military bases encircling the globe who are anything but a threat to it?

Which are the countries the Hegemon has promoted with democracy in last 70 years? On the contrary, how does she think the democracy of Iran, Congo, Chile, Algeria, Palestine, Middle East etc. has been mutilated by it? Is supporting military regimes and brutal dictators her idea of promoting democracy?

Clearly, the paid academicians would now look to whip up support amongst Indian citizens through propaganda for India to give up on Russia. Anastasia says as much in her piece: "I ask my Indian friends—academicians, journalists, lawyers, philosophers, schoolteachers and politicians—to condemn Putin's terror."

More than ever, India's neutral, law-based, peace-calling policy would come under stress. It would now be India's citizens who would be whipped up to go against their government's principled stand.

Reference:

[1] https://indianexpress.com/article/opinion/columns/dear-indian-friends-you-are-on-the-wrong-side-of-history-a-letter-8189659/

[2] https://www.counterpunch.org/2020/03/10/the-most-hated-man-who-ever-lived/

[3] https://static.poder360.com.br/2022/02/2014-Coup-1.pdf

[4] https://en.wikipedia.org/wiki/Ukraine%E2%80%93NATO_relations

[5] https://www.state.gov/u-s-security-cooperation-with-ukraine/#:~:text=Since%202014,%20the%20United%20States,and%20improve%20interoperability%20with%20NATO.

[6] https://www.washingtonpost.com/history/2020/06/26/russian-election-interference-meddling/

Link to Article:

https://www.newsbred.com/express-oped-incites-indian-citizens-to-rise-against-modi-govts-stance-on-ukraine/

Why US Wants to Take on Russia and China Together

October 9, 2022

The United States fears the world in its fist would be prised open by Russia and China if unchecked by 2030.

The greatest power in human history relies on its fake Dollar and military might to pin down nations who don't follow its script.

It happened to countless nations in Africa and Latin America, as it happened to closer your home with Saddam, Gaddafi, Assad etc. as its with China and Russia today—and India tomorrow!

The Hegemon relies on one-two trick from its code-book on independent States: (a) Either inflict a regime change—fund activists, minorities, politicians, bureaucrats, judiciary, media etc. to plunge the country into anarchy and then manipulate its own "man" into power who would gift them the "client state"; or (b) inflict a war in the name of "humanitarian intervention" to keep its boot on the throat of a recalcitrant State.

If the US doesn't do it, it can't control land, labour or resources (food, water, energy, metals) which makes others poor and them super rich.

The loosening of control would expose the fake currency that Dollar is which US prints whenever it wants to. As long as the dollar is world's reserve currency, it doesn't matter that Washington presently has debt to the tune of 30 trillion dollars.

But if nations bypass Dollar in bilateral and multilateral trade, the House of Cards would come crashing down.

The US has been trying the first trick of anarchy but in a single-party control that Russia and China are, it's not working. It has now dragged Russia down in Ukraine, as it would shortly do with Taiwan for China. It has encircled Russia with five NATO nations and it's in tearing hurry to create an Asian NATO to do the same to China in Pacific Islands.

Now look at Asia-Pacific region on the map and you would clearly see the United States has invaluable assets in Japan, South Korea, Australia and New Zealand to breathe down China's neck.

Why Pacific Islands Are Now In US' Eyes

Another test now awaits New Delhi: The United States wishes to rope in 15 Pacific Islands for its war games.

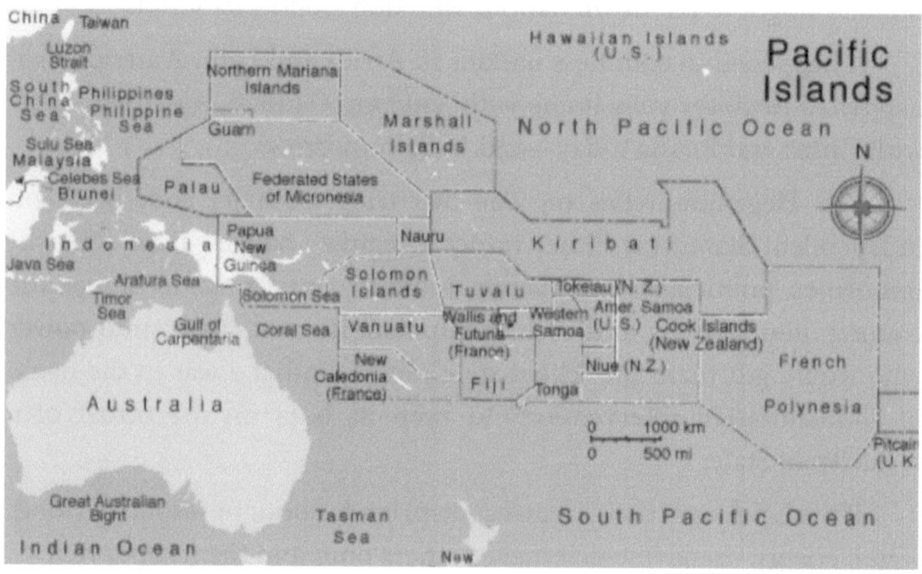

The White House held its first summit with Pacific Island nations (Fiji, Marshall Islands, Micronesia, Palau, Papua New Guinea, Samoa, Solomon Islands, Tonga, Tuvalu, Cook Islands, French Polynesia and New Caledonia) on September 28. Vanuatu, Kiribati and Nauru stayed away. The observers, no prize for guessing, were Australia and New Zealand.

The US played generous hosts— $810 million to the region, including $60 million aid to Pacific nations for 10 years which Kamala Harris promised in July. It didn't let anyone forget either that $1,5 billion have been provided in the past decade. The US biggies, including Secretary of State Antony Blinken, have been hopping on planes to this region this year. It's "Peace Corps—a volunteers' programme—is set to return to Fiji, Tonga, Samoa and Vanuatu.

Amidst the pompous gestures (recognizing the Cook Islands and Niue as sovereign states) and words by Joe Biden ("America…and the world depends on your security…") the US had to drop its insistence on new security relationships from the Declaration on the US-Pacific Partnership as Solomon Islands stood its ground.

US' Bloody History In Region

Most Islands obviously don't want to get caught in the Battle of the Biggies. Besides, there is that bloody history which is too painful for these till-now ignored Islands.

The United States during the 20th century organized scores of badly regulated tests of nuclear weapons and dumped nuclear waste in the Pacific Ocean which is prefers to call its "own lake." The military goals were more important for the Washington than the welfare of region's citizens.

We have it from the documents of a UN special rapporteur in 2012 that the US did permanent damage to the Marshall Islands through nuclear tests carried out for more than a decade.

A UN fact-finding mission found that citizens of the Islands continued to suffer in health from the 67 nuclear tests conducted by the US in the Islands between 1946-1958. And that it has permanently contaminated their land. (*Some have even suggested that nuclear pollution of the Marshall Islands is much worse than in Chernobyl and Fukushima.*)

These are organized and repeated human rights violations. The countries in the region want acknowledgements and reparations.

Military arrangements aren't good for them. They also can deduce that the fund offered is less than 6% of the $15 billion granted to Ukraine this year.

And then there is this elephant in the room: China!

Unlike the US' war games, China has promoted beneficial cooperation with regional players for decades now.

Between 1992-2021, the trade between China and the Pacific Island nations grew from $153 million to $5,3 billion—or in other words, expanding 30 times in 30 years.

Its BRI (Belt and Road Initiative) has clearly outshone the US, Australia, New Zealand and Japan for the region. It helped in Covid pandemic as it does with climate change through the Pacific Island Forum (PIF) board. It has already offered 10 Island nations support in policing, security, fisheries, data and a free trade zone. It has been attending the Post-Forum dialogue since 1990.

China, as we all know by now, is deeply anxious on Pacific Ocean. It has no deep access to it: cut off by these Islands and Australia. (*That's why letting go control of Taiwan would be a blow in the gut for the Beijing, a "Red Line" so to say.*)

The Pacific Islands are now aware of their geostrategic importance. But they want to be players and not pawns. It's aware that the South Pacific region is one of world's richest and most active fishery areas. It knows Beijing brings infrastructure, education, culture, tourism, science and technology—with no ideological strings attached—to the table. The US on the other hand, despite its excesses in the region, could hurt with "color revolutions" on Islands who step out of line. (*A case in point is that out of $1.5 billion provided in the past decade, as much as $180,000 went to support journalists and propaganda!*)

One problem to the US' goals is that its citizens know little about these Islands. In order to push its agenda, it needs to rope them in. (*Hence the Peace Corps to exchange students and professionals' visits, promote tourism: In other words people-to-people ties.*) It already occupies Guam, Saipan and Okinawa. A few more Pacific military bases would not hurt. It would play on Beijing's fears and anxiety and hopefully their preventive action—like Russia's Special Military Operation—could be sold to Western citizens for a counter military "humanitarian intervention" to commence.

The US-in-hurry wants to take on Russia and China simultaneously.

That's why they want to build an integrated system of alliances, between European and Asian allies, between NATO and "Asian NATO", if you may. That's why they invited its Asian allies to the NATO Summit in Madrid in June.

That's why NATO now openly says it deals with Asian affairs and aims to be a global alliance.

By projecting the Russian threat to Europe and China's fear to Asia, a dual threat, it could bring all of them together in a Bloc, much, much bigger than the one during the Cold War.

Link to Article:

https://www.newsbred.com/why-us-wants-to-take-on-russia-china-together/

Why Did India Stick with Russia on Referendums?

October 12, 2022

If you miss the first buttonhole, you will never manage it properly. Ask the wrong questions—expect to get useless answers.

– GOETHE

So the UN sought a vote from its 193-member General Assembly to denounce Russia incorporating four Ukrainian regions through referendums.

Moscow wanted "secret ballots" but 107 nations are for "open, recorded" ballots which includes India.

Moscow arguably wanted secret ballots for who would dare go against the Hegemon and side with Russia in open? No one fights a crocodile in water.

India went with the majority in asking for "open vote" but didn't vote against Russia by abstaining from it.

At a superficial level, India must have been peeved by recent US' moves: $450 million to modernize Pakistan's F-16s; US envoy in Pakistan Occupied Kashmir (PoK) which he referred to as Azad Kashmir; and Germany, a sidekick of US, looking for UN intervention in Kashmir.

But at a deeper level, India must have gone by UN Charter and international laws with which it always professes to abide by.

So what does UN Charter say on the matter?

Article 1 of the UN Covenant on civil and political rights not only stipulate the right of self-determination of all people but also they are bound to promote it.

Article 19 of the Covenant stipulates the right of all people to "freedom of expression."

There are any number of UN resolutions in its support.

This is the principle which led to Algeria gaining its independence from France through a referendum in 1962.

In 1991, a number of referendums were held such as in Kosovo. The Serbs, like Ukraine today, opposed the referendum. Serbs, like Ukraine today, also didn't recognize the referendum.

The UN had also held self-determination referendums in Sudan, Timor-Leste and Ethiopia/Eritrea.

The trouble is, UN allows or ignores these referendums as it suits the Powers, that typical who-fights-crocodile-in-the-water syndrome.

UN went for self-determination referendums in Sudan, Timor-Leste etc. only after tens of thousands had been killed.

It ignored referendums in Crimea in 2014; as it did in Abkhazia, Ossetia etc.

In the present referendums in Ukraine, neither the UN, EU nor OSCE (Organization for Security and Cooperation in Europe) showed any interest. (But when have the people's interest mattered to them?).

It's another matter that around 130 international election monitors were there who saw the legitimacy of people's vote in eastern Ukraine to join Russia in referendum.

However, UN, EU, OSCE—these "beacons" of democracy and human rights—didn't show any interest in people's peaceful exercise of self-determination.

Indeed, the UN should've held these referendums in 1991 itself when Ukraine broke away from the USSR, taking a large Russian minority (30% of the population) with it.

A referendum should've been held in 2014 after the illegal "coup" in Ukraine.

In the intervening eight years, UN itself has documented 14,000 killed in Donbass region.

What did this supreme global body do to stop the endless killings?

Wasn't a referendum then in order?

Why didn't it stop NATO from compromising Ukraine's neutrality?

Wouldn't its interventions have saved humanity from coming to such a sorry pass where it faces nuclear extinction?

The truth is, when ethnic groups can't coexist in peace, it's the duty of global bodies to protect their life and well-being. They should rise in unison and not be partisan.

The principle of territorial integrity can't override the right of people to their lives, to self-determination.

Or how would you describe the 78-day bombing of Yugoslavia by NATO in 1999 which were completely in violation and illegal in the eyes of the UN Charter?

NATO had attacked a nation without the approval of the Security Council. (We would let go Yemen, Afghanistan, Iraq, Libya, Syria etc. for the moment.)

The truth is, world is jungle and the sweet words of "democracy" and "freedom of expression" are mere weapons in the hands of the powerful.

They have never meant the good for humanity and they never would.

The precedent was set way back during the Nuremberg trials after the Second World War which only held Germans guilty of excesses but ignored completely the one of allies and what they did to civilian population of Germany, for example, razing Dresden, the then cultural capital of Europe, to ground.

What about carpet bombing of tens of other German cities?

Or should we recall the obliteration of Nagasaki and Hiroshima?

It's the same story in our times when the Iraq War of 2003 was fought on lies and neither Bush nor Blair have been termed as "war criminals", never mind millions who have died, pillaged, raped or been rendered homeless.

Or for that matter Afghanistan where the US wanted Talibans to hand over Osama bin Laden without providing the evidence.

Who accounts for tens of thousands lives similarly uprooted and extinguished in over two decades of boots on the Af ground?

Remember, it was the West which supported the apartheid in South Africa.

It was the US which had placed Nelson Mandela—hold your breath—on its international terrorist list.

And Osama Bin Laden never made it to FBI's Most Wanted Terrorist List even after 9/11!

The simple fact is: The legitimate right of people to secede through a popular, overwhelming will can't be twisted as "annexation" by Russia.

Modi's India has been stoic in standing with justice, truth and process on the Ukraine Crisis.

It would only get hotter in the kitchen; and for the sake of humanity, let's pray India doesn't look to save its skin.

Link to Article:
https://www.newsbred.com/would-india-vote-against-russia-in-un-on-ukraine-referendums/

So Did Russia Commit Genocide in Ukraine?

October 21, 2022

This man peering at you in the image (below) has ruled that war crimes, made graver by torture and rapes, happened in parts of Ukraine which is now with Russia.

Obviously, it's not a trifle judgement which tomorrow the chamber of assassins would use in an ad-hoc tribunal to implicate Putin if Russia was to lose; like it was with Slobodan Milosevic (Yugoslavia), Jean-Paul Akayesu (Rwanda), Charles Taylor (Liberia/Sierra Leone) and Khieu Samphan (Cambodia) etc.

All of them were judged to be evil by such tribunals, created while Bill Clinton occupied White House, where he mixed work with pleasure between 1992-2000.

Erik Mose, head of Commission of Inquiry on Ukraine

That's where it's leading to in the case of Putin for this man, Erik Mose (above), head of Commission of Inquiry on Ukraine, brings weight to his findings by visiting dozens of sites and hundreds of witnesses, never mind he was duly escorted and entertained by one of the parties itself, the Ukrainian armed forces.

In boxing parlance, that's not being a referee but sitting in the corner of one of the two fighters.

But I am only starting.

Mose is beholden to the Hegemon which spends hundreds of millions in creating tribunals, populate it with its own men, often mandated by the UN bodies which itself live on the crumbs tossed by its host in New York.

Why you need ad hoc tribunals when UN itself was created to stop wars and punish war-criminals by the world, fresh from the horrors of World War II in 1945, is a good question.

It's best answered if you pay attention to who creates tribunals and what they fear—obviously convincing 190-odd nations is a lot more difficult than putting all the king's men in a handpicked court.

So the route often taken is through UN Security Council which has 15 members and a simple vote gets you the tribunal you want. (Don't confuse it with UN veto-Powers which is invested in only five nations.)

Now back to our Commission of Inquiry on Ukraine, mandated by UN Human Rights body, and its head who has a history of standing with the war criminals.

So let's relive Erik Mose in Rwanda where he did a thorough job for his Masters first as deputy and then head of what else but a tribunal by the name of International Criminal Tribunal for Rwanda (ICTR), between 1999 to 2007.

Rwanda of course registers in our minds as a nation in Africa but for a further help on its geography, view the map and do make a mental note on its neighbours as I set about recalling that dark history.

The Background to Rwanda Genocide

Rwanda had Tutsis and Hutus, sub groups of the same clan, the former only 15% of population but elites and holding the levers of power; Hutus majority but only farmers.

A Tutsi king not surprisingly ruled, as it did through its history even when they were under the benevolence of first Germans and then Belgians. After Hutus rebelled strongly enough in late 1950s, independence came in 1961 but by way of bifurcation of land between Rwanda and Burundi, the former now under Hutus and the latter still under Tutsis.

(We Indians know the colonialists' rulebook, don't we. First, grow the majority and minority apart, divide the land, and put your own men in power so that even if the land is relinquished, the loot of the land continues unhindered.)

In this case Tutsis were favourites of colonialists for their loot-agenda. Tutsis in power in Burundi led a genocide of 200,000 Hutus in 1972. (Where was UN? Again, a good question.)

Now was the question of cleansing Hutus from Rwanda. The colonialists did two things: In 1989, nine colonial powers, let's call them West, withdrew from the International Coffee Agreement. Now coffee was Rwanda's main revenue but as the prices crashed worldwide, the government was on its knees. State-owned companies went bankrupt, health and education services vanished, child malnutrition surged and hyperinflation ruled.

The Rwandans now begged the IMF who, true to their genetic make-up, offered loan with savage conditions which only made it worse for the poor Africans. There was famine and social despair.

Then in 1990, a wing of the neighbouring Uganda military, known as the Rwandan Patriotic Front (RPF) invaded Rwanda. The RPF was led by Paul Kagame, a Rwandan Tutsi leader, trained by the US at Fort Leavenworth, Kansas. They went on rampage against Hutus in Rwanda. It was naked aggression but the West painted it as a "civil war." (As for what did Security Council do, not even authorizing an observer mission, I would say again: Good Question.)

The RPF rampage over next three years gave them much of northern Rwanda. Several hundred thousand Hutus were driven out.

Now the US officially made an entry. In 1994, even as a genocide was unfolding, president Bill Clinton successfully led out most of the UN peacekeepers who were already in Rwanda. The US also blocked subsequent UN reinforcements.

More was coming. On April 6, 1994 Rwanda's president was slain in a rocket attack on his plane. (The French anti-terrorist judge, Jean-Louis Bruguiere was to tell a UN secretary-general that it was CIA who were involved in the shoot down.)

This was the flashpoint which launched the Rwandan genocide of hundred days. Tens of thousands were killed. Hutus lost the power. A tribunal was now set up to judge the guilty between the period of January 1 to December 31, 1994. (Who brought them to this point of course was conveniently left from the tribunal's brief.)

A little diversion here to give you the full picture. Burundi had permitted 600 US army rangers to be around to help RPF. Tanzania had a role in planning the plane's shoot down and no less invaded Rwanda from the east and south blocking escape routes for the Hutus refugees, fleeing RPF's atrocities. In the spillover of war, millions of Congolese were killed and Congo itself broke into fragments to be exploited by the Western mining companies. The great lakes region of Africa was drowned in blood.

How Rwanda Tribunal Butchered Justice

Now let's look at what the tribunal did in its existence of subsequent 17 years.

First the UN Security Council invested the chief prosecutor with the power to indict, arrest and prosecute suspects. The defense prosecutor stood no chance to prepare his case for he needed the approval of masters of Rwanda who were Tutsis. So the power to judge who was guilty and who was not was gifted to the winners of the war. Witnesses thus appeared and disappeared just as in a script. Further which defense witnesses could've logically appeared against the powers of the land?

Thus no RPF leader was ever persecuted. NONE. Even as a US State Department document tells us that RPF was killing 10,000 Hutus a month and were responsible for 95 percent of the killing.

Jean-Paul Akayesu, the Rwandan leader who was convicted for genocide, complained of the one-sided judgements of the tribunal. This is what the Rwanda tribunal said in reply: You have made the charge but what's your evidence to prove the alleged partiality of the Tribunal? And that was that!

The chief prosecutor, Carla Del Ponte, was terminated of her job for probing RPF. She was later to write in her memoirs that the United States and Britain were behind her firing in order to protect RPF.

Nobody was held responsible for shooting down the plane carrying Rwandan president.

And what happened to those who were acquitted, convicted or released after conviction? They are still under house arrest in Niger, without a country, without papers and without the right to join their families. Abandoned by the fake international justice. Others were sent to penal colonies like Benin, Mali and Senegal.

And now we have the same man pronouncing "war-crimes' in Ukraine territory which has by an overwhelmingly popular vote joined Russia. Another farce is unfolding while the justice itself is hung upside down. The judge who never said a word on perpetrators in Rwanda has now pronounced a scripted verdict on Ukraine.

As for Paul Kagame, the Tutsi leader of RPF, he is still in charge of Rwanda after nearly 25 years, feted and hailed as Human Rights hero in Western capitals and their lackey media. He duly visits the genocide memorial in Rwandan capital Kigali to lay wreath on innocent victims on whom apparently he had no role to play.

Listen to David Scheffer who himself was main negotiator for the United States during the creation of tribunal on Rwanda: "It (the tribunal) was like a battering ram in the implementation of US and NATO policy."

Link to Article:

https://www.newsbred.com/this-man-un-mandated-on-putin-russias-war-crimes/

Next Time US Quotes "human Rights", Remember Cuba

November 7, 2022

Today I want to tell you how little you know about the world you live in.

Almost the entire world barring two have condemned the US sanctions against Cuba for 30th straight year in the United Nations this week.

I am sure you didn't know.

Figures might drive home the point better: In the UN General Assembly of 193 nations, 185 voted against and two in favour of US sanctions against Cuba.

The two who haven't are naturally the United States and Israel who are but two sides of the same coin.

Ukraine, as it could be understood, abstained.

This is almost the entire humanity on this earth against the US Sanctions on Cuba which are 60 years in the running.

These Sanctions might just be a term for you for nowhere you read how hideous they are. So let's give it half a minute.

Cuba, before the US sanctions kicked in in 1962, depended on almost everything on its Big Brother: Trucks, buses, bulldozers, telephone and electrical equipment, industrial chemicals, medicine, raw cotton, detergents, potatoes, poultry, butter, most canned goods, and even such staple items essentials to a Cuban's diet as rice and black beans.

Cuba was nothing better than an economic appendage of the United States.

But then a revolution happened in this little country in late 50s which has a population a little over 10 million less than the one of Delhi and an area (1.08 lakh sq.km) lesser than that of Telangana.

The US didn't want communism in its backyard which might appear reasonable to you, never mind you aren't inclined to apply the same logic in case of NATO in Ukraine for Russia.

But we would let it go for the moment and stick to almost a genocide of Cubans all these years.

So by its Sanctions, the US presumed the revolution of Fidel Castro won't last long for the measures amounted to leaving the Cubans in a coma.

Cuba couldn't import for Sanctions restricted the use of US dollars. Assets were frozen; freight insurance shot through the roof, Cubans abroad couldn't send their earnings home without a higher cruel tax, inflation soared, jobs lost, money vanished—and all this spiralling effect meant the citizens were denied the most basic needs of food, clothing, education, housing, water and sanitation etc. Agriculture and tourism, vital for its economy, was paralyzed. (Kennedy banned Americans from visiting Cuba). Third world countries were deterred from investing in Havana. Latin American countries were pressured to severe their ties with Cuba.

But Cuba didn't bow. It held its ground. The US now turned the screws further.

In 1982, Ronald Reagan placed Cuba on the US "State Sponsors of Terrorism list" — its illegitimacy you could gauge in that no less than Nelson Mandela, for number of years, was a "terrorist" for US State Department as Washington supported the Apartheid regime in South Africa. (Remember this when next time you hear any intervention by the Hegemon as champion of "Human Rights" in this world.)

In 1992 Congress passed the Cuban Democracy Act which, among other measures, stopped any international ship from coming to US for 18 months if it had docked in Cuba on the way.

The 1996 Helms-Burton Act came down heavily on any company which had invested in properties nationalized by the Cuban government.

Any reactionary group that sought to overthrow the Cuban government were—and are—provided with utmost funds. Any Cuban who fled the country was granted US citizenship. No questions asked.

President Donald Trump exceeded all. He slapped 243—yes 243—new sanctions on Cuba, 90 of which cruelly came in the year of the Covid-19 pandemic.

Cubans responded by almost being heroic in delivering a vaccine of its own against the pandemic. But Sanctions took away the supply of syringes for them.

The rest of the world, all along has been watching. As recently as this September, it watched Hurricane Ian batter Cuba, cutting out electricity island-wide. The world was privy to what the UN agencies and others were saying about the genocidal nature of US Sanctions.

The UN ECLAC said: "…the numerous United States sanctions constitute the most severe and prolonged system of unilateral coercive measures ever applied against any country…it obstructs the access of Cuban citizens to basic goods and violate their rights."

Under US president Joe Biden things have only worsened. As Cuban foreign minister Bruno Rodriguez said in the UN: "The US administration has escalated the siege around our country, taking it to an even crueler and more inhumane dimension, with the purpose of deliberately inflecting the biggest possible damage on Cuban families."

The US blockade has cost Cuba over $144 billion in six decades. It costs Cuba $15 million daily. Only this year under Joe Biden, the loss amounts to $6.3 billion. In the first quarter of this year, Cuba earned $493 million—but its import bill was over $2 billion!

So why the United States does what it does against a hapless Cuba?

The excuse of Communism doesn't cut ice: Neither there is USSR alive, nor is it US' business to interfere in any other sovereign country, never mind capitalism, communism, socialism or any other system it prefers.

Just after the Cuban revolution in 1959, even before official US sanctions kicked in, this is what an internal US State Department memo defined the US goals in Cuba thus: "The only foreseeable means of alienating international support is through disenchantment and disaffection based on economy dissatisfaction and hardship… (and that) every possible means should be undertaken promptly to weaken the economic life of Cuba."

Further, Washington's goal ought to be, the memo said, to make "the greatest inroads in denying money and supplies to Cuba, to decrease monetary and real wages, to bring about hunger, desperation and overthrow of government."

Let's now check the merit, if any, which made the US believe that Cuba was a terrorist state.

Nelson Mandela was a fan of Cuba all along his life: For one, how Havana assisted Angola in its self-defence against the CIA-backed rebels, against a number of sovereign nations which left 1.5 million Africans dead at the turn of this century. When Mandela, the modern apostle of peace and non-violence died, South Africa invited the Cuban president Raul Castro in his memorial service to honour his memory.

(All hell at that time broke out in out "civilized" world. How could Cuba sit with others in international comity? It's not dissimilar to how India's deep system reacts when a Pranab Mukherjee visits RSS.)

Cuba's medics are humanity's heroes. It sent more than 4,000 medics in 40 countries to help fight Covid-19 pandemic. It's one of the frontline states in fight against global warming and rising sea levels.

This is what Nerys Dockery of Saint Kitts and Nevis island said when the world stood up against US sanctions on Cuba recently in the United Nations: Only five months ago she was facing losing her right eye. But was saved by a Cuban optician.

I write this piece to let you the reader be aware of what is sold to you in the name of "Human Rights" and "rules-based order" by your media, at the behest of West.

What more proof do you need that you haven't heard a bit about how the world opposes the US Sanctions on Cuba for 30 years now.

And that US has never been closer in breaking Cuba's resolve than it is now. Cuba's economy is in very, very bad shape. So-called freedom protests, at the behest of allegedly USAID and National Endowment for Democracy are taking its toll. There are shortages, power outages and long lines for food items and fuel. Emigration has reached a number of 140,000 Cuban citizens now in the US in October itself. To top it all, there is a kind of power vacuum at the top.

I would leave you with a titbit which could disgust you.

The United States, through a treaty more than a century old, has Cuba's land—Guantanamo Bay under its possession. This is the same 118 square kilometres in eastern Cuba which is known world over for the cruelty US inflicts on its prisoners of war (POW).

Guantanamo Bay is home to around 3,000 permanently stationed US military personnel. It's annual rent—hold your breath—is a mere $4,085, so around one cent per square metre of land.

That's not all. Since 1959 and the triumph of the Revolution, no cheque has ever been cashed. Cuba has been demanding that the US return the base since 1959. There are resolutions passed in every Non-Aligned Movement summit.

But predictably, the US don't care and your media makes sure you don't know

Link to Article:

https://www.newsbred.com/the-world-has-just-voted-against-the-us-but-you-dont-know/

Media is No Better Than a Puppet of the West

November 9, 2022

Indian Express has given a completely different spin to our foreign minister Dr. S Jaishankar's meet-up with his Russian counterpart Sergey Lavrov in Moscow.

"Global South in acute pain, return to table: Jaishankar to Russia"[1] is its screaming lead headline in three decks on front page today.

It's a lie.

And I take it up for it concerns you and me, indeed the well-being of our entire nation of 1.40 billion plus.

You think I am reacting over the top? Well, let me present my position.

1. Russia has all along looked for a peaceful settlement. They sent the peace proposal to West much prior to it put its boots in Ukraine. Even in March, a few weeks into its Special Military Operation (SMO), its talks with Ukraine were closer to a settlement before Boris Johnson flew in and scuttled the negotiations (Why, I would explain later).

2. Indeed, Russia had persuaded the West to sign Minsk Agreements, the UN-mandated, way back in 2015 against a hostile Kiev government which was wreaking havoc in Russian-dominated eastern part of Ukraine;

3. Russia hoped against hope for seven long years but nothing changed on the ground, the eastern Donbass region continued to suffer

shelling and murderous attack by Kiev which the UN itself has documented as 14,000 killed in this time span.

These facts would let you know that Russia has sought a peaceful solution to the problem all along.

Russia even now is ready for talks but how little Ukraine is could be gauged by its leader Volodymyr Zelenskyy insistence it wouldn't as long as Vladimir Putin is at helm in Moscow.

So, Russia is all for peace. As for the newspaper's insistence: "Jaishankar to Russia", it's a lie. Even the Indian Express copy doesn't support its headline.

India, like everyone else, knows it takes two to tango. And that's why India has never supported any resolution on any global forum which holds Russia guilty all these months. It has resisted the incessant pressure from West to join it against Russia.

Further, Russia allows Ukraine's grains to leave the ports for supply to Global South. Does it show its concern or intent to inflict "acute pain" as the Indian Express has indulged in its forgery? (This was before the grain deal fell through.)

For if Russia is at fault in this existential crisis, most of the world would've joined US' sanctions against Russia which they haven't: None in Latin America or Africa; only three in Asia (Japan, South Korea and Singapore) etc. Just a handful of Western nations have banded together to destroy Russia forever, a mission they have been pursuing for centuries.

For the uninitiated, I would briefly present the reasons why the US-led West want Russia to be extinct forever:

★ Russians pursue Orthodox Church branch of Christianity, different from the Catholic/Protestant one: For a general idea, visualize Sunni vs Shia in the Muslim world;

★ First the United Kingdom and now its foster child the United States have never wanted peace in Europe. A united Europe was once bad for an island power like the United Kingdom: The historians called it "Balance of Power." Now it's the US which has taken over the baton from the United Kingdom. It's policy all along has been: **"Keep US in; Germany down and Russia out" in Europe.** Without Europe in its bag, US won't be able to control Middle East and its oil; its influence in Eurasia would be over in a blink. Without Europe, US is only an island, 6,000 nautical miles away from the heart of the world.

★ And then there is this resource-rich Russia which is in the eyes of the plunderers that West has all through been in its living history. You only know of Russia's oil and gas and fertilizers etc.; yet there is an unimaginable wealth in Arctic which Russia is beginning to get serious about.

★ **If this all is too complicated, look at the map. You would notice that the sea lanes of the world are dominated by Western powers while the inner land is led by Russia, China and India largely. If this landmass gets together, and breaks the stranglehold of sea powers circling it, the game would be over for the West.**

Ukraine is a bait which the US threw it at Russia and the latter was left with no option but to take it.

Ukraine was being armed to the teeth; there are allegedly US biolabs; and NATO was offering its membership to Ukraine which meant a direct threat to Russia's existence: A promise which the US had made to Russia after the USSR imploded and which it never kept by offering NATO-membership to all and sundry around Russia.

And now we come to the India part and why it concerns a billion-plus Indian citizens.

1. To begin with, there is this little matter of cooperation in military and trade in Russian energy. We all know that India's military is

heavily dependent on Russia which unlike US is not shy in providing its tech know-how: BrahMos for instance.

2. India is getting cheap energy from Russia which is vital for its growth. India is a low-income country. So any energy bought at exorbitant prices would mean further crushing debt on a nation which is world's third biggest energy guzzler. So without Russian energy, The Modi government would pass on the shooting energy debt on its citizens who can't afford it;

3. India desperately wants to break free of its geographical constraints. Pakistan and China hold it back on its West and East frontiers; in the North, Himalayas block the access to the world. Its best hope is in cooperation with Russia which has made INSTC (International North South Transport Corridor) and Chennai-Vladivostok Eastern Maritime Corridor possible. Better accessibility would allow India to export more at a lesser transport cost and faster; it would also mean import at a vastly cheaper rate.

So what do we make of Indian Express and media of its kind which lie on the subject?

★ The agenda of course is to keep India and Russia apart which is the naked goal of West. Indian Express, by distorting truth, is showing itself to be a foot soldier in this mission;

★ That the United States is nobody's friend and would hurt any nation which wants to be independent, as is the case with China, Russia and India. And which was the case with Iraq, Syria and Libya, Cuba etc.;

★ That they fuel unrest and anarchy so that a free nation's governing class submits to its demands. Financial control, through IMF and World Bank, leaves such nations powerless.

★ Yet India wants to be independent which displeases the West. It's not happy that India is buying Russian energy and thus negating the effect of Sanctions; that India is "shaky" in Quad against China; that its dumping dollar in pReference: to trade in rupee with Russia.

It's imperative for the rest of the world to have alternative to Dollar in trade; and unbroken supply chains where every nation could pursue its interests. Under dollar, you are subjected to whims of the Hegemon and never free from the shackles.

India and Russia, to my mind, are two of the strongest forces capable of unshackling the world from this serfdom.

They must build bridges not just for business and security interests but also at a people-to-people level where a growing understanding would grow the roots deeper and not just at the governmental level.

It would mean not just promoting trade but also tourism and cultural awareness between India and Russia much of which is strikingly similar, such as reverence to nature and godliness.

There is much to be done by both India and Russia. And there is much to be done to counter evil propaganda.

Reference:

[1] https://indianexpress.com/article/india/global-south-in-acute-pain-return-to-table-jaishankar-to-russia-8257206/

Link to Article:

https://www.newsbred.com/how-indian-express-has-twisted-jaishankars-meet-up-with-lavrov/

UN Asks for Reparations from Russia When It Can't!

November 16, 2022

We the Indians still see a halo around the UN.

It's time we see it as a rigged body.

I provide the lowdown below in as fluid a manner as possible so as those unawares are not bolted away from the piece out of boredom.

I seek the attention of masses for informed citizenry alone can help India stay the course of approaching multipolar world, now at our doors.

***

We have learnt that the UN General Assembly, with a 94-17 vote, has asked Russia to pay reparations as war-damages to Ukraine.

Russia has termed it as an attempt to legalize the seizure of its hundreds of billions of dollars and assets by the "Anglo-Saxons", in the words of its ex-president Dmitry Medvedev.

For good measure, Medvedev added: "We will do without such a United Nations Organization."

***

The United Nations came to life in 1945 and then went to sleep.

We didn't notice it was in slumber for the US-NATO war crimes in **Americas** (Guatemala, Nicaragua, Cuba, El Salvador, Bolivia etc.), **Africa** (Rwanda, Angola, Congo etc.), **Asia** (East Timor, Korea, Japan,

Iran etc.) and **Europe** (Greece, Yugoslavia etc.) escaped us in their enormity.

We knew what happened in Vietnam wasn't funny, or in Korea, but somehow the UN didn't seem someone which had failed in its duty. It remained desirable, almost divine.

The nodes of information in media and academics did a good job in the cover-up; selling us the United States' wars in the name of curbing Communism, as these days it's in the name of "Human Rights".

When Soviet Union slipped into history in the 1990s, and China was nowhere to what it is now, the US had the entire field we call planet to itself. Almost immediately it went for Yugoslavia, bombing it for 79 days through its war-arm NATO, dropping 20,000 bombs, quite a few of cluster and depleted uranium kind, killing more civilians than they did soldiers.

Of course, this campaign didn't have the approval of the UN Security Council. But it did nothing to nail the Western lies such as 500,000 missing Kosovans or Albanians which after the war turned out to be no more than 10,000 persons. In the end the US had the mafia state of Kosovo it wanted, a geo-strategic nugget in the heart of Europe, with its natural resources such as black coal at their disposal, and boots stationed.

All of this escaped us, as was the fact that within a few months, President Bill Clinton had bombed four countries: Sudan, Afghanistan, Iraq and Yugoslavia.

Afghanistan and Iraq we would hear more often in following years, almost welcomed by us after the horrors of 9/11 which came to our drawing rooms; the barbarians who had violated the land of liberty and equality, the beacon of free world as we thought the US to be. It needed to be set aright: "The Axis of Evil" as it was sold to us by then president George Bush Jr.

***

Afghanistan was immediate and lasted until now, a good 20 years. We are told that the Talibans wanted proof of Osama bin Laden's involvement in 9/11 before they could hand him over—never mind the US had created him in the first instance—but the Hegemon didn't brook any questions.

We now have the evidence that even after US unleashed its fury, the Talibans were willing to strike a deal to end the war quickly (*The Afghanistan Papers* by Craig Whitlock); as did the word from *The Guardian* (October, 2001) that president George Bush rejected the Taliban offer as "non-negotiable."

We still don't know enough of the massive tragedy. Over a lakh of those killed were civilians. Successive US presidents—the Bush, Obama, Trump and Biden—lied from both sides of the mouth. When the US withdrew—with a parting, horrifying drone strike on civilians to boot—they made sure Afghanistan's assets were frozen; and aids dried down out of concern for "human rights."

Millions of Afghans today are starving.

The US did all those right under the nose of the UN, for 20 long years, and the global body kept sitting on its bum.

***

Oh yes, Iraq.

To begin with the US first imposed inhuman sanctions on this Middle East oil power for 12 years. Saddam Hussein might have been a psychopath but the US nurtured him for long before 9/11 presented an opportunity too good to miss for its oil control.

The US went to UN but its weapons inspection team turned up nothing. When the UN Security Council vote was taken, only 4 of 15 concurred with the Hegemon. Yet NATO launched a war on what we know now was the bogus claim of Weapons of Mass Destruction (WMD) in Iraq's arsenal.

A former Amnesty International board member, Francis A Boyle, tells us that all in all 1.5 million Iraqis died which included 500,000 children. Some 200,000 of them met a violent end, often blown to pieces by coalition airstrikes or suicide bombers, the last creation of a nincompoop named L. Paul Bremer who knew no Arabic and never set a foot in Iraq but here he was the US-appointed Iraq's Czar. Amongst his most hideous blunders was disbanding of the Iraq army. "We created half a million angry, armed, unemployed Iraqis in 48 hours," remarked Bremer's predecessor.

Medical system collapsed as doctors fled in droves, children mortality hit the roof as malnutrition and starvation hit the land. The effect of depleted uranium is still felt in Fallujah among a generation of orphans. The radioactive substances caused malformations, sterility and infertility.

Here is *The Independent* of London on the Fallujah horror: "Dramatic increase in infant mortality, cancer and leukaemia… exceed those reported by survivors of the atomic bombs that were dropped on Hiroshima and Nagasaki in 1945…"

But the US was only starting in the Middle East. Libya, Syria, Yemen etc happened in quick succession, indeed there are too many to recount in this piece. I would touch briefly on Libya and the rest you could look up.

UN, of course, was AWOL.

***

The US-NATO carried out 10,000 air strikes and several hundred cruise missile attacks on Libya for seven months in 2011. The US-NATO claimed Libya's leader Muammar Gaddafi was about to unleash a genocide on its own people in Benghazi.

The US secured a UN Security Council Resolution which authorized a no-fly zone to protect civilians. It soon morphed into a full-scale invasion, and then into an avowed mission to unseat Gaddafi, clearly an illegal war but the UN wasn't outraged. As for the threat of genocide, an independent British parliamentary inquiry determined that "Gaddafi wasn't planning to massacre civilians. This myth was exaggerated by rebels and Western governments…"

And what did they destroy? The CIA World Facebook noted Libya had a literacy rate of 94.2%. The World Health Organisation (WHO) was gushing on country's health care service in 2011. Life expectancy was 75 years (better than India's). Libya had the highest GDP in Africa. Less people lived below the poverty line than in the Netherlands.

That this havoc in Libya had its horrific consequences in Niger, Tunisia, Mali, Chad and Cameroon is better left unsaid for some other day.

***

I do think that a few of us, thanks to social media, have a bit of an idea of suffering humanity in the last two decades. But the early years of an impotent UN are shrouded in obscurity. I would seek your indulgence for a minute on North Korea.

North Korea, much reviled and a pariah in international community for the crimes we don't know about, has suffered as few nations have ever. It was virtually destroyed during the Korean War in the 50s. Every single family in North Korea lost a loved one during its course. No less than 30% of its population—some 9 million people—were extinguished. 78 of its cities and thousands of its villages were razed to ground.

General Douglas MacArthur, the architect of this annihilation, later admitted in US senate: "I have never seen such devastation. I have seen, I guess, as much blood and disaster as any living man."

Today, North Korea is said to be a "rogue nation", one of "axis of evil", a threat to world peace though we all know which nation justifiably be called the terrorist state of our world.

***

"[The US] is the greatest purveyor of violence in the world today."

– Dr. Martin Luther King (1967)

"[The United States] is the most warlike nation in the history of the world."

– Jimmy Carter, 39th President of the United States (2019)

The government bombs; the people shop.

The term, post-War is a misnomer. We know 15 million lives were snuffed out during the World War 1. It was 26 million during WW II. Since then, US-led wars have accounted for over 20 million dead. The induced anarchy has brought terrorist groups home to roost everywhere, be it in Africa, Asia or Europe.

So rigged is our world that the US president Barack Obama was awarded the Nobel Peace prize in 2009. A few years later he was bombing seven countries simultaneously.

***

Reparations? Of course, none to these and countless other suffering nations.

Such is the disdain for international laws that president George W. Bush once reacted thus to if US had violated the international law on Iraq: "International law? I better call my lawyer; he didn't bring that up to me."

To be fair, the United Nations evokes as much sympathy as it does disdain.

For the last 30 years, the UN General Assembly is unanimous in voting against the inhuman sanctions on Cuba, but for the US and Israel. [1] Yet these inhuman sanctions have lasted for over 60 years.

Palestine is recognized by 138 of the 193 nations. Only last week, the UNGA passed a resolution—98 in favour, 17 against—to request the World Court to urgently weigh in on Israel's "prolonged occupation, settlement and annexation of the Palestinian territory."

But nothing happens say on Cuba or Palestine because the UN has been reduced to impotency by the financial muscle of the West. The Security Council has a fractured vote on dire issues; the UNGA can't move a fly. It's only used as a tool by West to push its globalist agenda.

***

This call on Russia to provide reparations to rebuild Ukraine is a joke.

Neither the UN Charter nor other international laws authorize the UN General Assembly to demand reparations.

UN has shot itself into foot for now reparations could be sought from a Cuba to Serbia, Iraq to Libya to Serbia to North Korea.

It indeed looks a ploy to legally seize the huge Russian assets in the shadow of UN.

The West has created a task force for the purpose, called REPO (Russian Elites, Proxies and Oligarchs) as a mechanism to loot Russia's assets which is upwards of $300 billion as of now.

The REPO—made up of the US, Australia, Britain, Canada, France, Germany, Italy, Japan and the European Commission—has its hands in the honey pot.

The lion's share in this $300 billion of course is frozen reserves of Russian Central Bank in various European banks.

There is embargo on gold imports from Russia so that the latter can't make up for the loss in revenue due to sanctions.

The Spanish authorities have seized a $90 million super yacht of Russian billionaire Viktor Vekselberg. Fijian law has managed to lay hands on a $300 million yacht owned by another oligarch, Suleiman Kerimov.

Since Volodymyr Zelenskyy has quoted a figure of $600 billion for postwar recovery of Ukraine, it's clear how the West intends to supply the funds. Ukraine has demanded frozen Russian assets and has had vocal support from several European nations, such as Lithuania and Estonia.

***

So do go beyond the propaganda which is served by lackey media, academics and your think-tanks etc.

Reference:

[1] https://www.newsbred.com/the-world-has-just-voted-against-the-us-but-you-dont-know/

Link to Article:

https://www.newsbred.com/un-diktat-to-russia-pay-reparations-to-ukraine/

False Flag Attack from Poland is Copybook Us

November 17, 2022

A missile attack struck a village in Poland[1], killing two, which the media rats were quick to blame on Russia before US-NATO ruled that out, never mind their rogue vassal Ukraine still clung on to its blame-Russia game in the hope of World War III.

My first reaction was why would Russia blow up an old trailer and a tractor in Poland?

And whatever happened to NATO's air-defense system for its members, one of which is Poland?

I sure thought this is it, the formal roll down of World War III, for the blueprint is exactly the same which the US uses to justify the wars it can't do without for its loot and plunder.

Gulf of Tonkin

Your grandpa of course would be aware of "Gulf of Tonkin" fraud which caused the Vietnam War: The US claimed the North Vietnamese forces had attacked its ships in those waters on August 2 and 4 in 1964 and it had no option but to bomb them which escalated into a human tragedy like few in human history.

We now know that the so-called August 4, 1964 attack never happened once some 200 documents were declassified after nearly half a century in early 2000s. It showed that the US had distorted the truth about the Gulf of Tonkin incident, ostensibly to suit president Lyndon B Johnson and his political goals.

The cost? Americans lost 58,220 of its own men; Vietnamese some 3 million lives.

Media never asked the question and we never paused to think: What was US warships doing in Vietnamese waters? And what else North Vietnamese could've done if US ships were with the South Vietnamese attacking them?

Pearl Harbor

You must be aware of the Pearl Harbor incident of December 7, 1941 which brought the United States formally into World War II the very next day. The Japanese attack on this US naval base in Honolulu, Hawaii killed 2,403 Americans and wounded 1,178 others. But we now know that Americans all along knew the Japanese war ships were approaching their naval base but did nothing to thwart the disaster.

The US used the attack to "sell" the war to its people, much like it did with Vietnam, or in recent history with Afghanistan, Iraq, Libya etc.

It so happened that the far shores of the Pacific Ocean were important to Americans for its raw materials. The Depression years of 1930s hadn't left the United States. But here was Japan, a mirror-image, which was occupying lands in Asia for its own acquisition of resources. It had occupied China, and the rubber-rich French colony of IndoChina. It was eyeing Dutch colony of Indonesia for its oil-rich gains.

Thus began severe US economic sanctions on Japan (sounds familiar, eh?). The partners in crime, the British and the Dutch, lent a helping hand in an embargo on vital oil products. The Japanese offered US a share in the Asian loot, as long as it was allowed to extend its own sphere of influence in Latin America.

Predictably, the US said no.

The US wanted the war but it didn't want to initiate it. One, it would be difficult to convince its people; two, it would've brought Germany and Italy, as allies of Japan into war and the isolationist US Congress would've never approved of it.

Out came the same time-tested methods which we now know from Vietnam, and of course the ongoing Ukraine Crisis: Push your enemy to the wall for he would have no option but to come out throwing punches.

The strategy used in Pearl Harbor included the deployment of warships close to Japanese territorial waters.

Economic sanctions were bringing magic of its own.

These continuing "putting pins in rattlesnakes," as FDR was to say privately to friends, finally yielded gold.

The rattlesnakes in Tokyo finally had enough.

A Japanese warship set sail for Hawaii where the US had provocatively stationed its fleet.

The US had decoded in advance the Japanese move but they sat tight and let the Pearl Harbor incident happen.

The trophy was the world domination which came after the World War II, courtesy largely of Soviet Union and millions of Russian lives lost, an ally which they are now choosing to snuff out forever.

***

This is no place to dwell on how 9/11 happened; and how that incident suited the US to launch its endless wars in the Middle East.

Likewise, I won't rake up the start of the Spanish-American War in the closing years of the 20th century which gave US the control of the Caribbean and launched its Pacific plunder. The *casus belli* was the mysterious sinking of US battleship *Maine* in the Havana Harbour, an act which was immediately blamed on the Spanish.

I would rather also leave aside the shooting down of MH-17 in 2014 which killed 298 on board and endlessly blamed on Russia. So blatant were the disregard for facts that Russia left trilateral consultations with the "investigating" Netherlands and Australia after a while, claiming the other two were not keen in uncovering the truth, and had other goals in mind.

***

This Poland Missile thing seems to have fizzled out for the moment. But there is no mistaking the pattern or similar false flags which would keep plunging humanity into crisis.

Yet this is as important a moment as ever to know your media.

All that garbage we are fed non-stop on television and print media.

And that you should never believe its word if it concerns war and peace, democracy and human rights, and all those lovely ideals which seduce you into pinning for the Wrong.

They jumped the gun for that's how they know wars are manufactured: In this case Poland had been violated and NATO must jump to its protection against the perpetrator Russia under its Article 5 obligation of collective defense.

The US and NATO, as I said, have blinked but the danger hasn't gone away. We know of the sabotage of Nord Stream 1, the Crimean bridge bomb attack and the past history to know it's coming again.

Meanwhile, brush up on what's happening in Italy where a major "Nazi attack", linked to Ukraine's Azov Battalion has been foiled.[2] This is terrorism in the heart of Europe and we all know who smiles the broadest when a similar thing is wrought upon the Middle East. Sowing anarchy and reaping harvest have always worked, hasn't it.

And that the weapons in the hands of these terrorists could be the ones which had been earmarked for Ukraine should tell you about the bloody years ahead of Europe—a la how Libya's arsenals created the Islamic State (IS) etc.—irrespective of how Ukraine thing ends.

Reference:

[1] https://en.wikipedia.org/wiki/2022_missile_explosion_in_Poland

[2] https://sputnikglobe.com/20221115/italian-police-foil-deadly-plot-by-neo-nazis-linked-to-ukraines-azov-battalion-1104265416.html

Link to Article:

https://www.newsbred.com/do-wonder-what-russia-gains-by-attacking-trailer-and-a-tractor-in-poland/

Who Would Trust a Wolf But a Fool, Zelensky?

November 24, 2022

This is a tale of how Ukraine trusted West with its life but it is fast slipping away.

Here was a nation, albeit a constructed one, wanting to carve an identity away from its "motherland" Russia and was smitten by what the West could offer by way of market for its goods; jobs for its people, economic aid and all that glitter as its favoured child.

It didn't realize that Ukraine was no better than a bait for Washington in its persistent quest to destroy Russia, the first move being to delink Moscow from Europe. If the good fortune brought about the fall of Vladimir Putin, it'd be a double bounty.

Well, the Washington has succeeded in alienating Europe from Russia.

Europe won't have its energy from Russia, that adhesive which was joining the two from the hip.

Russia too would no longer be a Eurasian power and would now firmly be directed towards Asia where the West hopes it would irk China at some point in future, given how Central Asia would be prized by both.

Now Ukraine, for all the West cares, could go to hell.

Kiev is now finding out that the NATO could train its men as guinea pigs but won't get its own hands dirty on Russia. Worse, there is no certainty that funds and weapons would be supplied endlessly.

Kiev first learnt that the fire it lit in the form of a missile strike in Poland was quickly doused by West lest it leads to a NATO intervention and World War III.

It has learnt to its great sorrow that endless stream of Ukrainians fleeing to European capitals are unwelcome, for example the much-touted UK's "Homes for Ukraine" was nothing better than a false hope[1].

Further, the European Union (EU) is dithering on its ninth round of sanctions against Russia which has led to Ukrainian foreign minister lash out in public anger: "If the Ukrainians are not tired, then the rest of Europe has neither the moral nor the political right to get tired."

Moral and political right? Who but a fool would expect the West to swear by it. When has a trust in a wolf's words brought about a happy ending?

There is more to it. Ukraine's currency, the Hryvnia, has fallen by 70% against the Dollar/Euro/Pound; GDP has sunk by 40%, more than a million have lost jobs, nearly 10 million people have been displaced etc, etc.

Russia, having learnt from the playbook of West only in Yugoslavia, is busy destroying Ukraine's energy infrastructure. So traffic light isn't there to stop accidents at night; lifts don't work never mind you are climbing up to 15th floor with your grocery; winter has arrived but your boiler or washing machines can't whir; nobody buys your flat ground floor up for any missile could hit it at any time. Internet is unstable, batteries can't be charged like before, card machines don't work. Cash economy is all how daily life goes by.

The goods you used to get from Russia are no longer there; you don't have money to buy products from import.

Oh yes, the West seemingly is endlessly supplying funds but it's coming with a caveat. True to its time-tested method, the West would like to outsource Ukraine's public resources for "better management".

This is ownership—and Ukraine thought West is helping them forge an identity, secure its sovereignty. They are left with no leverage over their sponsors. How do you sell this kind of independence to your people? In the midst of pitched battle for survival, they don't find the Big Brother over their shoulder who had pushed them in the hole of hell in the first place.

The slightest hint from West of "fatigue" would throw Volodymyr Zelenskyy into the cage of growing dissidence in his inner circle. If he seeks a peace deal with Russia, after losing countless men, a land the size of a Hungary, a nation flattened, he would be torn up in pieces.

The sad truth is, one could know where Ukraine is coming from but they chimed the bell of a savage in search of refuge.

History teaches us that people of all colour and sizes seek to throw off the yoke of their masters. That's what you learn from freedom struggles in Asia, Africa, Latin America and even Europe where Poles, Lithuanians, Latvians, Estonians etc wanted to call the air they breathe their own.

Ukraine lies on history's faultiness where ideological and civilizational divergences—the West and East, the Catholic/Protestant and Orthodox Christianity, liberalism and conservatism—grow apart from each other.

Ukraine itself has its entire East of Russian lineage while its Western part, historically belonging to Habsburg Empire under the name of Galicia and Transcarpathia, always felt a tug towards the West.

There is a reason why Ukraine means "borderland." It was invented by non-Russian communist dictators for political reasons only in the 20th century. It's been in existence for only 30 years, a decade of which now as a vassal of the United States.

Washington used it as a pawn on its geopolitical chessboard, like it did with most of those satellite states in Europe which were once part of the Soviet Union, giving them NATO membership and positioning its nukes facing Moscow and St. Petersburg.

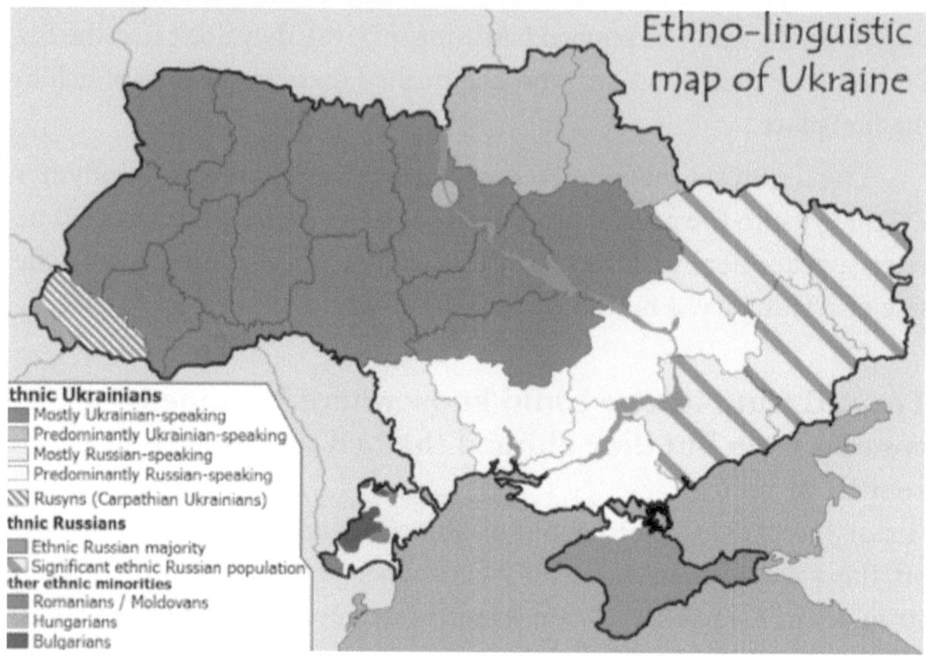

The West brought the existential question for Russia right on its door. Ukraine, more than anyone else, was a red flag for both historical and practical reasons for Russia as it contained its own people and access to Black Sea from where Moscow depends on its trade with Central Asia, and elsewhere.

Kiev saw a better future with West than with Russia, with access to capital markets, EU investment funds, larger trade, and emigration to Capitals of Europe and America for its workforce. They saw a future in Anglosphere who were all too keen to lure them into wonderland.

But as I said, West couldn't care the least about Kiev. Ukrainians mean nothing to them. They have got what they wanted: Severe links between Russia and Europe and turn the former firmly towards a narrower sphere of operation in Asia.

And now the end is in sight. Russia would move into top gear once the conscription of soldiers is complete. The missile drama in Poland has shown them that a direct confrontation is farthest from the minds of West. Their enemies are battling their own recessions and a seething citizenry could erupt any moment in the cold, freezing, bleak days of winter. Russia would be happy to settle this side of Dnieper river and bring about the collapse of Kiev regime by wrecking the infrastructure.

West, meanwhile is hoisted on its own petard.

In the longer run, Ukraine would be seen as a catalyst of a New World Order: the tragedy is it would've come entirely at its own cost.

Reference:

[1] https://sputnikglobe.com/20221122/why-is-west-eager-to-give-ukrainians-billions-worth-of-weapons-but-not-refugee-benefits-1104557861.html

Link to Article:

https://www.newsbred.com/ukraine-for-all-the-west-cares-could-go-to-hell-now/

Latest Joke: EU Calls Russia State Sponsors of Terrorism

November 29, 2022

Indeed, think about the terrorism that has originated in your lifetime and the names uppermost in your mind: Osama bin Laden, Al Qaeda, ISIS?

Well, Osama bin Laden was cultivated by the United States much before he hit headlines at the turn of the century, funded and armed to teeth, not just in Afghanistan against the Soviets but also previously in hapless Yugoslavia, eyed by the predators West.

Al Qaeda? Well its founder Ayman Zawahiri would've been nowhere without the support of CIA, NATO and the Turkish branch of terrorist network Gladio.

It's no secret to political elites but to we the innocents fooled by our media that Al Qaeda came into being in 1988 by the US special services to spread the brand of Islamist terrorism after they have had their fill with the Fascism/Nazism card in Europe or Communism anywhere else.

ISIS? Do find out about the al-Tanf American military base in Syria—yes, against the wishes of sovereign Damascus—where ISIS mercenaries are taught the use of missiles, drones, sabotage etc and parcelled to wherever they are needed by the West. Presently hundreds of them are in Ukraine to fight the proxy war against Russia.

While you wonder why terrorists are finding refuge under the Big Brother—obviously to be used at any given time and venue—do brush up on Abu Ghraib and Guantanamo Bay where horrific torture is inflicted on countless individuals without legal recourse or "human rights" by very those who swagger as its ultimate champions.

So when the European Union (EU) dub Russia as state sponsor of terrorism, implying doing acts so as to spread terror in the hearts of woeful Ukrainians, don't miss the irony for these very people bombed tens of German cities, killed and raped thousands, in World War II without as much as a courtesy call at Nuremberg or anywhere else since.

Anyone for the Vietnam War where US tested is Napalms, cluster bombs, rockets designed to enter caves, "dummy" bullets etc, reducing local peasants as no better than guinea pig? It drove the population into urban slums, and the mass murder soon extended to defenceless peasant societies in Laos and Cambodia.

In the process, most established norms and international obligations such as the UN Charter, the Geneva Accords (1954), the Nuremberg Code and the Hague Convention etc were cast in junk.

It also is nothing but state terrorism when you install oppressive and terrorist regimes across the world—the Banana Republics—which abounded in Caribbean and Central America (your Trujillo in the Dominican Republic or Somozas in Nicaragua) and the names such as Diem and Thieu (South Vietnam), Mobutu (Zaire), Pinochet (Chile) and Suharto (Indonesia) which readily come to mind.

Heavily armed by the West, these autocrats and dictators unleashed terror which if only it was to reach us—without the cover-up by the media—would shake us to the bones: Like a million killed in Indonesia in just a year, 1965-66 which, it's now proven without a doubt, had the acquiescence of the United States.[1]

Many more million lives lost could be added if one was to run through whatever happened in Argentina, Brazil, Chile, Paraguay, Guatemala, Nicaragua etc at a given time in their history through overt or covert US operations.

The events in Afghanistan, Iraq, Libya, Yemen, Syria etc are too recent to escape memory. These lands have suffered enormous human tragedy, infrastructure damage and environmental degradation.

Even in Ukraine, while Donbass or eastern part of the country was subjected to incessant bombing and killing, and Minsk Agreements amounted to little, there was no outrage in the European Union on state-sponsored terrorism for years. When neo-Nazis, in the form of Azov Battalion, were causing havoc, a blind eye was turned at their monstrous acts.

Closer home, in Kashmir, for decades now we have Pak terrorists soaking the pristine land with locals' and Indian soldiers blood but you won't hear a word against them in US Congress, EU parliament etc. But all hell breaks loose when a "temporary" provision of Article 370 is diluted.

The West does what it does is to ensure its economic interests through own intervention or from those who are installed for the very purpose.

Everything is a fair play in this exercise: creating terrorists, militias and use of money to bring recalcitrant voices to heel.

The servitude of media, and the obedience of bureaucracy, judiciary, academia is secured, whatever it takes.

So in terming Russia as a state sponsor of terrorism—of no value but for propaganda—the EU has dutifully followed its master the United States which has deemed Cuba, North Korea, Iran and Syria as state sponsors of terrorism.

As for its sanctity, just remember that Nelson Mandela himself was a terrorist in their books for several years!

Reference:

[1] https://www.theatlantic.com/international/archive/2017/10/the-indonesia-documents-and-the-us-agenda/543534/

Link to Article:

https://www.newsbred.com/the-latest-joke-you-missed-eu-has-called-russia-state-sponsor-of-terrorism/

The Iran Factor in India-russia Ties

December 3, 2022

How important is Iran for India?

In crude terms, probably second only to Russia.

Figures sure don't support it:

If oil is the biggest component in energy-deficient India—our 85% needs are imported—Iran factors nil.

So literally not a penny in $119 billion chunk of our overall $600-billion plus imports go to Tehran.

And if India exports $300-plus billion of its goods around the world, guess where Iran is:44th in the list when even Nepal is 10th![1]

Yet Iran is second only to Russia for its value for without it we potentially have no ground below our feet outside India.

If you look at the world map, you would understand it: We have Himalayas in north, China and Pakistan sit on our eastern and western shoulders and all we are left with are our sea routes to conduct business with the world.

So if India could literally hit the road, like China has with its Belt and Road Initiative (BRI), it could reach faster and cheaper to Central Asia and the rest of Europe and its trade ambitions could explode.

If we are still the 5th largest economy of the world, imagine how it would boost our chances to be the Top Three in the world in next decade.

Our infrastructure, technology, manufacturing, transport, agriculture, demography edge etc would hit the roof.

It would not only lift our 1.40 billion people to an envious lifestyle, we would also have the money to spare for Global South which prime minister Narendra Modi has set as priority for India's G20 role.

Don't we know that the Global South is beholden to China for this precise reason, its money which keeps them on their feet on all sectors of economy.

Iran offers that window to where we want to see ourselves in next decade and more; it's the node for which we built Chabahar Port and without which the INSTC (International North South Transport Corridor) is a non-starter.

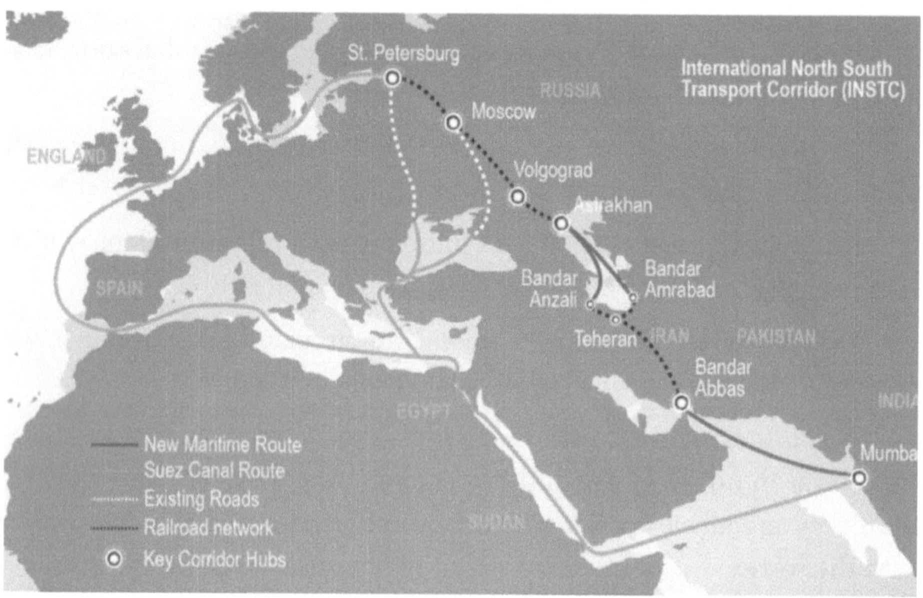

This land connectivity, through INSTC, is virtually the future India sees for itself.

It is what would make India a global power, and not just a regional player.

So if Tehran is this important, why don't India offers its money through the purchase of Iranian oil which till 2019 made it among New Delhi's top three oil suppliers?

More so when Tehran desperately needs friends and trade to alleviate the US sanctions, in force since 1979 but only intensified since 2014 on the drama around its so-called nuclear threat?

For a while India enjoyed buying Iranian oil under the US waivers which stopped under Donald Trump in 2019.

Tehran was rightly hurt, even took recourse to criticising India on Kashmir, and it appeared India had lost a friend forever with which it had shared boundaries till 1947, and a civilizational history for centuries.

A valid question now is: Why India fears US on Iran when it doesn't on the issue of Russia?

For one, India in 2022 is vastly different to what it was in 2014.

In 2014, it was just about coming out of the damage of Congress rule. In just eight years, it's a confident nation of nationalistic fervour and burning ambitions. A global player trusted by even antagonistic forces.

For last five years, India hasn't bought oil from Iran while it has seen China lap it up with both hands and yet no US sanction has come Beijing's way.

India has also tested waters with Russian oil in holding its ground against US pressure—a primer of which had come by buying the new age S-400 missiles from Moscow.

For a nation which can't survive without energy of which it produces little, India has no option but to buy the cheapest oil in the market for its people for whom even one-rupee hike is a matter to decide who forms the government.

Iran brilliantly fits this puzzle for its oil resources, for trade, for connectivity but there is also a bigger geopolitical necessity above all.

The two of world's biggest powers today are the United States and China.

India along with Russia provides that third vector as a balancing voice which allows Global South to not fall between these two rival poles.

Not to say that it allows both India and Russia also to project themselves as independent powers, and not a sidekick of either the United States or China.

This logic is not lost on New Delhi. But it's that big bully called the United States which doesn't take kindly for a friend or a foe to sidestep the road it lays down for them.

Henry Kissinger once famously quipped: "It may be dangerous to be America's enemy, but to be America's friend is fatal."

If this sounds chilling, there are good enough reasons for it.

★ How do you cope with secessionists who come from across the border and inflame your Sikh and Muslim population to keep trouble brewing?

★ How do you cope with domestic anarchy, whipped up on religious or caste lines, or gender and LGBT politics, taking the route of our Universities, to show the government as impotent, turning its popular base into open hostility?

★ How do you cope with a sold-out academia and media, the planted Human Rights groups and NGOs, a judiciary, bureaucracy and political parties fattened over decades, ready to use your own Constitution against you in the name of "democracy" and "individual rights"?

★ How do you cope with a Hegemon which has a doctrine of keeping you destabilized at your borders: Sometimes, its Kashmir and Punjab; or Uyghur, or Ukraine, or nurtured Kurds in Syria which bomb Istanbul and cause riots in Iran on the orchestrated hijab issue.

And if this is not all, the US has Dollar through which it could roil your financial markets; the beholden world bodies like IMF, WB and WTO to suck the last drop of your blood, the joined-at-hips EU who remains one of your two top trading outposts alongside the US.

(If still not convinced, give an answer to yourself:

★ *How do anti-CAA stir, or farmers' protest could sustain themselves for over a year?*

★ *How could penniless farmers squat on doors of Delhi without a worry on feeding families?*

★ *If tens of millions of funds were needed for that stir to be sustained, who provided that money?*

★ *If the judiciary first sat on the issue, and then didn't make public the report of the committee it had formed, what explains this dereliction of Constitutional obligation?*)

It should explain why India has been hesitant on Iran in the last few years.

Iran has been grumpy but they also understand India's predicament, listening to the Russian voice in their ears.

They hope India would come around with an open stance of affinity with Tehran—most probably when the US becomes an unbearable weight on New Delhi's shoulders.

Iran is also the card through which India keeps US in check. If New Delhi openly aligns with Iran, it would be game over for the US.

Washington knows it. The nightmare of US is Russia-Iran-China-India as four poles of a multipolar world which would bring curtains on its global supremacy.

All four, incidentally, are civilizational forces too.

Not that this New World Order is far off.

Iran is already part of Shanghai Cooperation Organization (SCO).

It has survived against all odds and is a power to reckon with in the Middle East today.

India also doesn't need to worry on account of Iran's rivals, such as Saudi Arabia, Israel or even Turkey as all have woken up to the changing dynamics of Middle East which drives the world through its oil.

The next US action would be either to withdraw itself in its own zone or open the Taiwan front with China.

It's unlikely US would withdraw: Its survival depends on its aggression for the world knows Dollar is nothing but a fake currency.

Only a servile world would let Dollar retain its pole position: A free world would reject it at the first opportunity.

So if US aggression is imminent, so would be India's distance from the Washington: And India-Iran ties would have warmed up a notch higher.

If India is to keep growing, fulfil aspirations of its billion-plus, sooner or later it would have to bite this bullet.

It's Washington only which would leave India with no other choice.

Reference:

[1] https://tradingeconomics.com/india/exports-by-country

Link to Article:

https://www.newsbred.com/the-us-question-and-the-next-step-on-india-iran-ties/

Serbia is Once Again in the Eye of the West

December 13, 2022

As Serbia is baited by Kosovo, no better than a pawn to West like Ukraine, we recommend readers the author's widely-acclaimed book on Yugoslavia's destruction — "HOW UNITED STATES SHOT HUMANITY"[1]*—which was the genesis of much of world's problem today, including spurt in terrorism.)*

Another Ukraine is unfolding in Europe, and likewise it is of West's making.

Kosovo is making life difficult for a large number of Serbs within their territory and Serbia can't be a spectator for long, as Russia couldn't be to what was happening to ethnic Russians in the Donbass region of Ukraine.

Serbia has the UN resolution and international agreements on its side, much as Russia had Minsk Agreements to protect lives of helpless fellow ethnics. But international rules and treaties in our world are bound to the little finger of West and are useless if it doesn't suit them.

If Serbia intervenes—and its hands are being forced—it would be portrayed as aggressor, like Russia has been, and the combined weight of West would strike and crush the Serbs for a very, very long time.

Unlike Russia, Serbia is a small, poor, non-nuclear European country and would've no means to defend itself.

The brutal West is unable to come to terms that Serbia hasn't sanctioned Russia on Ukraine and sees it as a sign of Slavic brotherhood between the two nations.

There are a clutch of other motives which the West has on Serbia to which I would come later. As of now, let me give a little background to the extremely volatile situation developing between Kosovo and Serbia in Southern Europe. For the Old Continent, this Ukraine 2—as if Ukraine 1 wasn't enough—holds the seeds to destruction of humanity on a much wider and worse scale than the two World Wars.

A brief background

If you look at the map, you would find Kosovo as a southern tail of Serbia which has Hungary in its north and Romania and Bulgaria in east.

Serbs, as people, suffered for 400 years under the Ottomans, Habsburg, Hitler's Germany and by the machinations of the West for the last 30 years.

They suffered under the Ottomans for they were not Muslims and were heavily taxed and denied ownership of property.

When the Habsburg monarchy fed itself on the decaying Ottomans in the second half of the 20th century, they found Serbia an obstacle to their designs on the rest of the Balkans.

Serbia then was a much larger entity, combining Bosnia-Herzegovina and Albanians and handed over the much-needed pretext to the Austro-Hungarian (Habsburg) Empire when the Archduke Francis Ferdinand was assassinated in 1914.

It sounded the outbreak of World War I, Austria-Hungary ended up as losers and Serbia found itself enlarged as the leaders of Slovenia and Croatia also chose to unite with them into a single kingdom.

(*Slovenia and Croatia did so to go from the losing to the winning side and avoid paying war reparations. Better still, enlarging themselves on the Adriatic coast at the expense of Italy.*)

This joint kingdom was renamed "Jugoslavia" in 1929. Croats and Serbia though engaged in fierce conflicts soon enough to plague what could be termed as the "First Yugoslavia."

In 1941, Serb patriots rebelled against the Kingdom of Yugoslavia who had joined hands with Nazi Germany during World War II. This led to a German invasion, bombing of Belgrade, and creation of an independent fascist state of Croatia (including Bosnia-Herzegovina), attaching much of the Serbian province of Kosovo to Albania, then a puppet of Mussolini's Italy. Croatian Ustashe followed it up with unleashing of a genocide against the Serbs.

After World War II, the Communist Yugoslavia broke up with Soviet Union in 1948. Josip Broz Tito was the helmsman in this own course of "self-management" and also made a few of Yugoslavia's provinces almost autonomous, like Kosovo.

Once Tito died in 1980, things took turn for the worse. Yugoslavia fell neck deep in debt to the West. The International Monetary Fund (IMF) arrived with austerity measures but Slovenia and Croatia, the two richer Republics within Yugoslavia, were not prepared to pay for other poor republics of the State.

The first multiparty elections were held in 1990—not in all of Yugoslavia but separately in each Republic. It was an invitation for Slovenia and Croatia to declare themselves as independent.

Internal administrative borders were now international borders. The defending Serbian army was now the aggressors. The protesting Serbs, within the fold of the two newly independent nations, were secessionists! The 1975 Helsinki Accord of inviolable territorial integrity was thrown into bin.

The demise of Soviet Union in 1991 was the trigger for the West—US, Germany, NATO and media in particular—to bare fangs in open against the "aggressor" Serbs. Russia in post-Soviet world was in its own existential crisis anyway. It was time now to punish their Slavic brothers.

The West's machinations led to one after another Republics breaking away from what once was Yugoslavia. Serbia was now a standalone nation but its woes were unending. An orchestrated insurgency was initiated in its Kosovo part between 1995-1998. When Serbia tried to quell it, NATO intervened, under the pretext of Human Rights, and bombed Serbia for 78 days. Yes 78 days!

Present Times

This led to creation of Kosovo. A "country' which is unrecognised by the United Nations; nor by India or China; and indeed not by half of all the nations of the world.

But it exists, for it gives the United States its biggest military base, Bondsteel, in the heart of Europe; Germany an access to Adriatic Sea; in Kosovo a dream of a greater Albania to Albanians, a Muslim nation within Europe, which is yet another tool the US could use to keep the Old Continent in torment. The Neo-Nazis in Ukraine and Jihadists, not to say refugees spilling over from the war-torn Middle East and Africa, is anarchy waiting to happen in Europe which suits the United States no end up.

This Kosovo card has now been brought out to drag Russia into a wider war if they rise in defence of fellow Slavs. Kosovo has intensified its persecution of Serbs within their territory and Serbia can't afford to look the other way, armed as it is with UN resolutions and international agreements.

There is UN Security Council Resolution 1244 which provides for Serbia to send its security forces into the province to protect ethnic Serbs if required.

The 2013 Brussels agreement envisioned the autonomy for the remaining ethnic Serbs in Kosovo.

Under the Washington Agreement of 2020, Kosovo had agreed not to apply for membership in any international organisations.

Yet Kosovo has now gone back on its word and is applying for a membership in the EU in next two days on December 15.

In all this, the West has looked the other way on the matter of upholding international laws.

When Serbia suggested it would send its troops to defend ethnic Serbs within the Kosovo territory, as deemed legal by the UN Resolution 1244, Germany called it an "absurd" move.

Serbian president Aleksandar Vucic is saying his nation is "nailed to the wall." Serbia isn't being permitted even to be neutral in the Ukraine conflict—its' being forced by the West to come out in open and criticize Russia.

(It must make you marvel the nerves of India which has stood its ground against the overbearing West on the Ukraine conflict.)

Don't be surprised if there is a false flag attack in coming days—a bomb attack or a massacre—which would give the West a pretext to blame it on Serbia and widen the conflict.

On one hand it shows the frustration of West in failing to bring Russia on its knees. On the other hand, Serbs, the whipping boys of history, are finding their demons rise again.

Reference:

[1] https://www.amazon.in/How-United-States-Shot-Humanity-ebook/dp/B012O6QO48

Link to Article:

https://www.newsbred.com/another-ukraine-is-unfolding-in-europe-who-would-bell-the-west/

Russia Has Seen NATO and is Unimpressed

December 26, 2022

NATO, I have a feeling, is being found out in Ukraine.

It's one thing to bomb unarmed civilians in Libya or Afghanistan and quite another to square up to an enemy with chutzpah in the game.

For three generations, NATO meant obeisance by the world – the respect a wolf has in a henhouse.

Now no less than a Wall Street Journal says Europe is running out of weapons.

US anyway wasn't producing the tanks or planes, battleships or aircraft carriers at home but was outsourcing them to its minion nations.

So it is with putting its own boots on the ground, such as in Vietnam, Syria or Afghanistan, where the experience has not often been pleasant.

Often the US looks for a proxy—be it Ukraine or a Taiwan or Jihadis for that matter—to cut inconvenient regimes down to size.

And so it is with funding and arming Ukraine to the teeth: Trading the proxy regime's manhood in a bid to cripple Russia gravely.

Yet 10 months on, all we see is that Russia could bomb its targets at will in Ukraine.

Ukraine doesn't have the air defense capability to deter the Russians; its general Valery Zaluzhny is asking for 300 tanks, 700 infantry fighting vehicles, 500 Howitzers more to "beat this enemy."

Now all this Wishlist is much bigger than the total armoured forces of most European armies.

As for Zaluzhny, nobody is asking him: Sir, you had similarly predicted a similar outcome with a much larger armed forces and weaponry at your command in early summer. Why do you think we should take you seriously now?

Ukrainian forces, meanwhile, are relentlessly being drawn into a meat-grinder by the Russians on frontlines of thousands of miles.

Russia's tactics is to double down at different nodes of frontlines. It brings out the enemy's second line of defense from the hiding who are then minced in pieces for the other world.

Russia, deliberately, isn't attacking Ukraine's third line of defence which is their command centre, for it doesn't need to.

Russia, the masters of attritional warfare, is using minimum of its men, weapons and resources to suck its enemy—Ukraine and NATO—dry.

NATO being worked inside out

The tactics are also allowing Russian generals and military intelligence to work NATO inside out, as Putin observed[1] the other day.

So Putin isn't keen on winning in the strictest sense of the term; the West too has no better aim than to cripple Russia and the war is meandering along till one or the other can no longer keep standing.

Meanwhile the West, from time to time, keeps preening; lauding or inviting Zelensky on its lawns and stuffing his pockets with whatever it could.

The pretence would drop once Bakhmut falls in the Donbass region, and a desperate West tries to hurt Russia deep enough for the latter to launch its prized weapons.

For this is what we heard Putin saying the other day in Eurasia Economic Council: "I assure you, after the early warning system receives a signal of a missile attack, hundreds of our missiles are in the air (…) It is impossible to stop them (…) There will be nothing left of the enemy, because it is impossible to intercept a hundred missiles."

Pepe Escobar, the noted geoanalyst,[2] says: "Russia can knock out all NATO bridges, ports, airports as well as power stations, oil and natural gas storage, Rotterdam oil and natural gas installations, in a matter of a few hours. All energy production equipment across NATOstan would be destroyed…A dazed and confused Empire would be unable to move troops, any troops, to Europe."

Pivotal Moment of History

If it's really how things are as I have espoused so far, we are looking at a cataclysmic moment of modern history.

There is a latent fear that any miscalculation could lead to an Armageddon where there are no winners or losers left.

But if it's Father Time the two antagonists are playing out, NATO could irretrievably be hollowed out.

NATO began as a security alliance of Western nations before it spread its tentacles to most of Europe and then diversified to Asia stealthily for its Charter doesn't allow it to go beyond the Old Continent.

But the truth is, after the break-up of Soviet Union, NATO formed an informal connection with Japan in 1992. This has spread likewise to similar arrangement with other Asia-Pacific nations such as South Korea, Singapore, Australia and New Zealand.

When NATO waded into Afghanistan, it drew Central Asia in its ambit who were forced to offer assistance for transit and other purposes such as overflight and basing rights.

No less than eight non-NATO nations presently have troops in Kosovo; 14 non-NATO nations had their military forces in Afghanistan till the other day. NATO has a military-to-military relationship with Pakistan. (India of course won't touch it with a barge pole.)

But now its world is in tumult.

The humanity has a wool drawn across its eyes by the shameless Media who ought to have been alerting that we are no better than sacrificial lambs in this deadly game.

And that if Western citizens wake up even now, there is still some hope it could deter its notorious elites.

Reference:

[1] https://www.newsbred.com/nato-has-opened-itself-to-scrutiny-by-our-military-leaders-putin/

[2] https://strategic-culture.org/news/2022/12/17/news-from-the-natostan-imposed-meat-grinder/

Link to Article:

https://www.newsbred.com/russia-now-knows-what-nato-has-got-and-is-unimpressed/

How I Think the Ukraine Conflict Would End

January 1, 2023

Ukraine affects us all at the existential level.

We see that both sides—NATO with Ukraine as proxy vs Russia—can't see peace happening.

★ If Kiev gives up, NATO could crumble which means the West itself as we know it.

That hundreds of billions have vaporised towards sustaining a faraway regime would enrage citizenry enough to uproot governments the elections of which are due in Ukraine and the US in less than two years.

Right wing forces would be unstoppable, the nationalistic fervour would deal a death blow to European Union (EU), already beset with refugee crisis from the Middle East and Africa, and now millions of Ukrainians pouring in across the borders. Inflation and recession, the economic haemorrhage…I leave it to your imagination.

★ If Russia runs out of men and weapon, the hordes would surround Moscow in a blink; it could disintegrate into pieces and a civilization would sink into dark ages. The Muscovites would rather put everything on line, including a mutually assured Nuclear destruction than to let it happen.

So let's look into the future and take an educated view on how this all would pan out.

War, to West and East, mean two completely different things.

Russia which has seen many a times in its history Moscow being surrounded, razed and burnt to the ground, look at its protection from not just a military point of view.

It sees war as an existential matter, involving political, economic, social and even civilizational cost.

It's prepared to burn itself down—like it did with Napoleon—to ensure the enemy gets nothing and loses all its vitality.

The Eastern Front, the deadliest, most brutal and the greatest conflict on land in human history during the World War II, was decisive in ending the Third Reich and giving the world as a trophy to the West even though none suffered more than Soviets who lost 30 million of its men, mostly citizens.

So here is this thing to remember: War to Russia is not just its army. Its citizenry know the implications and are prepared to lose everything.

And like it happened in 1814 and 1945, it's prepared to chase the enemy all the way to Paris or a Berlin, to ensure the serpent isn't left with venom for a long, long time.

To the Russians, A War isn't better than just a battle if the long-term objective isn't factored in.

Their long-term objective in this Ukraine Conflict, to my mind, is leaving NATO exhausted and exposed, and the Western economies in a mangled state for its citizens to bring about a fundamental change in how their elites and media dupe them.

It would shape a new world, like it did after 1945, not in the image of a Hegemon but the one of a multipolar order in which Russia could rightly claim to be its architect.

China having sustained it economically, and India with its courage and buying spree, would be judged by history to have been of invaluable asset in this quest.

The Western approach to War, in contrast, is completely different.

But for the two World Wars in 1914 and 1945, they have never had to mobilize a large land force and resources.

They went out for their objectives, rarely had to defend their borders, a prerequisite for Russia with thousands of kilometres of vulnerable borders.

The West thus has never been forced to raise a large army, relied rather on technological superiority and quality of its weapons, and depended on proxies, peacekeeping missions, small expeditionary forces etc to achieve its objective.

Yes, it got bogged down in Vietnam, in Algeria or Angola, but it was all away. Beyond a point it wasn't prepared to lose the flower of its manhood once it realized the hopelessness of its mission, like it recently happened in Afghanistan.

It thus appears in Russia's interest to bog the West-NATO down in Ukraine till the latter sees the hopelessness of its mission for Russia to shape its borders, Europe and the World to its advantage.

Russians are in no hurry to end the Ukraine Conflict.

The way it fights its war is to lose its men and ammunition but ensure that the enemy is left with it neither, and since it has more men prepared to die, and more ammunition, it's they who are left standing in the end.

West fights its wars not for its borders but to satisfy the unlimited greed of its military industry.

Russia in contrast has all its energy and sinews geared only towards the protection of its borders and society.

Russia ensures the war materials and investments are for the State and its safety.

The West on the other hand does it for a private sort of caucus which takes precedence over nation's well-being.

The West fight its wars for its billionaires. Russia for its people.

Russia is being mocked for its old weapons which is both hubris and stupidity.

Russia always looks to have weapons which could be operated by conscripts or new recruits without much loss of time or advantage. The turnover is seamless.

The West in contrast goes for weapons which are complicated and need dexterity and experienced hands to be effective and once this corpus is exhausted, a like-for-like replacement isn't possible in a short time.

So even if the US-NATO spends 20 times more than what Russia does on its military budget, the former can't spare the number of men or long enough for that qualitative advantage to sustain itself over a long period of time.

So Russia is waiting for the West to reach that moment of helplessness and futility for it to give up on Ukraine.

West had thought it would suck Russia dry of its economy for the citizens to rise in revolt and replace Vladimir Putin but none of the sort has happened.

Once US give up on Ukraine—be sure it would not be without war clouds on Serbia or Taiwan with the shameless Media shifting the humanity's attention elsewhere—it would be the moment for Russia to demand and get what it wants.

From what one has gathered from the peace proposal it sent to the West before it put its boots in Ukraine, Russia would ensure Ukraine ceases to be a military threat for many decades.

Anyone can see that the reconstruction and rearming for Ukraine, as well as for the new manpower to emerge, would take years as it is now. For its infrastructure to be put in place, investment to come in—nobody could bet on it as nobody could if the Ukrainians would ever return to the wastelands which was once its home.

Russia, thereafter, would surely go for its other hostile neighbours, NATO or non-NATO, to be neutral henceforth. Where Poland and Baltic nations could have their armies but not significant enough to be a trouble in future.

The West, it seems, knows nothing about Russia. Erich von Manstein, the best general of Hitler, once said that only when you think you've killed all the Russians, another bunch comes over the hill.

Napoleon too learnt at the cost of losing everything.

Otto von Bismarck, the maker of modern Germany, had a warning for those bullish and foolish enough to take them on: "Don't fight with Russians. To every stratagem of war, they react with some unforeseeable brutishness."

So be ready. Ukraine conflict isn't getting over in a hurry.

But whenever it would be over, it's Russia which is likely to achieve its goals—at a tremendous cost of course.

But then it's nothing new.

Link to Article:

https://www.newsbred.com/how-i-think-the-ukraine-conflict-would-end/

How Our Truth Bishops Are Brainwashing Us

January 8, 2023

I have been in England for the last fortnight and can't access RT or Sputnik. The Blighty has resorted to legal means to fight what it terms is "Russian disinformation.[1]"

It's the same in the United States where the Biden administration created a Disinformation Governance Board[2] "focussed on Russia." (*Paused as of now*). The acronym DGB is eerily similar to KGB so please don't mind my chuckle.

Now of course you can't question these two Anglo-Saxons driving the world and must view the "truth" from "lie" as they tell us to do. Their forward agent, the mainstream media, glosses over the most logical lead which any self-respecting pro would rather pursue than ignore or die out of shame.

Sample:

★ Every day we hear that Ukraine is winning war. But then why millions of Ukrainians are fleeing the country? Why their flight from the killing-fields is completely blanked from our attention? Why no pictures, no heart-rending stories?

★ The Wall Street Journal reported that Ukraine is wiping out Russian soldiers and has neutralized enemy's missiles. And that Russians are ineffective as Western allies have transformed Ukraine's air defences. Anyone please then why most of Ukraine is without electric power?

★ The sabotage of Nord Stream 1 is the Pearl Harbor moment of world history. It severed Europe's dependence on Russian energy rather violently and ensured the Old Continent would be a vassal to the United States for a long time to come. Who did it? Apparently, our truth bishops show no concern, not even pretence of following up when one of Western Powers' own minister thanked[1] the United States for blowing it up.

★ Below is the image of dates when the mainstream media scooped the news that Russia is running out of ammunitions. From March '22 onwards till now. Clowns are still on with their pantomime act.

2022 "RUSSIA RUNNING OUT OF WEAPONS" HEADLINES

- March 25: "Russia running out of precision munitions"
- Apr 2: "Putin 'running out of missiles' "
- Apr 29: "Russia running short of precision missiles"
- May 6: "Putin 'running out of missiles'"
- May 9: "Russia Running Out Of Weapons, Can Be Defeated By Ukraine"
- May 15: "Analysts and media reports that Russia's missile stocks are running low"
- June 10: "Ukraine is running out of ammunition"
- June 11: "Russia 'running out' of precision weapons"
- July 1: "Russia Admits It's Running Out of Weapons"
- July 8: "Vladimir Putin running short of missiles"
- Aug 13: "Vladimir Putin humiliated as Russia warned weapons stocks running out"
- Sep 9: "Russia Is Running Out of Missiles"
- Oct 11: "Russia running out of weapons"
- Oct 13: "Russia will run out of arms before Ukraine"
- Oct 16: "Ukraine says Russia running out of missiles"
- Oct 28: "Russia runs out of missiles"
- Nov: 9 "Russia may be running out of missiles to use against Ukraine's infrastructure"
- Nov 22: "Russia is running out of missiles – Ukraine's Minister of Defense"
- Nov: 23 "Russia Is Running Low on Ammo"
- Nov 26: Russia Firing Old and Empty Missiles as Putin Runs out of Weapons
- Dec 13: "US: Russia is running out of ammunition"
- Dec 15: "Russia Is Running Out of Missiles, Ukraine Security Chief Says"
- Dec 26: "Russia Is Running Out of Missiles – Ukraine's Ministry of defense"

★ Oh, Hunter Biden. Now the **Twitter Files** have shown how it "rigged" the US presidential elections of 2020. If you look at the sequence of US' pull out from Afghanistan and how the neocons have manipulated Ukraine to bring the world to a brink, who knows if without Hunter Biden's cover-up job by our sinful media Donald Trump would still be president and we would have been spared Biden the dad.

★ We have been flooded with "Russia's unprovoked aggression in Ukraine"—google it—but the cowboy Bush flattening Iraq and destroying millions of lives on false premise of WMD (Weapon of Mass Destruction) finds no mention as an act of "unprovoked aggression."

★ How does it sound for free societies when the Espionage Act dating back from 1917 was dusted off in an attempt to indict Julian Assange for 175 years? If the media isn't protecting one of its own, what makes you think it speaks for people? That Assange was kept for years under the conditions amounting to torture, confirmed no less by the UN Special Rapporteur on Torture in 2019, has no takers?

So a man who has only been faithful to his profession, who is not even a US citizen, could be extradited under the Espionage Act. Where do you think it leaves us if we ever stumble upon any classified information and feel it deserves public attention? Anyone, anywhere in the world could be imprisoned for committing the crime of telling the truth.

We now know that all along Twitter was at the beck and call of the US government even as its public stance was one of commitment to thwart covert propaganda of the government. And that the Pentagon used Twitter to shape opinion in Iraq, Kuwait, Syria and Yemen for good five years.

We are now privy to the fact that in 2020, Facebook and Twitter executives were attending classified briefing from the top attorneys of Pentagon.

But the media won't touch the matter with a barge pole even as we the people are duped of truth all the time.

The ruthless empire, which has spread anarchy, genocide, wars, vaporizing lives and nations relentlessly since World War II, how come it's always shielded from the attention of media? How gullible do you think we all are?

That our "free press" has turned its back on Assange, one of their own, the most consequential journalist of our times, doesn't it tell you what we read, see or hear is nothing but only propaganda?

Powers can only thrive in dark

But then propaganda has been essential to the US since the Spanish-American War in the 19th century in which the US blamed the sinking of its battleship Maine to manufacture the war when it was a malfunctioning boiler which had caused the explosion.

To anyone who cares to look, Walter Lippmann and Edward Bernays used propaganda to shape Americans opinion in facilitating US' entry into World War I on fake premises. From a pacifist and isolationist country, the Americans were successfully turned into a German-hating nation.

Some 350 years ago, David Hume in his "First Principles of Government" wrote that MANY are government by a FEW and the trick is to shape the citizenry to their opinion.

Samuel Huntington once famously observed: "Power remains strong when it remains in the dark; exposed to the sunlight, it begins to evaporate."

That's why manufacturing consent is a prime concern of powers. And that's how free societies are run of which we are so proud. Government are said to run on people's will even as the truth is completely opposite.

And so we must be shielded from "Russian propaganda" even if it means pining for falsehood and not truth. Not reading the other side, we are told, is for our good only.

Those who question, you've been warned, would suffer cancel culture and whataboutism. Those who are a threat would be extradited and even eliminated.

This method of our rulers, one has to admit, has been wildly successful.

Or why else the US citizens would happily give consent to billions of dollars going down the drain on Ukraine even as they suffer a sky-high inflation and recession which could last years?

Reference:

[1] https://theowp.org/reports/uk-to-strengthen-internet-laws-to-fight-russian-disinformation/

[2] https://www.washingtonpost.com/technology/2022/05/18/disinformation-board-dhs-nina-jankowicz/

Link to Article:

https://www.newsbred.com/if-russia-is-losing-the-war-why-are-ukrainians-fleeing/

Why We Don't Hear a Word on Fleeing Ukrainians

January 17, 2023

You leave your home one day.

That is, all the womenfolk and children with their cats or dogs you won't leave behind.

Elderly you would like to but they could turn into corpse by the exertion in freezing winter, not to say a destination where neither the warm bed, food nor medical care is guaranteed.

Men of course aren't allowed with the caravan, directed as they are to the front often perforce by a pitiless State. They head East to their family's miles on West, different roads but identical future, preordained doomed.

Ukraine, like all other wars, shows humans at their ugliest worst. Some nine million Ukrainians have fled homeland, most likely never to return. Majority hitch themselves to Poland or Germany, quite a few to France where social security system is most generous. They no longer call it "asylum" but "protection" in France. Besides, Frenchmen pride themselves for welcoming the persecuted.

The European Union has done everything to live by its religion of "human rights." It has offered temporary protection to fleeing Ukrainians and every European state under its umbrella has to oblige. For a year at least, possibly three, Ukrainians get their residency rights in whichever State they choose to stay and have access to labour market. There is financial support, education and free energy.

Only, if things were as easy as it appears on paper.

Volunteers, who opened their doors in compassion, are showing fatigue for guests haven't left after months and there is no end in sight either. Energy bills, already a drain, have only shot skywards. States, such as Germany, were already beset with a crippling housing shortage. Berlin has turned its abandoned airports into temporary housing; France has lined up ferries, Ireland has managed hotel rooms. But all of it appears no better than band-aid to a gaping wound.

Housing is one of multiple issues. How do you address the language part in schools or jobs? Child care when a single woman answers the call of her employer? A reluctant employer who isn't sure if his new recruit would still be around in a year or three?

Most know these sorry Ukrainians would never return home. The Kiev government itself has asked its fleeing citizens to not return home.[1]. Ukraine has no economy left; its living off Western loans which it surely would default on. Even International Monetary Fund (IMF), beholden to the United States, is dithering. If so is the case with IMF, which investor would be pouring his money into a black hole?

There is little business so little job. Tax revenue, as can be guessed, has dried up. On its own, Ukraine simply can't raise money on the market. Donors, both individual and institutional, could only do as much despite their bleeding hearts.

Ukraine's debt, even before Russia's intervention last year, was spiralling. It now is mammoth. Its budget shows a deficit of $36 billion and much of expenditures are headed the way of army, police or military sustenance.

Ukraine has gone dark. Once the guns fall silent, it would have the kind of debt which won't be repaid for generations. Zelensky, but for his Western donors, isn't anyone's man of the year.

The pity is all of this was avoidable. A war hoisted on citizens by ruthless elites in the name of ideology, security, call it what you may, when all you needed was respect for each other's space.

All Russia wanted was the Kiev regime not to run on neo-Nazis who had made life hell for Russian-speaking eastern Ukraine. If the coup on an elected government in 2014 wasn't bad enough, the Minsk Agreement, I and II, were signed in bad faith by the West. As Angela Merkel and Francois Hollande, the then leaders of Germany and France have confessed, the Minsk Agreements were only a ruse to arm Ukraine to the teeth. It was deceit, treachery, fraud from those who are expected to walk the talk on "rules-based international order."

Ukraine is a classic example of how meek citizenry, like rats, are slowly fried lifeless on a tub growing hot by the minute. It ought to have reacted when oligarchs were siphoning off Western aid, political opponents were being jailed, books of Russian authors were being burnt in thousands, media was silenced and hell was raining on their fellow citizens in Donbass for the only crime of being Russian in origin. Now generations, and not just the present ones, would live on doles and taunts, with little human dignity or rights, in slums of their Western hosts.

The worse, we all know, is yet to come. The European citizenry, or the one in West, appear no different in letting their rulers run away with its agenda. They all have fallen for the propaganda that Russia is eyeing Berlin, London, Paris or New York when all Moscow wants is protection on its endless borders, the same as the United States desires in its neighbourhood under the Monroe Doctrine, or China yearns for in Taiwan.

So prices have hit the roof. Industries, transport, supply chains have all taken a hit due to economic downturn. The money which ought to have been a shield for Europeans is cascading down the bottomless pit of Ukraine. And when employment takes a hit, we all know crimes spiral, the ethnic mosaic turns into ghettos, the cultural and religious animosity of centuries come to the fore.

Ukraine is today Afghanistan, Iraq or Libya of Europe, overnight turned into a failed state. Like it happened in Kabul, Baghdad, Mosul, Basra or Tripoli, the seeds have been sown for extremists and terrorists to take hold of the rump of an Ukraine. We already know that weapons meant for Kiev are ending up in black market[2] and into the hands of anarchists who won't let Europe live in peace.

This has few parallels in European history. Of course there were two World Wars in the 20th century; for sure we have read on 30 years and 100 years wars amongst the British, Germany and French antagonists; there were Napoleon and Hitler; Genghis Khan once overran its plains and Ottoman Empire was a nemesis at door for centuries. But migration of this scale, of Europeans within Europe, possibly happened only when Rome ceased being a power[3] between 300 and 800 AD.

A burning Europe of course suits the United States, as it did for them in West Asia, or by lighting chaos on borders of India and Pakistan in the form of Taliban's Afghanistan. They won't let Europe or Asia, or for that matter Africa and Latin America live in peace. War feeds its financial czars and military-industrial complex for, as we know, nothing is more profitable than war. It doesn't lose its men nor its dollar is affected, fake as it is, subject to only print command of its treasury.

What is happening to Ukrainians could happen to rest of humanity. Elites don't give a damn if we live or die. They rely on a sinful media to take hold of our mind with propaganda. So it has been endlessly for the last few centuries, first under the British Empire and later with the American Century.

This though is no other war. Any loser in this conflict, the fear is, could resort to Nuclear option. And that's because neither West nor Russia could afford defeat. West would lose its hegemony of last 500 years for once Dollar goes so would its hold on the world. Russia, if it loses, would be carved up into many states, its resources up for grabs by imperialists who have instincts to loot and plunder, bred over centuries.

Citizens, on their part, could make a last-minute effort to rein in their rulers. They alone could stall the approaching doomsday. For once in graves, six feet below the surface, they won't matter.

Reference:

[1] https://www.theguardian.com/world/2022/oct/26/ukraine-refugees-told-not-to-return-yet-as-energy-crisis-looms#:~:text=Ukraine's%20government%20is%20advising%20refugees,cope%20with%20demand%20this%20winter

[2] https://www.reuters.com/world/europe/russia-says-eu-party-conflict-ukraine-2022-10-20/

[3] https://en.wikipedia.org/wiki/Migration_Period

Link to Article:

https://www.newsbred.com/why-we-dont-hear-a-word-on-fleeing-ukrainians-9m-of-them/

World Economic Forum: How An Ngo Loots the World

January 21, 2023

(This is the first of the two-part series on World Economic Forum which has a dystopian philosophy about a world with less people where global resources are only meant for a handful. The second and concluding piece follows this article.)

You won't know what is World Economic Forum (WEF).

One, it's not an "**economic**" body.

It's also not a "**forum**" for it permits no discussion, no argument and no challenge.

As for it to qualify as "**world**", it ought to have been made up of independent nations or global bodies like the UN, which it is not.

So WEF is neither World nor Economic nor Forum.

(*How it got the affix of "world" is another story: not dissimilar to World Health Organization which is privately funded. And before I fuddle you that the Federal Reserve which prints US dollars, is an independent agency of the US government, not bound by the president, legislators or any elected official, let's stick to the WEF only!*)

The WEF is just an NGO, based in Cologny, a lush suburb of Geneva (Switzerland), in operation since 1971, formed by its eternal chairman Klaus Schwab (84), with origins linked to Hitler, which you would read about in the concluding part.

It's been held in Davos in the Swiss Alpine resort every year, its glass-steel headquarters looking out on Lake Geneva, where the world's richest and most powerful, the global elites of the globalism, meet and believe they run the world.

Here the wealthiest could meet dozens of heads of states in 3-4 days in sound-proof rooms, out of bound of regulators, journalists and other such nuisances. So it is with Consulting and tech giants looking for a contract, a preferential tax treatment and avoidance of anti-trust proceedings. That they have their cheques ready for donations to political campaigns helps.

All of it is done under the veneer of virtuous undertakings—like this year's "Committed to Improving the State of the World"—but in essence they are looking for unelected "one world government".

In Schwab's own words, **"If no one power can enforce order, our world will suffer from a global order deficit**."

The trick is to present to we-the-people the "eternal threats" to humanity, like climate change and pandemic. It makes us surrender to surveillance, to State control, to be "mapped" and those inconvenient "neutralized."

The famous political scientist Samuel Huntington coined the epithet of "Davos Man" for such entities. In his words, "Davos Man is an unusual predator whose power comes in part from his keen ability to adopt the guise of an ally."

Two examples—**Climate Change and Pandemic**—would bring home the truth how they plan to bring about this "one-world government."

The Climate Hypocrisy

The theme of "cut-fossil-fuel-to-save-climate-and-humanity" by now is firmly embedded in our minds.

The WEF clamours for global carbon emissions to be cut by 50% by 2030.[1]

Now Greenpeace International has found that during the last year's WEF, 1,040 private jets arrived and departed out of airports in Davos.

Some 53% of these flights were under 750 km distance, some 38% under 500 km and one private jet indeed travelled just 21 km to arrive!

These private jets for the WEF 2022 reportedly produced 10,700 tons of CO2—or roughly what 350,000 average cars emit in a week.

Indeed, the top 10% of global rich are found to be responsible for as much total greenhouse gas emissions as the bottom 90% combined.[2]

As Greenpeace's transport campaigner Klara Maria Schenk commented "Do we really believe that these are the people to solve the problems the world faces?"

Covid Vaccines "Plot"

There has been massive increase in unexplained excess deaths following the Covid vaccination.

It's the vaccinated, and not the unvaccinated, who are suddenly sick and dying.

Doctors have also reported a surge in cancer and a drop in fertility following the vaccination campaign.

Now thousands of medical scientists and doctors are of the view the mRNA vaccines are causing permanent health damages. They are calling for urgent halt to mRNA injections.

Yet, the US Food and Drug Administration (FDA) has stuck to its approval of mRNA injections.

Bill Gates, a regular[3] at WEF, and one who has an outsized say[4] in WHO, is the key promoter of Agenda ID2020 alongside big Pharmas.

Agenda ID2020 was designed/sponsored by Gates and set rolling in the WEF of 2020. It's an electronic program which uses vaccination as a mean to obtain your digital identity.

World's population reduction has been a long-avowed plan of Gates and propounded in WEF.

Dubious vaccines—meekly accepted by the scared humanity, on the "global threat" that globalists drum in our ears, are tools for such goals.

In the United States, some 44% of Republicans and 19% of Democrats believe that Gates plots vaccines to implant microchips[5] into people. Some 20% young Australians believe it too. There have been anti-Gates protests from Germany to Melbourne.

The belief in these doubters is that these nano-chips could be a tool to trace people's digital money—yes, that moment has as good as arrived for us—besides other intimate details.

That these vaccines could be a slow killer that acts up in a few years or a disease that hits the next generation or a gene that renders women infertile is feared.

(If the readers sense a repeat of Nazis' eugenics programme[6], well, it was never dead all these decades, only working in the background.)

Further, hasn't Dr. Tedros, DG of WHO, been wanting the humanity to shift to digital money as he claimed physical paper and coin money could spread diseases?

As those who live or visit Western nations would aver, cash is as good as banned. Even a candy could only be paid electronically.

Now let's look at the hypocrisy of a moral facade which is kept in WEF, promoted by a pliant media.

As said, WEF"s official slogan this year is "Committed to improving the State of the World."

Now one of the ways of doing is to promote peace negotiations between Ukraine and Russia.

The WEF on the other hand shows its bias by not inviting Vladimir Putin to Davos whereas Volodymyr Zelensky is not only allowed the platform but his belligerence and war rhetoric is met with thunderous applause.

The WEF 2022 indeed acted as a war-participant itself. It announced it had "severed all relations with the Russian government and president Vladimir Putin" and "scrubbed Putin from the WEF website".

Now this is not what you would call the "Commitment to improving the State of the World."

If anything, WEF has appeared no better than a mouthpiece for US-NATO propaganda in recent months.

But then what better you'd expect from globalists whose very survival depends on the globalisation agenda; where nations are supposed to lose their sovereignty and submit to globalism.

This is what Schwab said in WEF, 2022: "A new dividing line exists in politics and society…between globalism and nationalism, between cooperation and protectionism, between embracing the new and preserving the old."

So it's not a struggle between Left and Right—it's between globalism and nationalism.

The "new" that Schwab propagates is the "Great Reset" or the "New World Order."

The "old" is where you live with your heritage, your culture, your soil or your Gods.

This "Great Reset" is chasing you, the people, to oblivion.

Oxfam[7] says the 10 richest men in the world today own more than the bottom 3.1 billion people.

The 1% wealthiest of Americans have garnered 25 trillion dollars in the last 40 years: The bottom half, in comparison, has seen their wealth fall by 1,000 billion dollars.

Since 1978, corporate executives have been compensated to the tune of 900%: The wages of a typical American grew just by 12%.

The average earning of world population is less than 3 dollars per day.

As the "Davos Man" has his way with tax-reduction and anti-trust blocking, and as the government's revenue drop, the social welfare programme takes a hit, the wages sink, you and I are reduced to margins.

This is the way to unrest, anarchy and even civil war and not the Democracy we hear from elites as sweeteners.

Huntington again: "Global elites have little need for national loyalty, view national boundaries as obstacles that thankfully are vanishing, and see national governments as residues from the past whose only useful function is to facilitate the elite's global operations."

With their jets and yachts, manifold mansions and private islands, the "Davos Man" of course is unmoored from the rest of humanity.

Every year, the WEF chooses hundreds of Young Global Leaders, a global network which comes to dominate large corporations, politics, academia and media in due course. Justin Trudeau has been one of the boys as has been Raghav Chadha, the AAP's very own.

These globalists are the unelected world government where the people are nothing but a nuisance.

This "Davos Man" failed to see the debt crisis of 2008 and is clearly unaware of the deindustrialization of the West. All it has done is to pillage the global economy, exploit workers, looted what was meant for health care, social welfare etc and yet demanded they be supported by their labour.

The history since World War II has been a tale of wealth flowing upwards in the United States, Europe and other major economies.

It's a tale where a select few have subverted democracy and replaced it by a new global class which shapes our future on the basis of their own interests.

The lobbyists, such as in World Economic Forum, have been in power, directing policies which affect the lives of we the people.

But Ukraine could be the catalyst which could bring this sinful conduct to an end.

I leave you with these paraphrased words from Putin on WEF:

The era of the unipolar world, led by America and the WEF's Great Reset, is over. The future world order, already in progress, will be formed by strong sovereign States...The future world order, already in progress, will not be the one plotted by America and the WEF, but will be formed by strong sovereign states. It is a lesson that the godless West will be made to learn the hard way.

(For those interested in diving deep on the matter, I suggest[8].

POSTSCRIPT: So what do we make of India's spirited presence in WEF every year? Now for a developing nation, investment is a requisite. But India under Modi is a nationalistic and doesn't conform to a globalist agenda. India also showcases its growth for technological cooperation with the world. WEF is nothing more than a bazaar for India—it doesn't see the world like the Davos Man does.

To be continued...

Reference:

[1] https://www.weforum.org/agenda/climate-change

[2] https://academic.oup.com/nsr/article/3/4/470/2669331

[3] https://www.weforum.org/agenda/authors/billgates

[4] https://www.swissinfo.ch/eng/politics/does-bill-gates-have-too-much-influence-in-the-who-/4657052

[5] https://pesquisa.bvsalud.org/global-literature-on-novel-coronavirus-2019-ncov/resource/en/grc-740780

[6] https://en.wikipedia.org/wiki/Nazi_eugenics

[7] https://www.oxfam.org/en/press-releases/ten-richest-men-double-their-fortunes-pandemic-while-incomes-99-percent-humanity

[8] https://www.amazon.in/Davos-Man-Billionaires-Devoured-World/dp/0063078309

Link to Article:

https://www.newsbred.com/world-economic-forum-how-an-ngo-loots-the-humanity/

Man Behind WEF We Know Little About

January 22, 2023

(In the first[1] *of the two-part series, you read about how World Economic Forum operates. This concluding one is about its founder Klaus Schwab.)*

Klaus Schwab indeed has succeeded beyond his wildest dream in building World Economic Forum (WEF) where the world's most powerful line-up in Davos every year in search of material salvation.

It's an extraordinary journey which began with his birth in 1938 in Ravensburg, Germany, in the household of Eugen Schwab, a mechanical engineer who was on the wrong side of history in aiding Adolf Hitler's atomic bomb effort through his company, Sulzer Escher Wyss. For good enough reason, this Nazi connection has been scrubbed clean from public attention.

Schwab Sr had no doubt that Klaus would only be something if he attends Harvard which the latter duly did in the 1960s and his life was never the same.

His professor in Harvard was Dr. Henry Kissinger, also born in Germany, who had been earmarked for bigger role by the American establishment, keen as the US was to hold sway over Europe at a weak moment of its history after the Second World War.

Henry had arrived in the United States as a Jewish immigrant fleeing Germany in the same year Klaus had been born, in 1938. He had been born Heinz Kissinger but changed it to Henry once on the American soil. He took part in World War II in the military intelligence wing, hunting down Nazi and Gestapo officials. Once the War was over, he returned to academics, completing his MA and PhD degrees from Harvard and yet sought recruitment as a spy for FBI (Federal Bureau of Investigation). Kissinger remained in the University campus long after, serving as director of the Harvard International Seminar between 1951 and 1971.

Kissinger was leading a 22-man panel of advisors to help shape "European Policy" and Klaus Schwab caught his eye early. It was later revealed that the Central Intelligence Agency (CIA) had been funding Kissinger's Seminars to the tune of $135,000.[2]

Harvard then was known the world over as playing a pivotal role in Cold War policy-making targeting Europe. Destiny placed Klaus Schwab right amongst its early proponents. The method used was to play on the Nuclear annihilation fear of the Europeans, now that the Soviet Union too had its N-bombs.

Kissinger saw in Klaus a potential future leader and the young German was introduced to John K. Galbraith and Herman Kahn, the two other intellectual giants of the American establishment.

Kahn had made his reputation on thermonuclear deterrence, Galbraith on Public Policy and Kissinger, as we know, in shaping the foreign policy of the United States, and of the world.

The one common thread in all three was their connection with the Council of Foreign Relations (CFR), the American branch of the Anglo-American imperialist "Round Table" movement. Galbraith was closer to Kissinger and together their goal was to ensure Europe is beholden to the United States, the new world power. The gambit was fear of Nuclear bombs. The agenda was to control Europe's social and economic policies.

The year 1973 was described by Richard Nixon as being the "Year of Europe". It was a willing ally in the project of European Economic Community (EEC), formed in 1957, which has now evolved into European Union (EU).

Kissinger was quick to grasp the essence of "Year of Europe" and revived the dying North Atlantic Treaty Organisation (NATO), working on the war-fears of the Europeans.

Klaus Schwab was chosen to be the vehicle for such a goal. In 1970, Klaus wrote to the European Commission about setting up a "non-commercial think tank for European business leaders." Galbraith was to fly over to Europe, along with Kahn, to help Schwab convince the European elites to back the project. The European Commission came aboard to sponsor this so-called "European Management Symposium" which within a year was to transform itself into the World Economic Forum.

On the face of it, the World Economic Forum was a European project—in reality, it was the handiwork of the US establishment for the CIA after all had been funding Kissinger for the same.

Galbraith was the keynote speaker in the first edition of World Economic Forum in 1971 but the second one lacked fizz. Klaus, at this stage, took a gamble which continues to pay huge dividends to this day.

The Club of Rome Gamble

Some three years ago, in 1968, the Club of Rome had been founded by Italian industrialist Aurelio Peccei and Scottish chemist Alexander King at a Rockefeller family residence in Bellagio, Italy. It had quickly become an influential think tank of the scientific, technocratic and wealthy elites. It promoted a global governance model by the elites.

As the WEF was tossing up and down in its second edition, the Club of Rome had published a controversial work, "The Limits to Growth" which claimed the burgeoning population won't have enough resources available by the year 2000. Klaus Schwab approached Peccei if he would be available for the keynote speech at the 1973 World Economic Forum which the latter duly did. This risqué public relations strategy was the steroid which pumped up the WEF. There was no looking back.

It was a controversial association for the Club of Rome was obsessed with reducing the global population which was described by its critics as influenced by Nazi's eugenics. In its another book, "The First Global Revolution", the mention was made that "**the common enemy of humanity is Man himself.**"

Below is this entire passage in the book which sounds eerie familiar to the WEF of modern times:

"In searching for a common enemy against whom we can unite, we came up with the idea that pollution, the threat of global warming, water shortages, famine and the like, would fit the bill...all these dangers are caused by human intervention in natural processes, and it is only through changed attitudes and behaviour that they can be overcome. The real enemy then is humanity itself."

The WEF today uses the same issues of climate, environment, pandemic etc to what its critics believe is the agenda of "one world government" where the majority would willingly surrender itself to surveillance. The imbalance in flow of money would make the majority lose life's essentials and livelihoods and the depopulation of the world would be set in motion.

The WEF "recruits" in due course would embed themselves into the system, generation after generation; the Big Business, political honchos and academia virtually would be running the world.

These "recruits" are the "stakeholders" which Klaus Schwab is so fond of referring. All powerful attract similar forces and these "stakeholders" gradually take the power away from democratic forces without the blood of common people on their hand.

This breed has only multiplied over the years and the so-called free society is beholden to them. They hold all the aces while common people live under the illusion of democratic processes and petty distraction by the media.

Klaus Schwab in subsequent years was to aid the nuclear ambitions of the South African apartheid regime through the same company,

Sulzer Escher Wyss, which had been the creation of his father, Eugen. That South African regime was the closest to Nazi-style governance reveals a habit of Schwab family to work with the genocidal dictators for immense profit and power. Its an Orwellian doublespeak that while the WEF today advocates nuclear non-proliferation, its Maker at one time apparently loved the bomb. The depopulation theory, of course, has a common link with the eugenics policy of the Nazis.

The man, un-scrutinized while sitting on the globalist throne, unsurprisingly has whims and could take offence quickly. The Vanity Fair[2] describes a moment when a Forum employee mistakenly pulled her car into Schwab's spot in the parking lot. She was duly fired.

Audi reserves its fanciest vehicles at a steep discount for Schwabs. His globe-trotting, catering, security services etc bills are footed by the Forum.

His nephew, Hans Schwab, now uses the Forum's own funds to manage its logistics through his Global Events Management company—again acquiring the start-up capital from the Forum. He hosts Forum's all events, a deal worth several million dollars a year.

(A fair number of facts in this piece have come through the tweets[3] tweets and pieces Johnny Vedmore has run on his blog, Unlimited Hangout.)

Concluded

[1] https://www.newsbred.com/world-economic-forum-how-an-ngo-loots-the-humanity/

[2] https://timesmachine.nytimes.com/timesmachine/1967/04/16/90327325.html?pageNumber=53

[3] https://twitter.com/JohnnyVedmore/status/1501965542697095171?s=20&t=9kHt8UHIxmnz2qfbjQbI2w

[4] https://unlimitedhangout.com/2022/03/investigative-reports/dr-klaus-schwab-or-how-the-cfr-taught-me-to-stop-worrying-and-love-the-bomb/

Link to Article:

https://www.newsbred.com/the-man-who-runs-the-world-economic-forum-you-know-nothing-about/

If Indians Ignore Ukraine, History Would Bite US Again

February 1, 2023

Indians have suffered gravely for shutting themselves out from the world in its history.

They went far and wide for trade but didn't learn how to protect its riches though reminders came often from an Alexander or Muhammad bin Qasim; a Ghazni or a Ghouri, or the Baburs or Abdalis.

If they couldn't shut the one passage of land from its northwest, they stood no chance on its thousands of kilometres of coastal borders against the rapacious colonialists who arrived in Calicut on May 20, 1498 in the person of Vasco da Gama.

Over the next 500 years, the Mughals and Englishmen took turns to mutilate our culture and heritage; disfigure our education system, strip the land of its bounty as flourishing industries gave way to droughts and famines.

This auto-mode didn't disappear with the independence in 1947, the collective memory took little note of some one-third of our land lost, or otherwise we would have put our best foot forward when the Dragon came breathing fire in 1961.

Kargil, till as recently as two decades ago, showed India could be easily fooled by smiles and hugs.

We trusted the enemies when the best friend we had was we only.

***

I suspect we Indians are similarly dolt on Ukraine Crisis.

Smug that if a Nuclear War breaks out, we are too far and thus safe from the scene of action.

It was same when colonialists were experimenting with their voyages and guns in South America in the medieval ages—that they would never drop their anchor on our Indian shores.

Or that the Covid-19 is China's mess and we might be neighbours but are blessed with different fates.

So this Ukraine matter is a crisis if we are daft; an opportunity if we have our ears to the ground.

That if we could free ourselves from the propaganda in media, and remember from history what happens in the Old Continent affects the entire humanity, we could stand as one behind the Modi government in the difficult choices it has made on India's destiny; in its quest to make it India's golden era.

So I write to engage my fellow Indians; to draw their attention where they could be indifferent; so as history's tragedies don't revisit us again.

To remind all of us that yesterday's invaders and imperialists, and today's superpowers, don't have our interest at heart.

That they would create a Hindenburg Report, as they did with anti-CAA or anti-farm-laws stir, to scare your admirable government into compliance.

***

So, Ukraine.

What's the real story behind what all you read?

So first what you read the latest: Germany is supplying 14 Leopard 2 battle tanks; the United States would send 31 M-1A1 Abrams tanks to Ukraine. Bravo!

Now tanks on its own are worth little if air defense support is missing as we know is the case with Ukraine. If operated in isolation, says military analyst Scott Ritter, it's simply an expensive mobile coffin.

Besides, these tanks won't reach overnight—it could take months.

There is this little matter of training the crew, and not just the one with the tank but the combined armed team which is further additional few months required.

Now tanks, even the best ones, break down regularly. These would need to be sent to its origins to be repaired.

The Leopard tanks were tried out against Kurdish and ISIS mercenaries in West Asia twice, in 2016 and 2018. Just IEDs, suicide car bombs and anti-tank missiles were enough to destroy dozens of them. How they stand a chance against Russians with hundreds, if not thousands, of rockets, missiles and other munitions is anybody's guess.

It's said that Russia has 5-1 advantage in terms of tanks they possess. Imagine how high the stock of Russian defense forces would go if images of these charred tanks is splashed across.

Last month Ukraine had asked for 300 tanks, 500 infantry vehicles, 500 artillery pieces from their West's sponsors to "win this war." So far NATO and its allies have only partially agreed. There is little knowing if it would be done next week, month or even next year.

Ukraine has also asked Germany to send across one of its submarines to "kick the Russian fleet out of the Black Sea." Now how do you do to a power entrenched there since the 18th century with just a submarine, Reuters doesn't tell us.

***

And so this tragic-comedy goes on endlessly.

The Western powers and media are stuffing us with all noise and little substance.

Meanwhile, Ukraine the country has been destroyed, millions of lives lost or uprooted, the economy world over has taken a hit, howsoever you may adorn the comedian with awards or promise of a bust in Capitol.

The truth is post-War order is in tatters; European Union is on its last leg; NATO has appeared all bluster and little beef; and Dollar as a currency has run its course.

The Modi govt has been astute enough to catch the headwinds and is one of the flagships in the armada shaping the New World Order.

Yet this crisis might outlast Modi as it could Vladimir Putin.

But if we the citizens know what is at stake, no puppet installed could throw India off course on its march to be a great power.

It's time to remember what we ought to have from History.

Link to Article:

https://www.newsbred.com/if-indians-ignore-ukraine-history-would-bite-us-again/

So did the US sabotage the Nord Stream?

February 10, 2023

So did the United States sabotage the Nord Stream-2, the gas lifeline of Europe?

Now the source is Seymour Hersh[1], a celebrated journalist like few, who lifted the lid from cover-up of My Lai Massacre[2] and Abu Ghraib prison.[3]

(Next time anyone goes delirious on the US army and how it's protecting human rights around the world; or that Hersh is a stooge of Russians, just gently bring up the two events to have the last word.)

It's possible you could be fooled by how the United States always "looks after" Europe.

You would be told they "saved" the Old Continent during the two World Wars, Marshall Plan thereafter, and NATO of course which is the "security shield" around the Western Europe, the heart of liberal world.

What you won't be told is that without Europe under its thumb, the United States can't secure the oil-rich Middle East, which is a springboard to Africa and the rest of Asia, hugely dependent on energy and makes up some 60% of humanity.

The truth is, without Europe, the United States is nothing but an island some 6,000 nautical miles away from Eurasia which holds most of world's population and works as a factory for the financial Czars of the western world.

(Actually, I don't like the word Czar which is demonizing the Tsars of Russia, never mind its nothing but a take on Latin "Caesar" who we swoon about for his exploits, both military and amorous kind.)

There is also a US policy you might be unaware: **Germany's technology and Russia's resources could rule the world and so the two must never become allies.**

And that the NATO's primary goal is to keep the Soviet Union/ Russia out, the Americans in and the Germans down.[4]

So, it should tell you that it's in the US' interest to keep Germany and Russia apart to control the levers of world and that it's a motive enough to sabotage the Nord Stream-2 pipeline.

That it also brings tons of money in the form of inflated LNG gas sales to Europe from across the Atlantic is a big deal too.

It should also tell you who gains from the Ukraine gambit which has secured a terrified European flock hanging on to the coattails of Washington.

In passing, I should also post how the biggies in the US administration were lusting for some time to reduce Nord Stream – 2 to nothing but a piece of junk metal in the bed of the Baltic Sea.

So here it is:

"(To stop the energy cooperation between Europe and Russia) A first step would involve stopping Nord Stream-2," — then US secretary of state, Mike Pompeo in 2020.

"There is still time to stop it…Kill Nord Stream 2 now, and let it rust beneath the waves of the Baltic." — US senator, Tom Cotton in 2021

"We have made clear to the Russians that pipeline is at risk if they move further into Ukraine." — Jake Sullivan, US National Security Adviser in 2022

"The pipeline must be stopped and the only way to prevent its completion is to use all the tools available to do that," — Senator Ted Cruz in 2022.

"There will be no longer a Nord Stream 2. We will bring an end to it." — President Joe Biden, standing next to German chancellor Olaf Scholz in 2022.

"I want to be very clear: If Russia invades Ukraine one way or another, Nord Stream 2 will not move forward." — Victoria Nuland, undersecretary of state for policy.

After the Nord Stream – 2 was sabotaged, the former Polish foreign minister Radek Sikorsky tweeted: "Thank you, USA."

The very next day, leaders from Poland, Norway and Denmark were present to open the new Norway-Poland Baltic pipeline as an alternative to the Nord Stream.

Nuland was ecstatic. "I am, and I think the Administration is, very gratified to know that Nord Stream 2 is now, as you like to say, a hunk of metal at the bottom of the sea."

Now the MOTIVE is established.

But is there enough EVIDENCE that it's the US only which has sabotaged the Nord Stream?

Now the investigation that Sweden has carried out hasn't been shared with Russia, a country whose lifeline, virtually, has been sabotaged.

Worse, Sweden hasn't even shared the findings with Germany and Denmark as its' "too sensitive."

So how do we know that its' US involvement in the sabotage and not a work of "conspiracy-theorists", a charge which is heaped upon those who question who-caused-9/11 since 28-pages of official inquiry[5] were not released for years.

The same fate befalls those who question how Osama bin Laden could survive for years, hiding in mountain caves, terribly sick and yet unable to be picked up by the US intelligence which could know of any activity even in a basement, never mind even if the mobiles are off.

Or the assassination of John F Kennedy who was naive enough to launch a new Dollar in place of Federal Reserve Notes and was bitterly opposed to "free trade" which today is imposed on rest of the world through financial and military might of the Hegemon.

(This New Dollar-thing of Kennedy if course is little known: Search as you might your Google, you won't find it. Here's a link[6] to save you the trouble.)

So we would never know.

All we would read in the media is denials.

Media of course would be the prime mover in this conspiracy of silence.

So, fellow Indians, please find out the world in which you live in and not as told by the sinful media.

It would make you realize the unspeakable tragedy of Ukraine with which Russia was baited and which has secured the vassalage of Europe for the United States for decades to come.

And of course the Nuclear Holocaust to which the humanity is slipping into every passing hour.

Reference:

[1] https://geopoliticaleconomy.com/2023/02/08/us-nord-stream-pipelines-seymour-hersh/

[2] https://en.wikipedia.org/wiki/My_Lai_massacre

[3] https://en.wikipedia.org/wiki/Abu_Ghraib_prison

[4] https://unherd.com/2017/10/keeping-russians-americans-germans-hows-nato/

[5] https://en.wikipedia.org/wiki/The_28_pages

[6] https://www.globalresearch.ca/the-rise-and-fall-of-the-international-gold-standard/13559

Link to Article:

https://www.newsbred.com/so-did-the-united-states-sabotage-the-nord-stream-2/

A Classic Orwellian Doublespeak

February 21, 2023

I have been a journalist since a teenager and my default position is to treat everything I read on politics and economics; history and war with a pinch of salt.

It's not that things don't happen. But causes and culprits are nearly always flipped upside down. The narrow gauge of mainstream media shields one party and vilifies the other under an agenda.

This branding of liberal vs illiberal; good vs evil—a classic Orwellian Doublespeak—has the sole intent of fooling citizens so they are no impediments to robbers who pass off as our rulers.

So these so-called liberals control the so-called free societies by co-opting so-called free media with three favourite tools of "democracy", "human rights" and "liberty."

All this while, they neither have human rights nor democracy nor free media on their mind.

***

Uff...Bored by the above preamble of some 100 words?

But stay with me and be sceptical of what you see or read as I demonstrate soon.

It in turn could make you vigilant on your elites—and come down hard on your mainstream media which essentially are their foot soldiers and work overtime against you, the land of your ancestors and future of your kids.

***

We read today that the US president Joe Biden dropped by in Kyiv and hugged Volodymyr Zelenskyy, the man who had visited the former's White House only during the Christmas.

It's a lead in Hindustan Times, the two leaders are clasping each other on front page of Indian Express and we are told the sirens in the background couldn't deter these wartime heroes.

While our media is gung-ho about the US president's moral code, nobody has asked why he hasn't yet reached Ohio in his own country, some 370 miles compared to nearly 4,000 miles to Kyiv, where carcinogenic chemicals have been released over hundreds of miles.[1]

The residents are reporting headaches and burning eyes; pets and chickens are falling down; and thousands of fish corpses float in waterways. Indeed, a mushroom cloud of poison is presently spread over eastern Ohio.

Look at the image of this tweet below

Now ask yourself just two questions:

- ★ One, why you haven't read about Ohio disaster in detail at all?
- ★ Two, what you make of a president who ignores own people while dashing off across continents in defence of "human lives".

Now much as your media is plastered with the images of the two, pick up your newspaper tomorrow and see how Vladimir Putin's important address to the nation is covered and how the Russian resolution in the United Nations on the sabotage of Nord Stream is displayed.

Both events are scheduled for today, February 21, and ought to be big stories for any neutral media.

If nuclear holocaust is the biggest danger humanity has ever faced, don't you think we deserve to know the viewpoint of the other party?

And if the sabotage of Nord Stream has ensured a split between Europe and Russia for ages; and Europe's citizenry is now paying through its nose for the energy which is supplied across the Atlantic by the US at exorbitant prices, why the media is sleeping over this historic divergence and human gloom?

All this while, the media couldn't stop plastering its pages on the "spy balloon" from China which we must believe is foolish enough to do so in open public gaze!

***

Do you know that the United States just had one of the biggest anti-war rally in years[2] in Washington this Sunday?

Thousands protested in front of Lincoln Memorial against weapons to Ukraine; raising slogans to disband NATO and join China and Russia in creating a multi-polar world. One was worried that "we have just shifted from Afghanistan to Ukraine" without a tear on how the US killed millions in Iraq or Libya and how instead of manufacturing cars or ships, "we are leading the world in making enemies."

Elsewhere in Germany, and mostly in Central Europe, protestors are hitting the street almost every week[3] against their hawkish rulers but it's being buried by the media.

This is the same media which wouldn't let go a single story that tugs the human heart if the fear of an Islamic State (IS) is to be embedded in readers' mind. But tell me if you have read a word on what's happening to millions of Ukrainians who have fled across the homeland borders. For highlighting the Ukrainian misery would add fuel to anti-War protests and force the rulers to seek truce when all they want is war, possibly nuclear war.

***

Something extremely alarming happened in Germany a few weeks ago.

Germany's security services conducted the largest police raid in history; spanning 130 locations and involving over 3,000 officers last December.

Over two dozen individuals of a far-right group were arrested for plotting to overthrow the German government.[4]

They were accused of plotting to storm the parliament, arrest lawmakers and declare the restoration of the country's monarchy by force.

Now this was Adolf Hitler revisited: On February 27, 1933, the German parliament—Reichstag—was burned down.[5] The Nazis, citing threat of Communists, used the moment to abolish a number of constitutional protections and paved the way for Nazi dictatorship.

The coming of second Hitler, I am sure you would agree, is a Front Page story for days in running. But the media won't run it for it has come to light that among the individuals arrested, some were State's own officers working at the behest of German government. And that their job was to provoke events which would stoke fear among citizens and thus ensure their compliance and support. But since the covers of establishment were being blown up, the media has smoked the news.

***

This event was eerily similar to what happened in Capitol Hill ahead of 2021 US presidential elections. We were incessantly told that the supporters of then US president Donald Trump had instigated the attack on US' much cherished democracy which led to the move on his impeachment—second in his four-year-tenure by the way—and which possibly derailed his re-election.

Subsequently, it has come to light that various agencies of the "deep state" had infiltrated the ranks of those demonstrators and media was at hand to blow it out of proportion. That noise has still not died from the media after two years. (Compare this to the silence on the recent coup-attempt on Germany).

But since Trump was an outlier; and Biden is part of the Liberal Gang, one is besmirched as womanizer and buffoon and the other, despite Afghanistan and Ukraine, and the promise of war against China soon, not to say sexual misconduct charges against him[6] and excesses by his son, is constantly being whitewashed by the media.

***

The truth is, in the world we live in, our rulers secure our compliance and support by raising the bogey of evil and drugging us by chortling "democracy" and "human rights" in our ears.

The mainstream media is one of their conduits and history tells us that they have done a mighty good job in their subversive roles.

Only, we the citizens, could buck this trend. And we could do it by either seen on streets or amplifying our voice against those who hold us in thrall.

Reference:

[1] https://www.theguardian.com/commentisfree/2023/feb/18/ohio-train-derailment-biden-east-palestine

[2] https://sputniknews.com/20230220/protesters-descend-on-washington-demand-natos-dissolution-peace-negotiations-with-russia-1107600002.html

[3] https://www.ft.com/content/fedc259f-bf96-4a22-b032-bc181d4dd51d

[4] https://thegrayzone.com/2023/02/02/state-security-germanys-far-right-coup/?utm_source=substack&utm_medium=email

[5] https://encyclopedia.ushmm.org/content/en/article/the-reichstag-fire

[6] https://en.wikipedia.org/wiki/Joe_Biden_sexual_assault_allegation

Link to Article:

https://www.newsbred.com/biden-in-kyiv-shouldnt-he-be-seen-in-ohio/

Why Russia is for Pushing the Borders of Poland?

February 26, 2023

We, indeed the entire humanity, is in a dangerous phase of its existence. It would be a folly to rule out a nuclear war.

Russia knows it is hemmed in from all corners.

Japan and South Korea is in its rear; while the NATO—which was once 1,000 miles too far from St Petersburg is now less than 100 miles away.

All its members of the Warsaw Pact, erstwhile of Soviet Union, are now members of NATO: Albania, Bulgaria, Czechoslovakia (now Czech and Slovakia), Hungary, Poland and Romania, as are three Baltic states (Estonia, Latvia, Lithuania) and the reunified Germany.

Do have a look at the map below to have a sense of Russia's anxiety, made worse by it being painted as an imperialist power while NATO, much against the evidence, is hailed as upholder of free world.

Thus media wasn't going to miss yet one-more evidence against "aggressive" Russia when its ex-president Dmitry Medvedev was quoted this weekend of wanting to rearrange the borders even if it meant pushing the frontiers of Poland[1], a NATO member.

I am not sure if Medvedev needed to say the obvious: Those who know Russia's geography understand completely what he means while those who are only beholden to propagandists got one more chance to swear against the "rogue" Russia.

Russia's Geography

If Russia heads out of its western borders, there are only north European plains; Conversely, those who who are heading into Russia from its western extremes, they too fan out in a wide open Russian landscape. This North European plains stretch all the way from France to the Ural Mountains.

Russia's worry has a historical basis too.

It is from these humongous Western frontiers—stretching for nearly 2,500 miles across which are 14 sovereign states, mostly hostile—that its people have fought many existential wars in the last 500 years. The Poles swooped down from across the European plains in 1605, Swedes followed in the footsteps in 1707 and sandwiched between the invasions of Napoleon (1812) and Hitler (1941) was one more grave threat from the Germans in 1914, all emanating from these very Western borders.

(I know you would be relating it with India's own fate on its Western borders from Ghaznis, Gauris, Mughals and Afghans for a millennium but we would come to it later.)

Now how does Russia come to term with such an open space which makes defending its Western borders a living, everyday nightmare?

Well, there indeed is a narrow point in this stretch between the Baltic Sea and the Carpathian Mountains—and it's called Poland.

If Russia could keep its enemies behind this narrow window, before they spread out on the vast Russian plains, it increases the safety of its continental shelf manifolds. Conversely, if the enemies get past Poland, their task gets that much easier.

It's in this context that Medvedev referred to pushing the borders of Poland for Russia's security.

But wait, we are only warming up to the matter.

The idea of Russia began only in the ninth century. A federation of tribes, Kievan Rus, sprang up around the Dnieper River who often found themselves pummelled by the Mongols, even after it had relocated itself to the Moscow region in the 13th century.

Since the geography offered them little protection, they spread themselves towards East (Ural Mountains), South (Caspian Sea) and North (Arctic Circle). Gradually, they gained the access to the Caspian Sea, and then to Black Sea; and Caucasus Mountain was one geographical feature which came handy as a natural barrier against the Mongols.

So, now Arctic made it safe in the North; Urals took care of South but the West was still a recurring nightmare (This is rather a crude explanation by me without nuances but I hope the general readers get the picture of Russia's situation.)

The worry goaded Russia to do what the geography demanded from them: In the 18th century, it occupied Ukraine and so Carpathian Mountains was now a natural defense (see map below). It also took control of what is today known as Baltic states to defend itself if the attack came over from the Baltic Sea.

Finally, there was now a ring of safety around Moscow: Arctic above, downwards over the Baltic, sliding further to Ukraine and then Carpathian Mountains to Black Sea to Caucasus to the Caspian, rising upwards to the Urals which rounded up to the Arctic Circle; it indeed was a ring of safety.

This then is the geographical reality which offered some cruel historic lessons to the Russians; and this when we haven't even spoken about its East which faces the militarized Pacific Ocean completely in thrall to the United States, not to speak of their countless military bases.

How Russia has protected itself in the East, on the boundless seas, is another story which the space here doesn't allow me to dwell upon.

Meanwhile, just satiate your curiosity with the knowledge that its stock of nuclear submarines is massive, widely dispersed and almost untraceable at least where it's deployed in the Arctic zone. It has the power to disrupt the very trade across the Atlantic which is the lifeline of Western powers.

***

If you look at China, you won't find it much dissimilar to Russia.

China too expanded into its surrounding regions to create a buffer for itself on the continental shelf.

(*So did the United States but in the discourse of our times, one is expansionist and the other protectionist of its motherland even though both are pursuing a likewise objective.*)

As the Russians sought that cushion for its mainland around Moscow, China too looked to cotton its Han heartland. It occupied and sent millions of its settlers across the arc of Manchuria, inner Mongolia, Xinjiang, Tibet etc.

Like Russia too, China has its perennial worry across sea on its east which we call the Pacific Ocean.

It is Pacific Ocean which makes China survive on its needs and flourish through its trade.

It is Pacific too which brought in imperialists on its shores and a humiliation which lasted for a century, not too long ago.

It is Pacific again when China looks out and sees Japan, South Korea, Taiwan, the Philippines; and Australia and New Zealand on its tails; who would do the bidding for a hostile West.

If Pacific is blockaded, China would implode.

****

So would India.

If seas are not accessible as it accounts for 95% of India's trade, including 80% of its imported energy on which it runs.

How do you think the geography has treated us and how history's lessons of centuries of subjugation been learnt or ignored in our security doctrine?

We all know that in our passage upwards, we have Pakistan and China on our shoulders and Himalayas on top which is both a shield and obstruction to the world.

The rest of India is awashed by sea from three corners over a stretch of 7,516 km.

By the seventh century, India had all the elements to be a seapower: Thriving seaports, skilled sailors and Chalukyas and Pallavas commanding its southwest and southeast regions.

Then Chalukyas, under Pulakeshin II, made its move, conquering Konkan Coast between the Gulf of Khambhat and modern Goa; and crossing the Narmada River to bring the region we call Orissa and Andhra Pradesh under his heels.

Pulakeshin II thus came to be known as "Lord of both the eastern and western seas" even though Chalukyas in southeast were never completely subdued and the conflict between the two, sucking in lesser southern kingdoms of the Pandyas and Cheras, as it did the kings of Sri Lanka, lasted for more than a century.

All of it though didn't affect India's pole position. It sat astride the shipping lines which linked the Middle East and Africa with Southeast Asia and China. (Overland trade too wasn't an issue since there was no

Pakistan and Indian traders could spread themselves even though the volume wasn't as big as on the seas.)

The story of Mughals was completely different from the ones Europeans pursued around the same epoch.

Mughals were happy with the "command of the coast" whereas the Europeans looked for "command of the seas", a distinction which the fear is we haven't appreciated in full to this very day.

So Mughals had competent navy but all it looked for was to come on top of littoral and riverine warfare.

There were no big ships but only fleets of war galleys.

The Mughals devoted itself on nodal points—ports, fortresses and coasts—and never ventured on to open sea lanes.

Then Portuguese worked out the passage to India; being outnumbered resorted to war and brutality with our coastal kingdoms and were successful enough to sail on for profits till Java and Sumatra, part of present day Indonesia.

Mughals then took the help of Dutch and Englishmen who were all too eager to clip Portuguese wings before supplanting their European pioneering sea power with more of the same much to India's misfortune.

In due course, Indian Ocean came to be known as no better than Britain's Lake.

Today India has the second largest army in the world: **But if the two World Wars were continental wars, and the next one is Ocean World War, how prepared do you think we are?**

History tells us that civilisations and powers don't emerge without a hold on seas and oceans.

And as long as imperialism is a fact of our lives, sea power is essential for a country like India which seeks a global presence and leadership of Global South.

History also tells us that imperialists have that big stick in the form of dominance at sea which we witnessed in instances of Korea and Vietnam, Greece and Panama and countless other countries who sought liberation or a free choice under the sun.

It surely is not lost on India to do more than just guard its coasts: It can't have a navy like the United States but it has the example of Russia which relies on no less than 11 nuclear-powered ballistic missile submarines for its defence.

India has one nuclear submarine—INS Arihant—and it has taken us over a dozen years though admittedly the cost (Rs. 900 billion) is prohibitive too.

The memory of United States' sending its nuclear-powered USS Enterprise into Indian waters on the onset of Indo-Pak 1971 war is still acute. It was then a Soviet Union nuclear-submarine, leaving Vladivostok and trailing the moving US threat, which deterred the Americans from unleashing its fury on us.

This is not a piece to dwell on Indian navy at length but the other day Raja Menon, a former rear admiral of Indian navy, and a submarine specialist, lamented in an article[2] that India still doesn't have a grand oceanic strategy.

Russia had a similar predicament for much of its history, and after much yo-yo, the existential threat still drove it to leave its coasts and be a threat to its enemies in open seas, not just in war but also in disrupting the trade—and communication (in naval parlance intelligence)—which is the lifeline for Atlantic powers.

India hasn't yet spelled out its National Security Strategy, like Russia does periodically, but it would be presumptuous to believe it doesn't know the wages required for its onward growth.

India won't grow to its potential if it's not prepared to pay the cost imperialists would demand in due course.

History is witness that seapowers don't become great if its citizenry haven't been co-opted in the process. It's part of culture for seapower nations.

The Modi government's Agniveer scheme, in this respect, is a step in the right direction.

We the citizens on our part too need to wake up to our history–and geography.

Reference:

[1] https://www.reuters.com/world/europe/russias-medvedev-floats-idea-pushing-back-polands-borders-2023-02-24/

[2] https://indianexpress.com/article/opinion/columns/india-must-update-its-security-strategy-and-shed-obsession-with-pakistan-8461381/

Link to Article:

https://www.newsbred.com/why-russia-is-talking-of-pushing-the-borders-of-poland/

If Bakhmut is Not Key, Why Thousands Are Losing Lives?

March 9, 2023

Bakhmut is in news so I believe you know about it.

Still, it takes little to share: Bakhmut, or Artyomovsk, is part of a 70-km defense line of Ukraine in Donbass, the eastern Ukraine the securing of which is the stated goal of Moscow.

Now it is conceded even by the West that Russia has all but secured Bakhmut but the Pentagon is saying it won't mean the tide of the war has changed.[1]

Kiev is saying it has only symbolic value and media is telling us it would be Russia's first major victory since it put its boots in Ukraine in February last.

Now it can't be symbolic if the fighting has raged on in Bakhmut for months and tens of thousands have been killed. It also can't be Russia's first candy since Mariupol is still fresh in mind but for those in amnesia.

The premium on Bakhmut is for good reason since Russia would now surely look to secure Kramtorsk and Slaviansk (see map), only 30 miles on its west, which would give it Donbass (Luhansk and Donetsk).

With Zaporizhzhia and Kherson regions already in kitty, together with Luhansk and Donetsk now, the four regions which chose to go with Russia in September last, Moscow would look at the map (see below) and see a neat symmetry aligning itself into Crimea, home of its Black Sea Fleet; which reducing Azov Sea to as no better than a pond in its backyard.

So it's a bit of a stretch to claim Bakhmut means nothing for this is where Ukraine had dug themselves in for nine years with all those trenches, fortifications and camouflages.

But these defenses have now been blown away; Kramtorsk and Slaviansk are next in queue for Russia would be controlling all the major roads and train routes of this region: And as we all know, supply lines are the lifeline of any military operation.

That's the reason Volodymyr Zelenskyy is refusing to pull out of Bakhmut:

★ *Even though no less than 10,000 of his troops have been encircled and would either surrender or die;*

★ *Even when his commander-in-chief Valery Zaluzhny is at odds with him* [1] *against continuing to throw his men in the "meat-grinder" since the life expectancy on frontline is only four hours presently;*

★ *Even when Washington reportedly asked Kiev to give up Bakhmut in January itself.*

It's not that Zelenskyy is buying time in wait for an imminent supply of promised tanks from the West.

- ★ *First, how do you bring the tanks to the scene of action? There are hardly any functional bridge left to carry their weight;*
- ★ *Secondly, how do you repair these tanks? For that could only be done hundreds of miles away either in Poland or Slovakia;*

It's also not as if Ukraine is blessed with unlimited supply of ammunition or men either.

The European Commission itself concedes that Ukraine presently is firing only 5,000-6,000 artillery shells a day compared to 50,000 by Russia.

Estonia, which is one of largest contributors on the ground to Ukraine, confesses Ukraine fires no more than 7,000 rounds compared to 60,000 by Russia daily.

That is no more than 200,000 shells fired by Ukraine compared to 1.8 million shells Russia fired last month!

This is a 10 to 1 advantage to Russia; and which also explains the Ukrainian casualty is 10 compared to one Russian on an average.

The truth is, Russia fires in a day what artillery Europe produces in a month.

Scary is the prospect, by Estonia's own estimate, that Russia could increase its ammunition production sevenfold in no time.

So why is Zelenskyy holding fort? Why is he rushing towards the bitter end in Bakhmut?

A few things are obvious:

- ★ *One, it would be difficult for West to justify billions of funds and arms to its citizenry, already simmering below the surface, in case of a major reverse;*
- ★ *Two, it could seriously affect the morale of Ukrainian army for they know the significance of Bakhmut;*

★ *Three, it could lead to a revolt within the inner circle of Zelensky where no less than his commander-in-chief is tipped as the new man in charge.*

***

One does wonder if all of this was worth for Ukraine.

They had signed Minsk Agreements with Russia, through the offices of France and Germany in 2015, promising to "prevent the prosecution and punishment of people[2] in eastern Ukraine but as we all know now, didn't mean a word of the international contract;

They had the opportunity to sign the peace deal before being dissuaded by the ex-UK prime minister Boris Johnson, not to say multiple approaches Russia had made for peace, leading up to its foray into Ukraine last February;

It now stares at a land which is reduced to a rump, possibly to-be-gobbled up by its neighbours, like vultures do to carcass;

Its people have run away; economy has drowned; government is but a collection of oligarchs who are fattening themselves on blood money while pushing the world to its date with nuclear extinction.

Does it really think it would wave a magic wand with a few extra tanks, a few extra aircrafts, a few more bodies strewn on the killing fields?

Of course, we won't read it in the newspapers who would furnish some comic relief in the form of a "spy balloon" or other such nonsense: Only meant to distract and take our attention away from the writing on the wall.

And all this while we thought Goebbels is dead!

***

Bakhmut of course doesn't mean that the Ukraine Conflict is ending anytime soon.

In coming day we would hear more often of "terrorist attacks" on Crimea and one could also not rule out that Russia would roll up its sleeves to take care of Romania and Poland, all but hostile Ukraine by other name.

The war would only get wider unless the other neighbours get rid of the death-wish to become another Ukraine.

More on this, soon.

Reference:

[1] https://www.rt.com/news/572541-artyomovsk-bakhmut-ukraine-austin/

[2] https://en.wikipedia.org/wiki/Minsk_agreements

Link to Article:

https://www.newsbred.com/if-bakhmut-is-not-key-why-1000s-are-losing-lives/

Xi's Peace Mission: But US Won't Let Kiev Accept

March 22,2023

If miracles happen, Xi Jinping would manage to bring Zelensky and Putin together on a Ukraine peace plan.

It would be welcomed by India, Global South, Middle East and even Europe, running low as the last-named is on ammunitions and the patience of its citizens.

German chancellor Olaf Scholz has already visited Beijing; French president Emmanuel Macron is due soon enough; and China's reputation as a peace-broker is vouched by two most unlikely neighbours on either side of the Persian Gulf, Saudi Arabia and Iran.

Meanwhile, Putin has welcomed Xi's 12-point peace proposal[1]; Zelensky says the fact that China has proposed "is not bad"[2] which is some progress since it's not a rejection of Xi's proposal.

I know we could be cynical but let's look at it this way: A time would come when negotiations would happen. Parties would sit across the table, a UN Security Council resolution would guarantee it, to be registered under the UN Charter. And it's also given that one or the other party would have a better deal.

And that's because all conflicts throw up one or the other in the driver's seat.

We know a large part of Ukraine is already with Russia; that the cream of Ukrainian forces have been wiped out; that what's appearing in print bears no relation to the footprints of men or munitions on ground;

that the best option for Ukraine is to salvage whatever it could, more so when China is offering hand in its reconstruction.

The carnage must stop; the utter ruin of Ukraine be prevented; and the humanity be saved from a potential nuclear blow-out.

But then America hates peace.

President Joe Biden has bitterly said that he hasn't seen if the peace plan is "beneficial to anyone other than Russia…"

"It's the idea that China is going to be negotiating the outcome of a war that's a totally unjust war for Ukraine is just not rational," Biden said. (Could Ukraine decide that please.)

John Kirby, a spokesman for the National Security Council, has said the administration does not "support calls for a ceasefire right now."

We have heard US Defense Secretary Lloyd Austin say the war must go on to "weaken Russia."

Peace, you see, is hated by the United States.

It wasn't there when a coup was engineered in Kiev in 2014; it wasn't in Minsk Agreements which were just a ruse; it wasn't when Russia fervently sought peace without claim on an inch on Donbass before it put its boots on the ground last year; it wasn't when Turkey tried to play a peace-broker; or before Boris Johnson guided Ukraine out of negotiating table.

In the intervening period, nearly two lakh Ukrainian have died; its economy has gone up in smoke, and millions have fled the homeland.

But then America doesn't want peace.

It can't see Europe getting its energy from Russia; it can't reconcile if Europe blooms with the integration of Eurasian landmass that China, and India, are intent upon; it can't see Russia survive even if Putin doesn't.

It now has its man in Japanese prime minister Fumio Kishida in Kiev[3], hours after he was enjoying golagappas with Indian prime minister Narendra Modi in New Delhi, to do its bidding.

Both Zelensky and the West are hoping against hope: Even their trusted media is giving up on their chances in the Ukraine Conflict.

Sample this from the Washington Post[4] (compressed for space here): "Ukrainian army stands degraded now; there is basic shortage of ammunition; and that the soldiers with combat experience are either dead or wounded."

Further, "An Ukrainian official says the tanks promised by the West is only 'symbolic'; 'we don't have people or weapons'; 'we are on the frontline and we have nothing to shoot with' 'the newly-drafted soldiers just drop everything and run when under fire'; or are afraid to leave the trenches."

And this from the New York Times[5], no less: "Russian forces are attacking along a 160-mile arc in eastern Ukraine; in Bakhmut, Wagner Group has seized control of the eastern side of the city; in other areas, Russia has stepped up shelling; the control of roads and rails that Kremlin considers so important to its goals…"

The West sure has hi-tech weapons but is afraid to supply: What if it falls into Russian hands; what if it triggers a nuclear war which Ukrainians won't mind initiating at this stage?

That Zelensky hasn't rejected Xi's proposal could be a ploy to buy-out time; not to say to cause panic among its Western allies who've emptied themselves on funds or arms. This is a war for which the West prepared for eight long years; now if the peace was to happen through China's initiative, it would be akin to death a million times over.

The West would have other reasons to hold its breath over what transpires between Xi and Putin in Moscow over the next few hours.

It's not that the two giant neighbours would announce a new digital currency as an alternative to recently mauled dollar.

The image of Xi and Putin together has a symbolic value of rallying the non-Western world against the US hegemony, 40 of whom, the African leaders, were in Moscow just a day ago, delighted no doubt that Russia has decided to waive off $20 billion of their debts.[6]

Peace would be a humiliation for the United States, not that Vietnam wasn't or Afghanistan wasn't or Saudi Arabia-Iran handshake through China isn't more recently.

We are presently in the most tumultuous times in human history of the last few centuries when the dominance of Anglo-Saxon bloc could be coming to an end.

Sure, it won't just fade away but would exact a price which the rest of humanity can't escape.

Reference:

[1] https://news.antiwar.com/2023/02/26/china-releases-12-point-peace-for-ukraine/

[2] https://www.theguardian.com/world/2023/feb/24/zelenskiy-open-to-chinas-peace-plan-but-rejects-compromise-with-sick-putin

[3] https://edition.cnn.com/2023/03/20/asia/japan-ukraine-kishida-zelensky-intl-hnk/index.html

[4] https://www.washingtonpost.com/world/2023/03/13/ukraine-casualties-pessimism-ammunition-shortage/

[5] https://www.nytimes.com/2023/03/13/world/europe/russia-ukraine-attacks-donbas.html

Link to Article:

https://www.newsbred.com/xis-peace-mission-in-moscow-why-zelensky-isnt-rejecting-it/

Why the Russian Ambassador Has Got US on Our Feet!

March 24, 2023

It's only hours since Denis Alipov, the Russian ambassador to India, called out "reputable Indian experts" dreaming of India-Russia rift in the wake of Chinese president Xi Jinping's visit to Moscow.

The first name to come to my mind was Indian Express who between C Raja Mohan and Shubhajit Roy produce more lies than is good for anyone's health.

I once wrote on Ukraine Conflict that the Indian Express takes its readers to be dumbs or idiots or both[1]; how they twist Jaishankar-Lavrov meet up[2]; why they want to force Modi's hands on Russia[3]; how they incite Indian citizens to rise against Modi's stance on Ukraine[4]; etc, etc.

Then I gave up on them as hopeless. It's not my job to be Russia's spokesperson as perhaps it is for them to be of the United States. I would cite numerous instances later in this piece to convince you it's not just they have a different point of view but rather it's guided by a partisan agenda.

Then my attention was drawn to a piece by Andrew Korybko where he has, point by point, taken apart an edit by Times of India which he has described as "malicious information"[5] on Xi's catch-up with Putin. I have no illusion about this newspaper either but in case you are still innocent on them, dive into Korybko's article.

I am into this piece not for stating the obvious. The people in South Block know about Lutyens' Media which the Russians know too; it's only that Alipov has now decided to say enough is enough.

A couple of things about Alipov's tweet before I move on to the central theme of my piece. One, Alipov has sensed there is a traction to these propagandists agenda lately; and two, he has described India-Russia ties as "strategic alignment."

The first opening for these hackers was the G20 finance and foreign ministers' meetings in India where Ukraine Conflict was broached upon and the mainstream media reported that but for a recalcitrant Russia and China a joint communique[6] was possible. India, as a host, could have done better than cut-and-paste the Ukraine passages from the Bali Declaration which one could explain but it's not a place to do so.

It ought to have upset our Russian guests and Sergey Lavrov was anything but diplomatic of what he thought of the organizers of the Raisina Dialogue, and the assembled audience, who didn't take any note of his scathing assertion[7]: *Why bring up Ukraine in a G20 meeting which is primarily on economic matters? And if it indeed is a platform for such discussions, what did G20 do in all those years on Iran, Afghanistan or Syria*?

This G20 affair was early this month: Since then China has hogged the headlines with the breakthrough they managed between Saudi Arabia and Iran; and now this Xi's visit to Moscow whose symbolism against the unipolar hegemony is still reverberating in Western capitals.

That all this happened within three weeks was too good a moment for these propagandists to let go by. They were out in force, sensing an opening in causing discord between Russia and India. Denis Alipov is too seasoned a diplomat not to get the drift; he has not only stepped in but for good measure also described Russia-India ties as one of "strategic alignment."

This "strategic alignment" is important to understand for those who are caught between the US-China binary. There are 191 other countries who matter more than you think they do. **Africa**, for one, appears a continent whose time has come. Resources were always there, now their economy is growing, as is the rebellion against West for it overbearing manners. (The Israelis had turned up in the summit of African Union last month and were escorted out for being uninvited.) **Central Asia** is important beyond words for the integration of the Eurasian landmass being sought; **Latin America** is coming out of slumber; **Mexico**, cheek by jowl to the US, is calling out the latter as "liars.[8]"

This is the world that is being shaped; a comity of nations who just don't want to be caught in one camp or the other. They dream of a day where they could pursue their interests with pressure from none. Russia and India offer that "strategic alignment"; offering cooperation and no coercion. It's a long road to "freedom" from the Anglo-Saxon yoke; and Russia and India in lockstep would only reassure the rest of humanity.

And now on to the propaganda of our Indian media which you don't spot.

1. Give it a thought: Those who talk about "press freedom" how are they treating Julian Assange? Have you read any piece on how the West has virtually murdered this shining light of journalism?
2. Those who tout for "freedom of press" why are they silent when you can't access RT or Sputnik media outlets in Western capitals such as London?
3. If West stands by "democracy", how come they have at least 45 military bases[9] in regimes—from Central America to Africa to Asia to Middle East—which are repressive and authoritarian?
4. If the West is a guardian of "human rights" where is that to be seen in Abu Gharib where prisoners are rotting without trials?
5. The media which doesn't get tired in mouthing Russia's "unprovoked" aggression in Ukraine; why they don't tell us if US wars in Iraq, Libya or Syria were indeed "provoked"?
6. If Russia has violated Ukraine's sovereignty what about the United States which still has occupied a part of Syria with its troops?

7. If Putin is a war criminal, why not Bush Jr or Tony Blair who drummed up fake WMD (Weapons of Mass Destruction) to invade Saddam Hussein's Iraq and ruined millions of lives; destabilizing the world to our misery;
8. If the United States indeed is for peace, why reject the peace proposal offhand which Xi has flouted and Putin has sounded amenable to?

Etc.

None of this of course is mentioned in our mainstream media. A media which neither means good for India nor Indians; nor for that matter Russia which is heroically standing alone against the might of West and NATO, against crushing sanctions and loss of lives of its manhood.

This media is part of the "information warfare" that is beholden to the West. How I wish they are exposed and citizenry freed from their matrix.

It ought to be endeavour of our governing classes: To go beyond the diplomatic cloak and provide light of truth to our citizenry.

It's my conviction that howsoever good the Modi government has in mind for India; till it has an informed citizenry, it would find itself against the headwind. Remember what they did with "surgical strikes" and turned heroism of our soldiers into skullduggery.

Denis Alipov, in this respect, has us on our feet! May we take a leaf out of his book.

Reference:

[1] https://www.newsbred.com/indian-express-takes-it-reader-to-be-dumb-or-idiot-or-both/

[2] https://www.newsbred.com/how-indian-express-has-twisted-jaishankars-meet-up-with-lavrov/

[3] https://www.newsbred.com/ukraine-crisis-why-indian-media-is-trying-to-force-modis-hand-on-russia/

[4] https://www.newsbred.com/express-oped-incites-indian-citizens-to-rise-against-modi-govts-stance-on-ukraine/

[5] https://korybko.substack.com/p/the-sino-russo-entente-can-produce

[6] https://www.newsbred.com/g20-foreign-ministers-meet-what-you-all-dont-know/

[7] https://www.newsbred.com/lavrov-at-his-cutting-best-in-raisina-dialogue/

[8] https://www.reuters.com/world/americas/mexican-president-calls-us-state-department-liars-after-rights-report-2023-03-21/

[9] https://en.wikipedia.org/wiki/List_of_United_States_military_bases

Link to Article:

https://www.newsbred.com/why-denis-alipov-the-russian-amb-has-us-on-our-feet/

Is Russia Really China's Junior Partner?

March 26, 2023

I am amused at how synchronized "Russia-is-a-junior-partner-to-China" chorus has gone up in West in the wake of Xi Jinping's visit to Moscow this week.

John Kirby spoke of Russia "certainly are the junior "partner[1]" in the regular daily White House briefing; Antony Blinken too was adamant that Russia is "very much the junior partner."

Then the Western mainstream media went into an overdrive: Foreign Affairs has called Russia as China's "new vassal"[2]; NBC[3] says Putin occupies only the "back seat"; Financial Times[4], MSNBC[5]… you name them, all have chortled at the lesser Russia in the alliance.

Then I heard Pankaj Saran, former Indian ambassador to Russia and ex Deputy National Security Adviser, say in a show that Russia would never accept to be a "junior partner"[6]. And further, that "I don't think Russia will mortgage its foreign policy to China."

Then why has this orchestrated noise on "little Russia" ratcheted up this week?

One, of course is to hurt proud Russians enough to make them revisit every move China makes vis-a-vis them; two is to prod the national scar which Russia suffered at the hands of the Mongols in the 13th century; three, to arm the considerable West-sympathizers who abound in Russia.

But this aside, is Russia really a "junior partner" who won't matter without China's benevolence?

History tells us that those who matter either have money or weapons: Those who have money can buy weapons and those who have weapons—well, they could have anyone's money!

Smile over, let's look it from the natural order of things: No two things are equal, not even identical twins. Synergy happens when two forces bring their best on the table. It makes both of them stronger: just as it happens in between two organisms.

Russia today has weapons to envy; China has the economic beef to matter. Which of the two components matter more in the synergy? Let's examine.

Russia presently is years ahead of the United States in quality if not quantity of weapons. It's hypersonic missiles today gives it years of advantage against anyone on the planet.

What are Hypersonic Missiles?

Well, Russia has three types of them: Zircons, Kinzhals and Avantguards.

Kinzhals have a speed of 12-15 mach (the speed of sound is 3.5 mach). All the Anti-Ballistic Missiles (ABM) which the United States has, or it has deployed along the Poland-Romania axis, could only work against missiles less than the speed of sound.

Very early in the Ukraine Conflict, Russia showcased Kinzhal hypersonic missiles to let the US/NATO know what they are dealing with.

Barely a few weeks into its Special Military Operation (SMO), Russia unleashed Kinzhal on a formidable Ukrainian weapons depot built to blunt a nuclear strike. The depot was way down into the guts of Mother Earth, some 500 ft below the surface, and fortified with several layers of armoured concrete.

That Kinzhal first rose up to 40 km on the sky, and then dived perpendicularly at the speed of 15 Mach; triggering scary kinetic energy before piercing through the seemingly nuke-protected underground weapons depot as a knife would through butter.

The impact on the depot was fatal but perhaps not as nightmarish as it's on the wiseheads of Pentagon and NATO.

Now Kinzhals are specifically meant to neutralize aircraft carrier strike groups. The United States has 11 of them and at best it could use six at one time. Russia last week fired six of its Kinzhals in one go—implying it could wipe out active US aircraft carrier groups in one strike.

Presently, Russia has 50 Kinzhal missiles. It has the capacity to build 200 Kinzhal missiles a year. It could be delivered from all platforms conceivable: Air, sea, submarines etc. It would take the United States/West many years before they could have a weapon of this quality. Much would have changed by then.

Now Kinzhal missile has a range of 2,000 km. And it is here where the China-senior-Russia-junior narrative could be put to bed.

Presently the US aircraft carriers are stationed at CBG -1,2 and 3 (in shaded rectangles), some 1,500 km away from Shanghai. China does have a DF-21 ballistic missile and claims it could strike up to 1,500 km. But with Kinzhal missile, the touch-and-go distance don't matter.

I happened to glance at the purchase power parity[7] in 2022 and found out that Russia's was $31,962 and China's $21,291. This after the devaluation of the Ruble after 2013.

Russia has all the things it needs for a modern life: energy, minerals, commodities, foodstuff etc. China, on the other hand, imports most of them. And does so through the sea routes which are increasingly becoming fragile. China's enemies could conjure up a blockade and cripple Beijing even without a nuclear strike.

Of course, it's there for anyone to see that China's buying of Russia's energy is a godsend for Moscow. But getting much of its enormous energy needs at a 70% discount isn't a bad deal for China either.

So this "junior partner" dig is rather shameless. I wonder why this "vassal" or "junior partner" tag hasn't been pinned on Germany, France, Italy etc. Indeed, they are no better than serfs. Such is their standing with Washington that the latter tells Olaf Scholz in public he would destroy Nord Stream gas pipelines. A Kishida is made to redraw his travel plan and dash to Kiev. It's the US which dictates to its puppets not to trade with Venezuela, Cuba or Iran.

No such thing is happening between Russia and China. The former isn't grumbling on a rather passive support to Moscow; the latter isn't stopping Russia from selling its energy to India and others, never mind if New Delhi is an integral part of QUAD against it. Nor do we find that China has blown up anyone's energy gas pipeline.

That's why I bristle at this crass stupidity of West in spinning the narrative. We hear Rishi Sunak of United Kingdom calling the AUKUS submarine deal against China and its "systemic challenge" as "brilliant." I can understand India or China's neighbours being fretful on Middle Kingdom. But how is United Kingdom endangered by China?

Who is a threat to peace here?

One who encroached the border of Vietnam last in 1978 or the one who is adding chapters in Iraq, Afghanistan, Libya, Yemen, Syria every day?

Reference:

[1] https://www.washingtonpost.com/politics/2023/03/21/white-house-knocks-russia-chinas-junior-partner/

[2] https://www.foreignaffairs.com/china/chinas-new-vassal?check_logged_in=1

[3] https://news.yahoo.com/chinas-drive-global-order-leaves-132358403.html?fr=sycsrp_catchall

[4] https://www.ft.com/content/73d50de6-53c8-4bf6-adf9-8cf108f82ca1

[5] https://www.msnbc.com/opinion/msnbc-opinion/war-ukraine-exposed-russia-chinas-junior-partner-rcna72003

[6] https://www.youtube.com/watch?v=gvb9BUO00DM

[7] https://en.wikipedia.org/wiki/List_of_countries_by_GDP_(PPP)_per_capita

Link to Article:

https://www.newsbred.com/is-russia-really-chinas-junior-partner/

Finland in NATO: Welcome to Thieves' Kitchen

April 8, 2023

Finland joins NATO.

Jens Stoltenberg of NATO says Sweden would join soon[1] too.

That would make NATO 32-nation strong.

In case, it's just a number to you, look at the NATO map below and how it would look to a Russian.

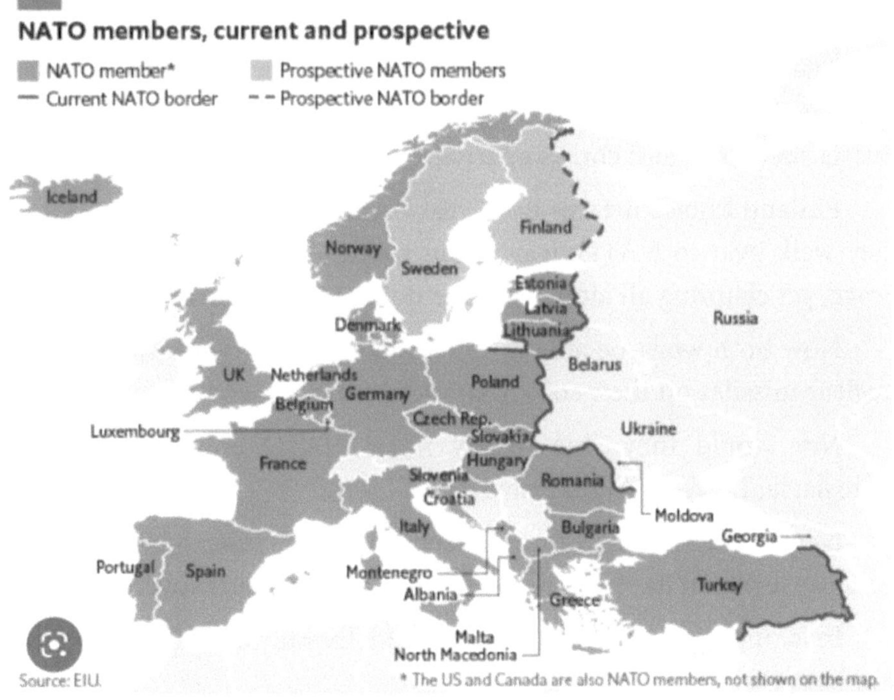

Both Finland and Sweden since 1945 were neutral countries.

At the height of the Cold War, when the Warsaw Pact around Soviet Union was 10 time stronger than NATO, they stuck to their neutrality.

It was in no small measure to leaders like Sweden's Olaf Palme (who incidentally was murdered) and Finland's Urho Kekkonen for they knew what war meant.

But over the last few decades, they have been part of NATO only albeit with other names.

Slowly but surely, the elites of military-industrial complex took over, the media began wagging tail for its piece of bone, and to draw from a romantic analogy, an engagement of two decades has now been formalized into a marriage.

Vladimir Putin would know it is NATO preparing for a war over Arctic where Russia has the first-comer advantage and which holds allure for its two main friends, China and India.

The West would love to drag them down on another front, entail a far nastier defense budget, to go with history's toughest sanctions, till Russia succumbs and comes apart at the seams.

Finland knows it faces no threat from Russia, as does Sweden, yet they walk over to NATO, leaving no room for neutrality, no room for peace, yet claiming all along they are doing so for humanity.

Now both won't be able to say no to the West if it wishes to set up nuclear missiles on their soils. (Norway and Denmark already do.)

Nor would they able to say no if NATO engages in another Yugoslavia, Libya or Afghanistan.

Never mind if their young are sent to far off lands to be slaughtered for a cause which has nothing to do with their nation's sovereignty.

In a moment of crisis, they would literally be occupied by US and NATO.

This crisis of course would be NATO's own making for Russia surely is not eyeing Europe.

And how the two forces stand against each other?

Nobody is talking of Nuclear War here—for it leaves no winners.

In conventional warfare, let's look at how NATO vs Russia theme could play out.

NATO initially was made up of national contingents. It no longer is the case. The US part of NATO force has long since gone home.

The European nations, one after another, have reduced their forces.

Only dimwits say "We would do war, whatever it takes."

For a real war isn't what you see on celluloid.

It involves a whole lot of things, not least brigades, headquarters, chain of transport and power, repair and replacements etc, etc.

And it is not as if you alone can hurt your enemy. You have to also factor in what your enemy could do to you.

Let's first see what Russia could do to the NATO before looking at the options the latter has.

If Russia was to set eye on just a few targets, which you got to concede it could very well do with its missiles from aircrafts, ships or submarines, the names of Pentagon, White House, CIA and NSA headquarters, NATO headquarters in Brussels, its military headquarters in Mons all look fair game.

As it could be with various European defence ministries, military headquarters, military airfields etc. Your ammunition storage, repair depots, naval bases, vessels, transport hubs etc all are potential targets.

In theory, military airfields are dispersed unlike ground forces which are mobilized. The spread out airfields mean use of civilian airports which of course would have to be shut down.

Most European military installations are near civilian clusters. The UK's military headquarters, for instance, is in a suburb of London. Hundreds of thousands of people live near seaports and airports.

How do you evacuate them (forget orderly phasing out)? Where do you hide them? In bunkers which you have already abandoned knowing they are no good against modern missiles? What housing alternatives you have? Which government could hope to have its citizens' support on such a matter? Do you think citizens' unrest in one won't spread across the borders? Who would risk announcing such a grave provision for its citizens, telling them they are under risk of air and missile attack? For what, Ukraine?

(Last week, when Zelensky gave an online address in Austrian parliament, dozens of MPs walked out[2])

Let's presume NATO has mobilized enough multinational forces to march towards Russia.

Now NATO has never deployed OFFENSIVE mechanized operations far from its bases. It all along has a DEFENSIVE orientation in that it would stop an enemy at the gate. They could thus fall back on their supply lines, reserves, maintenance depots etc, etc.

But here it's different. You are talking of moving thousands of miles towards your East. Training disparate forces takes weeks if not months. You also have to look at your reserve forces.

How do you get there? Is there any precedent in our times of moving such manpower and machinery over such a distance and not exposing yourself to enemy's air and missile attacks? How do you get them across the Channel, if I may ask?

We are talking of Western tanks, all still heavy and largely a leftover of Cold War, and mechanized units moving inside civilian infrastructures, a minimum of 10 km long convoy—for it would have all kind of recovery, repair, medical units etc, etc—damaging roads, bridges flyovers.

We are not even talking of regular supplies of spares, consumables, hospitals, workshops etc. Or evacuating casualties, reinforcements, replacing damaged weapons etc.

Then there is this basic question: How many Brigades could you spare? And if you send all of them towards Russia, who looks after your own Capitals?

Now let's address the question I am sure you have on your mind:

Why NATO has to move on the ground? Don't they have missiles and air carriers? Doesn't US-NATO spend many times over than what Russia does on its defense?

The truth is Western nations haven't paid much attention on long-range conventional missiles all these years. Yes they have Tomahawk cruise missiles with a range of 1,500 km. It has a warhead of 500 kg, no better than what was used in World War II. From a NATO's point of view, the targets need to be closer to sea since they are launched from ships and submarines. Where do you think Moscow is? And don't forget to look at the size of Russia, to begin with.

So even if you launch Tomahawk Missiles, let's say from the Baltic or eastern Mediterranean, you could reach Moscow, theoretically. Or that your aircraft carriers could drop conventional bombs on Moscow. But then we are talking of Russia which has one of world's most comprehensive air defence system. And I am sure nobody is forgetting what Russians could do in retaliation to a Buckingham or an Elysee Palace. No European government would look at such an option and still not tremble in its boots.

So there you are: You can't rely on your missiles, aircraft carriers and your mobilized mechanized units, at least in near future.

So who is winning war here in Ukraine?

Your best bet is to stretch Russia thin, which is where the Finland factor comes in, or drag them in the Pacific theatre to inflict damage on its eastern borders.

All this while hoping that the economic cost and loss of manhood would bring Vladimir Putin, and Russia, on its knees.

So far we have seen its' fanciful.

A defensive Russia, as it has no ambitions beyond Eastern Ukraine and the wellbeing of its local Russians, is impossible to beat by NATO.

PERIOD.

This simple truth is either not understood or fudged by mainstream media.

The present war, forget what your read in newspapers, is as good as lost for Ukraine.

One fine morning, you would have another walk-out from Ukraine like you had in Vietnam or Afghanistan, to a new theatre of a new adventure.

Unless of course Russia can't bear the cost.

But as long as China, and India, are picking the bills, Rubles is in business, isn't it?

Reference:

[1] https://www.youtube.com/watch?v=3exKfzkDYXs

[2] https://www.bbc.com/news/world-europe-65131744

Link to Article:

https://www.newsbred.com/finland-in-nato-welcome-to-the-thieves-kitchen/

Why the US Won't Supply Its Best Weaponry to Ukraine

May 9, 2023

Has it crossed your mind that in today's time when wars could actually be televised, we have had no such instances emerging from Ukraine.

There are few horrific images, few fleeing populace, fewer ruins even though the Conflict has lasted for over a year now and the casualties could soon near the figures of World War I.

We keep hearing about the Ukraine counter-offensive, that the delay is because of unusual rains and many feet deep mud on which little could move.

The trouble is where could Ukraine strike?

In Crimea or would they take on the four-five layered defensive Russian positions along a thousand km long border on the eastern side?

We have regular instances of Russian fighter planes moving over the eastern frontline and dropping 500 kg glide bombs at will which proves that Ukraine has no Air Defense System (ADS) worth its name.

We keep hearing about Ukraine summoning its reserves and its fighting prowess being boosted by the European and NATO weaponry but how do you move them when all the time you are in the prying range of Russian missiles?

The moment you move them, cobble them together, you open yourself to hell from the sky and at best you could have a window of 24-36 hours.

Yes, Ukraine has about 35 units of HIMARS rocket launchers but are there enough missiles to spread it over a 1000 km?

How do you amass fuel and ammunition? How to position forces, if they are of considerable numbers, secretly?

If you lose fuel, weaponry, transport, reserves in big numbers in first two or three days, how do you adjust your counter-offensive on the go? Which trench, tunnel or bunker would be able to protect the Ukrainian soldiers?

The entire Ukraine movement depends on rail and roads. Do you think they are out of bounds for the Russians?

We are talking of the unfortunate country without air defense, tank forces, little artillery and missiles, crippled electric grid and rail network, all destroyed.

We are talking of a country who would never be supplied by the US/NATO's best weaponry—for the fear if the Russians were to make a spectacle out of them, no other importing country would touch them with a barge pole even as they would line up for what the Russians could offer.

Yet Zelensky and his generals would need to do something to keep bloating the 158 billion dollars of aid in all forms they have already received. Without any tangible show on the ground, the Western populace would ask for accountability from their governments; opposition would go shrill and sinful media would run out of its sinister manipulation.

The trouble is, the moment Ukrainians launch something silly, it would be the end of it for the Russians would cast off all the restraint they have shown thus far in ensuring few civilian casualties. It would leave no Ukrainian soldier left standing.

Be sure, US/NATO are running out of options, they won't replace the Ukrainian men with their own, for talk is cheap. Why, we even have Henry Kissinger suggesting that the peace talks could begin before the year is out.

But a lot would happen before it comes to that stage. Russian foreign minister Sergey Lavrov has already declared they are in no mood to discuss peace with the puppet (Zelensky) and would rather hear from his masters (US/NATO) only.

Zelensky would either fall to his own generals or flee, the government eliminated and stripped of the fiction built all these months. These war criminals would be at each other's throats.

Zelensky would go down in history as a leader who lost his entire army, his country, for greed and hatred blinded him as he played into the hands of his masters.

Poles would keep vowing to come to assistance of the Ukrainians but who would they help when none are left?

Not that masters haven't suffered incalculable disaster.

Dollar is fast losing its sheen and without this fake currency, the US hegemony would disappear overnight.

Ties are forged, trade is being conducted in local currencies, BRICS and SCOs are beginning to amass the critical mass and the West Asia is primed to step into a life without the US.

All that the US has done is to reverse the gains they made through Nixon and Kissinger in 1972 to take China away from the orbit of Soviet Union. Now, Beijing and Moscow are blood brothers.

Sooner than later, the US would abandon Ukraine, and move on to their next project, possibly Taiwan. Nobody would question what happened to the poor country as nobody does today about Afghanistan or its infra.

We now know the truth of the world's finest fighting force the world has ever seen. It can't fight a sustained war; while we witness the Russian War Machine is unflagging still keeping a light hand without unleashing its full fury.

History tells us that it's fatal to assume Russians are weak; that they are running out of men or machines; on ground, in sky or under water.

The truth is the US or NATO bluff has been called out. Russia stays strong, despite sanctions, despite bombing its Nord Stream, despite the whole gamut of trickery and sorcery the West and its vassals and puppet media have unleashed.

Now is the turn of assassinations and terrorist attacks on civilians, to cause panic, in the vain hope of a regime change in Kremlin. Brace up for it in the coming days for the Hegemon won't let its hold of a century go up in smoke.

Don't delude yourself that Ukraine is still in the game. It's game, set and match to Russia. All we await is who is the next Ukraine the West would move on its chessboard to checkmate Russia and China.

Some, you see, are not genetically wired to see the writing on the wall.

Prudence has never been a gift to the bullies.

Link to Article:

https://www.newsbred.com/why-west-would-never-supply-its-best-weaponry-to-ukraine/

All Ukraine is Left with Are Terror Attacks

June 8, 2023

A dam (Kakhovka) is breached.

The outflow of water—the dam is as big as the Great Salt Lake in Utah, US—has risen by more than 10 meters; it has put thousands of lives, homes, wildlife, ecology etc in danger.

That's not all.

Water supply to Crimea is hurt.

Zaporozhye, Europe's biggest nuclear power plant too alarmingly loses the Dnieper water upstream, necessary to cool its reactors and its spent fuel rods.

Ukraine and the Western media are shouting shrill at this "act of terrorism by Russia."

Only nobody tells us what would Russia gain by bombing the dam it controls; putting its own people of Kherson and Crimea at risk; put a nuclear power plant under its control in red; and stretching itself thin while guarding thousands of kilometres of defensive lines in Ukraine's South.

Ukraine, on the other hand, has everything to gain.

It could divert the world's attention from its failed counteroffensive of a day before (Monday); delay Russia's advance on inundated earth; and hopefully drag this stand-off till winter for it to suck more dollars out of West' pockets and keep its shockingly apathetic audience indifferent.

Ukraine needed time to fall back from Kherson since they were running out of men.

Kherson is important for it allows the only access Ukraine has to the Black Sea.

Now both sides had to retreat and take positions on the opposite banks of the Dnieper River.

Sure, not the entire Kherson is with Russia. Part of it is with Kiev too. People on the other side have been endangered too. But if there is anything we have witnessed in the last year and a half, it is that the Volodymyr Zelensky regime has least concern for human lives.

Under the Martial Law, it has spared neither old nor young, even minors, and sent them effectively to meat-grinders of vastly superior Russia's air and ground presence.

Since the early days of Russia's Special Military Operation (SMO), one has seen how Ukraine wreaks havoc on its own people and territory, often by destroying infrastructure so as it doesn't fall into the hands of the enemy.

Nobody is pointing out that as far back as in December last year, the Washington Post, in a report, titled "Inside the Ukrainian counteroffensive that shocked Putin and reshaped the war[1]" had Ukrainian officials admitting they had plans to blow up the dam, "albeit as a last resort."

Ukraine's Major General Andrey Kovalchuk, who was commander of last November's Kherson counteroffensive, had admitted to the newspaper they had plans to execute this war crime.

Wrote the Washington Post:

"*Kovalchuk considered flooding the river. The Ukrainians, he said, even conducted a test strike with a HIMARS launcher on one of the floodgates at the Nova Kakhovka dam, making three holes in the metal to see if the Dnieper's water could be raised enough to stymie Russian crossings...the Test was a success, Kovalchuk said, but the step remained a last resort...*"

How then had Russia reacted?

It had gone to the United Nations, wrote to UN secretary general Antonio Guterres in October last, about the Ukrainian threat to the dam, but the global body didn't pay heed.

Russia is aghast that the UN secretariat which is adept at "politicizing" statements, hasn't condemned Kiev and instead throws up its hand at "insufficient information."

But then the stance of this global body, entrusted with the peace of this world, has consistently been to ignore Ukraine's war crimes in the last two years.

It has reacted neither to the bombing of the Crimean Bridge nor to the targeted assassinations of journalists Darya Dugina and Vladlen Tatarsky. It's conspiracy of silence to the sabotage of the Nord Stream 1 gas pipeline—which put the future of Europe at risk—is deafening.

The Russian envoy to the United Nations wasn't mincing words: "The Kiev regime has good teachers, responsible for destroying the Nord Stream and the deliberate targeting of the Tabqa dam in Syria. The West is used to doing the dirty work with other people's hands."

All It's Left With Is Terror Acts

By now, it's apparent that the Kiev regime would resort to terrorist acts as it stands no chance—nor does its NATO backers—against Russia on the battlefield.

It doesn't have to use F-16s or other fancy weapons for blowing up dams or pipelines or bridges is sufficient for the propaganda to work in its favour.

These are forces with a history of terrorist attacks—fire-bombing the Dresden; likewise with Tokyo; atomic bombs on Hiroshima and Nagasaki etc. Some still insist to include 9/11 in the list.

Many trace the birth and spread of terrorism in our times as a creation of the Hegemon: If not by affording funds or arms, then by creating conditions which give rise to extremism.

That's why the world fears them: They control the planet, they are everywhere: Be it governments, bureaucracy, judiciary or even labs.

Then there is that unsurpassable shameless servile Western media which would have you believe that Russians are attacking own Kremlin buildings with drones to spoil its own Republic Day parade.

That's why one hopes Russia is left standing on its feet at the end of this fight-to-finish. That Moscow is able to finish off the evil empire and free humanity from its bondage.

Otherwise, these history fabricators would cast Vladimir Putin as another Hitler and fraud narratives would be perpetuated as has been a few tales of World War II or Cold War.

Reference:

[1] https://web.archive.org/web/20221229064018/https:/www.washingtonpost.com/world/2022/12/29/ukraine-offensive-kharkiv-kherson-donetsk/

Link to Article:

https://www.newsbred.com/damn-kiev-regime-all-its-left-with-is-terror-acts/

The First Fake Coup of History Which Fooled the West

June 25, 2023

So the first fake military coup of the history is over.

Yevgeny Prigozhin's Wagnerites were 200km away from Moscow when hands were shook, a lot of credit went to Belarusian president Alexander Lukashenko, and it's now business as usual.

The idiots who were jumping up and down in Washington and Kiev missed a few obvious in their pathological hatred for Vladimir Putin.

- ★ How could 25,000 Wagnerites take over Russia without air support and anti-air defense, never mind the missing support of the people?
- ★ Who would've supplied these rebels with food and ammunition?
- ★ How is it that the long frontlines showed no skirmish, forget a long-drawn battle between the Russian and Wagner forces?
- ★ Who attempts a coup in open, marching hundreds of kilometres, almost for a full 24 hours, when it's always done in stealth, most likely in midnight?
- ★ What do you think is the possibility of such march going undetected?

How could Prighozin on his own decide upon a coup when he is not a military commander, in essence just a publicist for Wagner: I mean moving whole divisions involves the entire command staff, major generals and squad leaders etc. It's not as if Prighozin would issue an order and everyone would do his bidding. This is Hollywood stuff; it doesn't happen in real world.

It's well-known that Wagner has a considerable number of ex Russian officers and soldiers: A coup wouldn't have been possible without they being purged—and there was none in this instance.

It's been more than six months since Prighozin has been making noise: sometimes on lack of ammunition and often a rant against Russian defence minister Sergei Shoigu.

All of Prighozin's baits were taken hook, line and sinker by the West and its corrupt media and often with disastrous consequences: It buoyed the enemy into walking into a trap, sensing a discord or lack of weapons, and throwing themselves into the "meat-grinder" in thousands.

Come to think of it: If Prighozin indeed was causing trouble, why would Putin tolerate him against his own mission to the advantage of his enemies for these long months?

There is every likelihood this deception was rooted in strong logic: One, the blame wouldn't come squarely on Putin if the military goals were not met; arguably defense minister Sergey Shoigu would be the fall guy; and Putin would still be the charismatic leader to his millions of citizens, tragically betrayed by the very men he trusted.

The next logical question is: Why this antic at the very moment when Ukraine is in the midst of its counter-offensive?

First, it's important to remember that Prighozin and Putin met each other only nine days ago on June 14: A meeting they described as "productive."

Secondly, by taking "control" of city of Rostov, the "feeding" centre of frontlines, and marching in a straight line for Moscow, possibly Wagner was playing the act of drawing attention away from what Russia has planned in next coming days.

The involvement of Belarus—Prigohzin has been granted an access to this country—suggests a massive attack away from the frontlines, possibly Kharkiv, is in offing. Or it could be Belgorod they have set their sights upon. Chechens, we already know, are moving towards Wagnerites and joining the epicentre of tension. It's also an apt moment for Russia to mobilize its reserves.

All Putin has managed in last few hours is to successfully mobilize the support of his citizens: Possibly also identified the fifth columns who would've thrown off their cloak of patriotism sensing a coup.

In Russia, they call it Maskirovka, a deception too difficult for the enemy to understand. Putin, an admirer of Sun Tzu's Art of War, must have read that: *All warfare is based on deception—you attack when you appear unable to do so; you mobilize when your forces appear inactive; when near your enemy you make them believe you are afar; and when far away you make you enemy believe you are near.*

The weird coup most likely was no better than a PsyOp, intended to fool the enemy. Putin's short speech in the midst of "coup" was a giveaway: Hardly angry or pissed, as if he was reading a script.

And he is driving the West nuts.

Link to Article:

https://www.newsbred.com/the-first-fake-coup-in-history-and-the-west-indeed-was-fooled/

Wagner in Belarus: Making Sense of Rearranged Pieces

July 2, 2023

Russia's saviour Vladimir Putin has gone to length to describe the "Wagner coup" as a real one.

Within hours of Wagner Group's Yevgeny Prigozhin arriving in Belarus after aborting his march to Moscow while only 200km away, Putin was again addressing his citizens and hailing the "fallen pilots" for having saved the nation from the "mutineers."

It ran cross to my analsyis[1] that it was a staged event since you don't march for that long in the open without a reprisal; without a fallout in frontlines; without mutiny amongst fellow Russian officers; without food and other supplies; etc, etc.

If pilots have died, it certainly wasn't staged but who has seen the falling debris, dismembered bodies, wailing families, heart-wrenching funerals? Or Putin attending such funerals as is his wont?

An explanation has emerged that Wagner's convoys carried a mobile Pantsir-1 air defense system: Helicopters and plane which came within its range met their dreaded fate.

Now this itself would stretch credulity for why would Wagner have its own air-defense system when Russia, like others, have an integrated command structure and any force within can't take its own call on such a critical piece of weaponry?

Even if one presumes that Pantsir-1 anti-aircraft missile system was passed on between units in the thick of battle or Wagner might have acquired it during their operations in Syria, it still is a stretch since for many hours the internal security forces, the police and military, the border guards etc didn't twitch an eyebrow. And then within hours a three-way deal was struck between Belarus, Russia and Wagner while the convoys were on move!

Be that as it may, Prigozhin and Wagner are in Belarus which is a Russian gambit West and NATO are terrified with.

Belarus has had reasons to worry Poland, a NATO member, flanking its western wing as Ukraine is a threat to its underbelly in south. It shares a long 700-km border with Russia in east which can't afford its lesser neighbour to fall into the "hands" of West. It's close to Kiev, and was used as base by Russian troops to launch attacks on the Ukrainian capital in the beginning of their Special Military Operation (SMO). Not to say that to reach Kaliningrad, an isolated Russian territory on the Baltic Sea, Belarus is the shortest route for Russia.

Besides the historical links, Belarus' president Aleksandr Lukashenko is obligated to Putin on thwarting an opposition movement and its bid to topple him in 2020. Western sanctions pushed Belarus further into the arms of Russia who was generous with its money and energy resources. Belarus is lawfully bound to host Russian troops and weapons: And now Russia has stationed tactical nuclear weapons on its soil.

So clearly Belarus is critical if the Russia-Ukraine conflict was to spin out of control. Wagner's presence there now would force NATO and Ukrainian forces to rearrange their pieces on the geo-military chessboard. Wagner remains a formidable military presence, hardened like few armies are for its involvement for years in Libya, Syria, Central African Republic and Ukraine. Perched now within handshaking distance from Kiev, it's a mortal threat to the Zelensky regime. Not to forget it secures Russia's western borders; a call away if Russia in the guise of Belarus was to use them in West Asia or Africa. And yes it's a security to any threat emanating on freshly supplied tactical nuclear weapons to Belarus.

So Prighozin now has a deal with Belarus like it had with Russia: Already some 8,000 of Wagner soldiers are embedding themselves in the Belarusian setup and camps are said to being built for them in the Mogilev region, some 400-odd km from Kiev

So make what you must on the "coup"; on the "mutineers" and "betrayers" like Prigozhin, things as they stand today—Wagner in Belarus without any criminal charges on their heads; Belarus beefed; Russian intelligence in the process of identifying Ukrainian sleeper cells within its fold; Putin stronger than ever—these events have largely been in Russia's favour.

Staged or real, the "coup" has worked with clockwork precision.

Reference:

[1] https://www.newsbred.com/the-first-fake-coup-in-history-and-the-west-indeed-was-fooled/

Link to Article:

https://www.newsbred.com/wagner-in-belarus-making-sense-of-rearranged-pieces/

What If Russia Now Does to France What It Did to Them

July 4, 2023

History is a cruel bixch.

It wasn't long ago when France was actively involved in "maidan coup" in Ukraine, handing out from biscuits to bombs to rioters, and brokering a peace deal only to buy time for the UkroNazis to arm themselves to teeth.

If Russia was to do the same now to France—feeding the rioters with one hand while appearing a peace-maker with the other—how unfair would it seem?

All along, France has been treating Russia as an enemy when it was one within their own fold they prefer not to call immigrants.

The French first looted, killed, raped, pillaged and brutalised the peaceful North Africa—Algeria, Morocco, Tunisia etc—and then put their own pick in power after granting them independence in the second half of the 20th century.

Then cropped up the matter of rising from the debris of the Second World War: France needed men to go with resources. So young limbs were shipped across to plough in the reconstruction era, pittance offered for a life away from heat and degeneracy.

They thought they were smart in bringing over men who could speak French for assimilation (they still call them overseas Frenchman); the high ideals of "liberty, equality and fraternity" were held dear to offer them the best social security net in the world.

Yet all along this bunch carried their culture and painful history with them, building enclaves upon enclaves around Paris and Marseilles, staying close, distrusting their hosts.

The French elites, in their perfumed existence, drugged by high ideals yet blinded to reality, looked the other way. If anything, they offered them the knee, to borrow a parlance from the BlackLivesMatter. Riots became a matter of celebration and not concern. Those emboldened targeted the State and the natives who happened to be primarily Whites. The massive 2005 riots which lasted for weeks didn't break the French elites' slumber.

The truth is, a nation is easier to construct around culture, religion and heritage. The mere common language is as false a premise for a rooted society as is the notion that some vague ideologies alone could work.

In an ironical way, the French state only strengthened this "otherness" in their fold. The idea was not only to keep Marine le Pen and other ultra-rights in check but also have a captive vote bank in elections. (Shades of India, huh…)

All the "woke" ideologies, for example the so-called feminist warriors who celebrated the lawful abortion, and either vowed not to have babies or if at all a "brown baby", were blinded to the ballooning fold of immigrants who produce babies in profusion. (Pick out your India in this…)

France also offered the immigrant children the right to education. But who teaches them French in poor areas, in schools which are underfunded and in bad shape? Where are the resources to psychologically tackle the anger and betrayal fomenting in young?

So big is the size of immigrants that one-third of France today is made up of them. Every one person in 10 today is from an immigrant family in France.

You brought them over for your own selfish ends, bound by the greed of Capitalism which seeks to maximize profit on low wages, shunning, say a Portuguese or an Italian immigrant with shared cultural values but higher wages.

You thought ideologies and abstract concepts would tide over identities and customs; people and prejudices.

You wanted the immigrants to keep their individuality in the name of "multi-culturalism" as long as they show deference to some vague liberal and human rights ideology.

This is not how it works: You can't have your cake and eat it too.

This is the fate waiting to happen to all of Western Europe, and not just France: Immigrants as a block keeping the society on boil. The native Whites then gather under the wings of the ultra-rights; street battles ensue while an Emmanuel "Oedipus" Macron prefers dancing with Elton John than douse a burning Paris.

This is indeed a prototype of real "civil war" while you thought the Wagner-Prigozhin "coup" was the real deal.

Moscow indeed is humming a song today while Notre Dame is burning; France is falling.

Servile Mainstream Media of course would rush to take our gaze away from these riots and won't point out what is obvious to everyone: Western societies are in torment for the greed of Capitalism has infected its body. At times it would be economic woes, at other times ethnic groups pulling in different directions. Some woke ideology won't hide the blood on the streets.

If this was happening in India, the pen-hacks would lash out at the "fascist" State where minority is in trouble, democracy is dead. They won't let the matter die down, nor would their big brothers in NYT or Washington Post, unlike your newspaper suddenly taking France out between its covers.

Link to Article:

https://www.newsbred.com/what-if-russia-now-does-to-france-what-it-did-to-them/

Zelensky Ignored By the Suits in NATO Summit

July 14, 2023

Volodymyr Zelensky went to attend the NATO Summit. But the suits ignored him.

They promised him a NATO membership without a dateline which means nothing really.

Ukraine has got NATO weapons without being a member; NATO intelligence without being a member; NATO training without being a member; even covert NATO soldiers without being a member. Why the fuss?

If anything, Zelensky would've had a first-hand impression if the hired-hand like him has outlived his utility, a couple of pictures doing rounds barely concealing the contempt "the club" has for the beggar who got his billions, villas and yachts around the world for zilch results, now that the counter-offensive is an unmitigated disaster.

Ukraine had built up a powerful army; its masters had done everything what they ought to have been doing for their own citizens, in the hope that Russia and Putin would cease to exist. But nothing has worked.

Sure Zelensky has kept his part of the deal, sent his thousands to the meat-grinder, all but put Ukraine on its last breath but then the masters never take the blame, nor the puppet media ever admits it's the West, and not Russia, which is groaning.

Ukraine is left with few men to fight. Russia is ramping up frightening numbers in contrast. US itself has admitted it has run out of ammunitions.

Russia meanwhile is producing weapons and ammunitions, 24×7, 360 days a year. Sooner than later, something would give way.

At some stage, funds would stop. There won't be enough chests to wear the fatigues. West could send its storm-shadow missiles, even the cruise ones but the wars are fought over killing fields; on twitter and media it's just a deception.

When the penny would drop, Zelensky probably won't see the next morning. West can't afford a clown to spill the beans; there is no place in the world he could hide. The remnants of Ukraine would either go to Poland or Lithuania to which it historically belonged.

Zelensky ought to have known the rules of the game. These rules are adjusted on the go by the masters. They are there one day, not there the next. Hired hands have limited utility. Zelensky survives only to the day when Ukraine has run out of its last soldier.

West would either close the shop, cook up some excuse and move on to some new Ukraine, probably Taiwan, as it did with Afghanistan. Media would start singing new rhyme, a lullaby to us readers, never questioning, never training the lens on the West. You don't bite the hand which feeds, do you.

Yet, West knows the cost of losing this war. It would cede the stage to a multipolar world; it would be on the run once the fake Dollar comes to a grinding halt. Its drugged citizens could probably come out of their slumber. Neither the sanctions nor funds and conventional weapons has crippled Russia. The wolves are growling; the whispers are audible to ears.

The next step is Nuclear War: NATO's vague promise to Zelensky is an indication that card is still not on the table: For nobody wins a Nuclear War. That's also the reason why Putin is letting Ukrainians do all their antics in Donbass when it could swoop in an instant and finish off the clown's regime in Kiev. For Putin too doesn't want a head-on conflict with NATO. He knows nobody wins when the Nuclear button is pressed. He is happy to watch a flailing Ukraine sink in due course.

Zelensky's best hope now is if he could lay his hands on deadlier weapons to force a NATO-Russia conflict. Alarmingly, the United Kingdom has promised cruise missiles which is an old hubris trying to reinvent itself in a changed world. If all hell breaks loose, who is stopping North Korea from attacking Japan and who knows if Beijing won't reveal its fatigues underneath the businessman's suit?

Between dispensing with Zelensky (Ukraine) or choosing a Nuclear War, it's easy to make the right choice. The West could choose to go for broke for a mutually assured extinction or it could accept a reduced role and influence and leave the rest of world to its own mechanism, howsoever grudgingly.

The humanity is at the edge of a cliff, alarmingly close to where it has never been before.

Link to Article:

https://www.newsbred.com/when-zelensky-was-ignored-by-the-suits-in-the-nato-summit/

Russia-Ukraine Deal Was for Spanish Pigs and Not Poor

July 20, 2023

So we read in media that Russia has suspended the grain deal which could make millions in the Global South go hungry.[1]

Bad Russians, isn't it.

But your media won't tell you that Russia had extended this grain deal more than once, not just for the needs of Global South but also to earn revenue to buy products in return.

All this while Russia was fulfilling its promise but the other party wasn't and as we all know, it takes two to tango.

The Grain Deal, brokered by the United Nations and Turkey last year, entailed that Ukraine could export its grain out of the Black Sea ports but Russia too could send its grain and fertilizers around the world.

Now agreed that food and fertilizers are not part of the US sanctions. But the trouble is Russia's agricultural export bank, Rosselkhozbank, has been disconnected from the SWIFT, the main central payment provider mechanism of the world.

Russia also can't get insurance for its ships which is a no-no since Ukraine, by its own admission, had mined the Black Sea routes[2] in the initial months of conflict which had broken free in due course and have been floating all over.

What's the guarantee the enemy won't blow it up like Nord Stream pipelines have been or for that matter ammonia pipeline[3] in Togliatti-Odesa stretch?

Besides the grain, meant for the world's poor, were actually going to Spanish pigs![4]

An investigation by the Australian outlet eXXpress[5] claimed Ukrainian wheat and corn exports were feeding the pigs in Spain. As per this investigation, only 15% of the exports reached the nations in risk of famine. (e.g. Ethiopia got 167,000 tons, Sudan 65,000 tons whereas Spain received 2.9 million tons of wheat and corn from Ukraine!)

But our media is so devious and deceitful it would describe what is technically right but in essence laughable.

An AP report says that half of the grain from the deal was going to developing countries.[6]

Well, as per the World Trade Organization (WTO) classification, China and Turkey are still developing nations! So here you are.

The UN general secretary Antonio Guterres appeared magnanimous in offering Russia a subsidiary unit, attached to its agricultural bank, which could work around the SWIFT system.

Now this is again a smokescreen: One, to create a subsidiary unit itself would take months; Two, the payments to subsidiary unit would flow through the European Union which would know who all are involved in it to be punished later; Three, the payments would happen in US dollar and EU can't guarantee on the big boss' behalf.

How do we expect Russia to trust an enemy which slaps illegal sanctions and freezes your assets against all international norms and laws?

If Guterres really is so concerned about the poor and wretched humanity, why not do the right thing by declaring the unilateral Western sanctions against Russia illegal as it is under international law? Further, how about sanctioning those who implement these illegal measures?

The thing is the UN, on behalf of its Western masters, is worried that Russia would simply divert its grain to Far East and China—one more commodity moving out of the West's orbit of insurance and financial system, dealing a blow to US dollar as it were.

* * *

Time was when Ukraine was the world's third largest exporter of corn and fifth biggest exporter of wheat.

Blessed with enormous rich black soil, all of 32 million hectares of arable land—almost one-third of the entire fertile land of the European Union—Ukraine has always been a prized catch for the West's sharks.

It's no coincidence that one of the prime reasons why "maidan coup" of 2014 happened was because the then Ukrainian president Viktor Yanukovych had rejected to sign a EU agreement which was tied to a $17 billion loan from the International Monetary Fund (IMF).

Your media would also not tell you that as soon as the new government came in Kiev, three key positions were handed over to foreigners who had been given Ukrainian citizenship only hours before.

One of them was US-born Natalie Jaresko, overseeing a private equity fund created by the US government, who got finance ministry.

Two reports by the Oakland Institute document the "corporate take-over of Ukrainian agriculture" and the role of "the World Bank and the IMF in the Ukraine conflict."

The high stakes around Ukraine's vast agricultural sector could thus easily be understood.

In the name of reform, IMF nudged Ukraine towards intense private investment in the country.

Agriculture was the prime target: More than 1.6 million hectares were signed over to foreign companies.

Monsanto, Cargill and DuPont were the sharks who didn't take long in smelling the blood in the pond.

Cargill began by taking care of sale of pesticides, seeds and fertilizers and later expanded it to include grain storage, animal nutrition etc, including a stake in the largest agribusiness in the country, UkrLandFarming.

Monsanto invested 140 million dollars in building a new seed plant in Ukraine; DuPont was to follow suit.

In the name of vertical integration of the agriculture sector, the takeover of infrastructure and shipping was the next logical step.

Cargill now owned at least four grain elevators and two sunflower seed processing plants; it was to buy a grain terminal at the Black Sea port of Novorossiysk.

The floundering of the agreement EU was seeking and which was one of the reasons for "maidan coup of 2014" was now a reality.

Although Ukraine doesn't allow the production of genetically modified (GM) crops, the Association Agreement between Ukraine and the European Union, now committed both parties to "extend the use of biotechnologies" within the country.

That was the opening to bring the GM products into Europe, much to the delight of agro-seed companies such as Monsanto, though ironically most European consumers reject GM crops.

All aspects of Ukraine's agricultural supply chain thus increasingly came under the control of Western firms, actively promoted by the EU institutions and the US government.

It was virtually a takeover of Ukrainian agriculture by the European Union and the United States.

If that was not enough, the Conflict has now made only 45% of Ukraine's grain fields functional and the harvest is less than 60% of what it was in 2022.

So Eastern Ukraine has seceded; Western Ukraine is under the thumb of Western marauders who installed a puppet in Kiev to do all their bidding.

Meanwhile, the sinful media would evoke our vile abuses on Russia for keeping "millions of poor in the world" hungry; while a "humanitarian" West is moving heavens in the name of "democracy" and "peace" –never mind tens of thousands who have gone under the meat-grinder holding aloft banners which are nothing but a ruse.

Post-Script:

I leave you with a few headlines of our mainstream media which is symbolic of the rot modern journalism is:

★ Higher food prices and more hunger: Collapse of Black Sea grain deal poses a massive threat – *CNN* – Jul 18

★ World facing prospect of 'hunger games' as China hoards grains and Russia withdraws from deal – *Indian Express* – Jul 19

★ Russian Grain Deal: Why Moscow Is Being Accused Of Using Hunger As 'Blackmail' – *Yahoo* – Jul 18

★ Russia halts deal allowing Ukraine to export grain, in a hit to global food security – *LA Times* – Jul 17

★ Higher food prices and more hunger: Collapse of Black Sea grain deal poses a massive threat – *CNN* – Jul 18

★ Russia pulls out of Black Sea grain deal with Ukraine sparking hunger fears in poorest countries – *ITV* – Jul 17

Reference:

[1] https://news.yahoo.com/why-allowing-ukraine-ship-grain-063251188.html?guccounter=1&guce_referrer=aHR0cHM6Ly93d3cubW9vbm-9mYWxhYmFtYS5vcmcv&guce_referrer_sig=AQAAAJPvUJ6LIa7K-8CoPQhwfSMFfk8MlBBulteem24K1eigZq26VijtsVrKAgQGrklINT-kEeUFtKYEpYLDvcH_xbFQucL7njxPmDxZDnSOYKuONByR3g-mGeDYlPLq2lSnFFtMnLfMKUovocJfCuJVxL3EuB99XOuQECr-c1olMg-KgdTs

[2] https://www.euronews.com/next/2022/06/11/how-floating-sea-mines-are-stopping-grain-leaving-ukraine-s-ports-and-making-the-food-cris

[3] https://aurelien2022.substack.com/p/you-and-whose-army?utm_source=post-email-title&publication_id=841976&post_id=105837751&isFreemail=true&utm_medium=email

[4] https://www.feedandgrain.com/grain-supply-chain/news/15384273/report-ukrainian-grain-fed-pigs-in-spain

[5] https://exxpress.at/ukraine-weizen-schweinefutter-statt-essen-fuer-die-aermsten-der-welt/

[6] https://news.yahoo.com/why-allowing-ukraine-ship-grain-063251188.html

Link to Article:

https://www.newsbred.com/russia-ukraine-grain-deal-was-for-spanish-pigs-and-nor-poor/

Cluster Bombs: Whatever Happened to Ban of Its Use?

July 22, 2023

Ukraine has started using the Cluster Bombs[1] after its public appeal to the West to its supply was heeded by the Washington.

The allies, which includes media of course, are over the moon.

An AP report[2] quotes a defense expert that Cluster Bombs are an "attractive option"; more targets with fewer rounds, and since the United States has three million of them left in its storehouse, this is game, set and match for its puppet Kiev regime.

Whoa! But why wasn't it used from the word go?

Well, darling, it's so dangerous that way back in 2008, a Convention on Cluster Munitions banned its use, signed by no less than 120 countries which of course doesn't include the United States.

And how do we know it's so dangerous?

We have multiple examples of the Hegemon using it against the goat-herders and Arabs, none more horrible than the instance of Laos where between 1964-1973, the US dropped more than 2.5 million tons of bombs[3]—that is a planeload of bombs every eight minutes, 24×7, for nine years. It included Cluster Bombs.

So far 25,000 Laotians are dead and dying: No less than 40% of them children. And this is the Laos War which our media has all but wiped out from our consciousness.

What did the Laos do to deserve this punishment?

This question is little out of context but anyway: Laos turned Communist and the US decided to teach them a lesson; denying a free, neutral country the choice it made; never mind the "sovereignty" and "integrity" the Hegemon never stops mouthing for every nation of the "free world."

So what makes Cluster Bombs so dangerous that nearly every nation of the world is against its use?

Cluster Bombs open in mid-air, disperse hundreds of smaller bombs over an area the size of a city. Those which don't explode are even more dangerous: It's like landmines, and citizens keep getting maimed or dead decades later.

You could never be sure the ground has been cleared of the remnants of cluster munitions; it doesn't treat civilians differently from combatants and that's why the world is against its use.

We have the word of Hun Sen, the prime minister of Cambodia which suffered alongside Laos: He noted that half a century on, Cambodia still has not found a way to destroy all the explosives: "The real victims will be Ukrainians," he said.

But here we have the instance of a public appeal by Kiev duly responded to by Washington, and the entire West and media on its feet, applauding!

Interestingly, till now the United States was accusing Russia of the war crimes for using Cluster Bombs and so did the United Kingdom which rustled up the International Criminal Court (ICC) to haul Russia over the coals.

But now that the shoe is on the other foot, the silence is deafening.

The truth is it's not Moscow but Kiev which has kept dropping cluster munitions in eastern Ukraine since 2014. It's been reported by the New York Times[4] and Human Rights Watch claims one such strike killed eight civilians[5] in an Ukrainian town named Ilium.

We hear from the White House that the Cluster Bombs are being supplied in the vital "US national security interest." Imagine, turning the entire Ukraine into a killing field and terming it in the interest of national security when an average American can't place Kiev on a map.

Germany says it understands the need to send cluster munitions for otherwise, "it would be the end of Ukraine."

Did you spot the duplicity?

Now let's play a game: Suppose Palestine tomorrow demands cluster bombs to be used against Israel.

It could say that like Ukraine, our territory too has been seized by the enemy: And they have done it for longer years than Russia.

That we have been subjected to endless war crimes, illegal armed settlements have abounded and civilians are denied the basic rights.

How do you think the United States would treat this request from the Palestine? With all its claim to be the bearer of "humanitarian intervention" which would bring a scream of disapproval from Afghanistan, Iraq, Libya or Syria.

And suppose Palestine is able to lay its hands on Cluster Bombs, how do you think the West and NATO would react to it?

And if one may ask: What retribution came Israel's way when it used cluster bombs in south Lebanon during its 1982 invasion?

The United Nations itself has accused Israel of firing no less than 4 million cluster munitions in Lebanon in 2006.

In 2017, Yemen was the second deadliest country for cluster munitions after Syria, as per the United Nations. What was done to the perpetrator of this war crime?

The last we heard is that the US House of Representatives blocked the 2024 National Defense Authorization Act last week which would have banned the export of Cluster Bombs.

Russia says if the West wants it to be free-for-all, we too are ready with our Cluster Bombs.

The only factor which could stop this madness is if the citizens of the US and Europe bring down the doors of their war-hungry monsters.

Like lemmings, they all are committing suicide with their apathy–and taking us down with them.

Media could have been one powerful factor to rouse the people but they are sleeping in bed with humanity's enemy.

Truth alone could end this darkness and that's what goads me.

Reference:

[1] https://thehill.com/policy/defense/4108762-ukraine-starts-using-us-cluster-munitions-on-battlefield/

[2] https://apnews.com/article/russia-ukraine-cluster-munition-war-7332fa86b3c52d1ea8d63f92a7d5c2cb

[3] https://www.thecollector.com/war-in-laos-most-heavily-bombed-country-in-history/

[4] https://www.nytimes.com/2022/04/18/world/europe/ukraine-forces-cluster-munitions.html

[5] https://www.hrw.org/news/2023/07/06/ukraine-civilian-deaths-cluster-munitions

Link to Article:

https://www.newsbred.com/cluster-bombs-whatever-happened-to-the-ban-of-its-use/

When, and Not If, Poland Would Enter Ukraine

July 26, 2023

As soon as Ukraine is over, and it won't be long, Poland would step in.

Poles don't intend to fight the Russians—rather they would be like jackals who can't resist a carcass.

They lay a historical claim over western Ukraine, eye Lviv as one of its own, and after Ukraine gives up, they would arrive in the garb of peacekeepers, with a few other NATO wolves, notably Lithuania, and stay put forever.

At the beck and call of the West, of course.

The Poles look at war as an opportunity: Like they did during the 1st World War, which heralded the end of three empires: Austria-Hungary, Germany and Tsarist Russia (Ottoman, unrelated here, was the fourth.)

They sided with the Central Powers, swept Lviv and adjacent territories; forced the hands of civil-war torn Russia (Treaty of Riga, 1921) to cede its provinces; and also Vilnius besides other lands from Lithuania. A few years down the line, after the Munich Pact of 1938, a part of Czechoslovakia was added to its portfolio of acquisitions. (That they were sacrificed to Hitler by their malevolent masters in 1939 is another matter.)

***

The truth is Poland, and Ukraine, didn't exist on the world map before World War 1.

Poland was a historical region; Ukraine a geographical one, and that was about it.

By the end of the 18th century, the historical Poland was split between its three muscular neighbours: Prussia, Habsburgs and the Russians. Ukraine was a booty between the Habsburgs and Russians. It was the Russians, between 1795 and 1917, which held most of what we today call Poland and Ukraine.

The World War I was too good a moment to let it pass for Poland: Only if Russia could collapse. Ukraine was a natural ally in this quest. So Poles sides with the Central Powers (Germany and Austria-Hungary). Russia, riven with civil war between the Red and White, did end up giving Poland what it wanted. Jozef Pilsudski, who fought no less than six wars till his death in 1935, was Poland's man of the moment.

Ironically it was Russia, rather the Soviet Union, which gave Poland its life after World War II by consigning Adolf Hitler and his Germany to ruins. Not just life but Poland also acquired the German territory from the provinces of Silesia, Pomerania and the southern part of East Prussia.

The western Poland of today, one of history's irony, is nothing but a gift from Stalin.

***

Still, Poles suffer from a lingering sense of loss.

The World War II ended up giving Ukraine, then a part of the USSR, many Polish cities, including Lviv, a town of major military and geo-strategic value. (See map below).

Lviv is vital to East-West routes and passes through the Carpathian Mountains. Most railways converge on the city. It's an industrial hub of nodal importance and has a very strong ethnic presence of Poles to this day.

A "Balkanized Ukraine" would have great geostrategic importance for Warsaw as well as its Western masters.

***

Interestingly, the Zelensky regime is indifferent, if not a partner, to such designs of Warsaw-NATO in western Ukraine.

Zelensky vows to use the last Ukrainian to regain Russia-acquired eastern Ukraine but is not assailed by any such nightmare in western Ukraine!

Interesting, isn't it!

The present-day Ukraine has received weapons and mercenaries; its army is trained by NATO officers; all through the open borders with Poland.

Vladimir Putin says the present Kiev regime is no different to Ukrainian leader Symon Petliura[1] who sold out Galicia and western Volhynia to Poland in exchange for military support in 1920.

***

Yet Poland today could only spread itself in western Ukraine in the garb of a peacekeeper.

If it offers the alibi of an unstable border to put its armed soldiers around Kiev, or in Belarus, Russia could take it as a direct NATO intervention. In that case, Poland would open itself to attack from the Russians.

It would imply the Ukraine Conflict would spin out of control, putting the entire humanity at risk.

Poland needs a close watch: Whether due to its own revanchist claims or at the behest of its Western masters, its playing a dangerous game.

Post Script:

In passing, below is a map of Ukraine from a historical perspective.

Reference:

[1] https://en.wikipedia.org/wiki/Symon_Petliura

Link to Article:

https://www.newsbred.com/when-and-not-if-poland-would-enter-ukraine/

Russia-Africa Summit: Why India Should Pay Heed

July 30, 2023

The recent 2nd Russia-Africa Summit should interest India.

But for slaves from Africa which gave them the control across Atlantic (plantations and the new world of America) and its riches, the colonialists wouldn't have ventured around Cape of Good Hope, smelling India and using its opium to bring China and the Qing Dynasty to heels in due course.

Africa gave colonialists the world, the basis of its industrialisation, its technological breakthroughs—but for its uranium, Hiroshima and Nagasaki would've escaped atom bombs—yet in return got the title of the "Dark Continent" and a "coup" every 55 days in 90% of African states since acquiring "independence" in the 1960s.

The president of the Central African Republic (look for it in the map), Faustin Archange Touadera says the instability by militant groups is largely financed by western countries; the IMF and the World Bank, at the behest of "western powers" suspend financial aid; and such has been the loot of his country's vast reserves of gold, diamonds, cobalt, oil and uranium that after more than 60 years of independence, it remains one of the poorest nation of the world. "The Central African people have been taken hostage," he laments.

In all Africa has had 79 coups, one in Niger[1] just now as I write it, once every year on an average. There have been 40 French military interventions in the guise of humanitarian help in last 60 years. The loot is managed through kleptocrats the West puts in power, a continent-wide corruption pact. Dead? Millions and millions and counting.

The Rape of Africa, between 1445-1870, was carried out by eight European powers: Britain, France, Portugal, Belgium, Spain, Germany, Italy and Holland; the so-called democratic Europe which in essence promoted only thuggery in Africa. Those worthy calls of "Liberty, Equality and Fraternity" surely didn't extend to the Black Africans enslaved in the Caribbean and elsewhere.

In the modern times it's the United States which has too many instruments, such as the financial and global bodies, terrorists, muscles and deep pockets and local kleptocrats who do their bidding for their own cut.

The next logical question: What all this has got to do with the Russia-Africa Summit and the Indians?

Well, 49 out of the 54 African countries were in St. Petersburg for the Summit (July 27-28, 2023). It's practically the entire continent which as per our propagandist media is being denied "grain deal"[2] by the "inhumane" Russians yet come calling.

If Russia is so bad, how come almost the entire continent turned up? You'd have your answer in this piece of mine[3], if somehow it has escaped your notice that Russia is finding a way to supply food and fertilizers directly to the Africans, avoiding the Black Sea ports where it was servicing largely the well-fed Europeans and not the poor of Africa under the grain deal.

Not to say the $20 billion debt Russia has now written off of its African debtors!

The gutter media has also been telling us[4] that the Wagner Group had caused most of the instability in Africa, notably in Central African Republic, Libya, Mali and Sudan but you, I guess, now know better.

The above vision-correction for the Indian readers is not just to convey who is villain here: That it's not the Russian but the West, historically as well now, which has caused most mischief.

It's also to alert the coming of age of Africa so that we don't sleep over it. (It's not to say the Modi government is not alert on Africa—indeed, we are behind only West and China in being proactive across the Indian Ocean.)

Africa is home to 54% of the world's reserves of platinum, 78% of diamonds, 40% of chromium and 28% of manganese. Nineteen countries of sub-Saharan Africa have significant reserves of hydrocarbons: Its world's leading exporter of gold, platinum, diamonds, bauxite and manganese; the second for copper and crude oil. It's also the world's leading producer of cocoa, tea, tobacco, the second for sisal and cotton.

So young is Africa that by 2050, it would have 2 billion people, one in four being less than 25 years of age. It's tremendous work-force for the future of our world.

All the above is not intended to salivate at the business prospects with this Continent. Africa always has suffered at the hands of the exploiters: It's time to partner them to help them realize their true potential.

Russia in recent times has committed itself to alleviating Africa's energy and food problems: Indeed, 43% of the Africa still doesn't have energy.

India, on its part, is active on a variety of fronts, including technical know-how, infra, Line of Credit etc, etc. Our historical bond go back centuries, indeed much before the Europeans came into the picture. There is a general warmth between the people of Africa and India.

Today's Africa would be central to the oncoming multipolar world. Its enormous base of minerals, once its traded on a new currency, would liberate itself from the suffocating Dollar.

The West offers democracy—but that comes with a price of loot and compromised rulers. Russia, on the other hand, offers Africa sovereignty, a liberation from terrorism and mutiny and supplies it more arms than anybody else.

India, too, needs to keep building up its base in Africa; neither the West nor I suspect China would be a much help in its quest which is understandable. All those fetes and festoons on visiting White House shouldn't fool Modi; we are no better than use-and-throw entity in the eyes of the rapacious West.

Russia, on the other hand, is a power India could trust; a power which alone could stabilize Africa from the murderous machinations of the West and stop its war games.

Russia could prepare a stable Africa for India to go on an overdrive, and not suffer an Afghanistan where its decades of investment vanished overnight once the Americans left in a huff.

Africa is looking for genuine friends which India is. Africa would be critical in the emerging multipolar world and India could have no better friend than Russia on a common quest.

Reference:

[1] https://www.bbc.com/news/world-africa-66320895

[2] https://www.newsbred.com/russia-ukraine-grain-deal-was-for-spanish-pigs-and-nor-poor/

[3] https://www.newsbred.com/russia-ukraine-grain-deal-was-for-spanish-pigs-and-nor-poor/

[4] https://www.cfr.org/in-brief/what-russias-wagner-group-doing-africa

Link to Article:

https://www.newsbred.com/russia-africa-summit-why-india-should-pay-heed/

To Think Hamas Was But Only Israel's Creation!

October 9, 2023

I wish the once spokesperson of the Israel Defence Forces (IDF) hadn't equated the Hamas attack on its territory as the "Pearl Harbor type of moment[1]."

Now Pearl Harbor, as most know, was the moment when Japanese attacked the US naval base in Honolulu, Hawaii, killing 2,403 Americans and wounding 1,178 others. It formally brought the United States into the World War II the very next day and gave them the trophy we call the world.

Only, what most don't know is that the United States knew in advance the Japanese attack but did little[2] so as to justify their entry into a War they couldn't otherwise have "sold" to its people and Congress.

It also evokes the memory of 9/11 which still defies credulity to have been managed by a few hijackers hoodwinking the entire security apparatus of the mightiest nation of the world.

Be that as it may, let's look at what happened inside the Israeli territory a few hours ago.

That hundreds of Hamas fighters poured in from the Gaza which is an open territory, impossible to be hidden in their advance yet undetected by Israeli patrols, cameras, ground motion detectors and remote-controlled weapons.

That much vaunted air defenses of Israeli forces were overwhelmed by home-made hang-gliders powered by lawn-mower engines and box fans.

That the much-envied Israel's advanced surveillance technology (remember Pegasus?) were unaware of the Hamas operation.

The pictures tell us that literally a JCV tractor brought down the border wall, dozens of guys who even didn't have any guns walked past an Israeli military post, with an abandoned tank and all, taking selfies without any response, and killing and kidnapping hundreds of people.

Let's assume that Israel was unprepared for this moment: After all Sukkot celebrations were on; it was also the 50th anniversary of the October 1973 Yom Kippur War; but whatever happened to the ubiquity of Israeli informants? Their feared intelligence which could detect the bowel movement of an individual? If the defence is that their surveillance system was jammed, that's all the more damning for a nation hailed for its sophistication. Where was the security, the police, the army?

The allegation of a cyber attack by Iran also doesn't cut the ice. Did the Iranians also remove the IDF units? Are we to believe that Israel's border towns were utterly defenceless?

The Origins of Hamas

It's one of history's ironies that Hamas owe their origin to no other than Israelis who nurtured them to counter the secular Palestine Liberation Organization (PLO).

Once Israel took over the Gaza after the 1967 War with Egypt (remember this date, we would come to it later), it curated the Islamists to neutralize PLO and its dominant faction Fatah.

One of the activists Israelis encouraged was Sheikh Ahmed Yassin who was arrested once but released to continue his militant movement that morphed into Hamas in 1987. (Any resemblance to our own Jarnail Singh Bhindranwale and the Congress is only incidental).

Since the very first year of its inception in 1987, the first Palestinian Intifada or uprising, Hamas has had 12 such (1987-1993, 2002, 2005,

2006, 2009, 2012, 2014 and 2021) wars, the last one in 2021 involving the Israeli reprisal in Gaza which killed 256 Palestinians, including 66 children.

Now when it's said to be a "Pearl Harbor moment", you could take your pick if Israelis would drive out Palestinians out forever from their lands which from 1947 onwards has now been reduced to only a sprinkling of settlements (see image below). Ethnic cleansing of Palestinians that is.

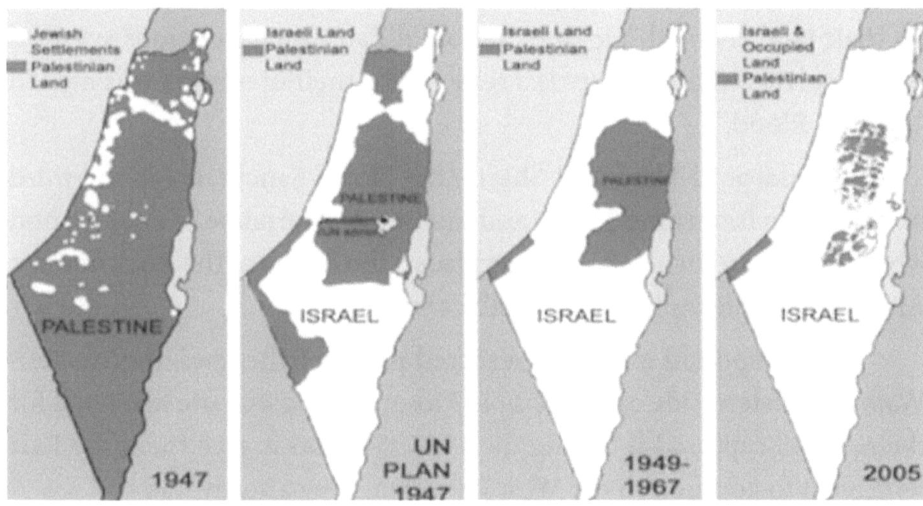

Or you think it's more likely to suit the United States, joined at hips with Israel, to plunge the Middle East into flames. The US neither can win in Ukraine nor leave Ukraine without a loss of face. Hence comes out the card of another major crisis which would seamlessly shift the attention away from Kiev.

Further, the US-West can't see a peaceful Middle East where Saudi Arabia and Iran are getting cosy, Syria is being welcomed in Arab League, China is the mediator Arabs are turning to, transport corridors are mushrooming by the minute, and the oil, the very basis of PetroDollar and US hegemony, is getting out of bounds. Did somebody mention Egypt, Saudi Arabia, UAE now a part of BRICS and ushering in multipolarity enveloping US' unipolar world?

Sure, the present crisis suits Israel and the US. Israel could justify the hell it's raining on Palestinians and wipe out whatever of latter is left. Why, only last fortnight, Israeli prime minister Benjamin Netanyahu was upholding a new map of the New Middle East without Palestine in the 78th session of the UN General Assembly in New York City Never mind Palestine is recognised by 138 of the 193 nations in UN.

Hamas, and its reasons, are apparent too. They can't see Arabs getting pally with Israelis as if the Palestinian cause doesn't exist. Further, the occupation, oppression and illegal settlements of Israelis on their land is one thing, desecration of Palestinian religious symbols is a complete red line. There is a reason why their operation was named "Al Aqsa Flood."

Al-Aqsa or al-Haram al Sharif (the Noble Sanctuary) is the third holiest site in Islam after Mecca and Medina. It's the name of a compound which is home to two holy Muslim places: the Dome of the Rock and the Al-Aqsa Mosque built in the eighth century.

This compound overlooks a sacred place for the Jews, the Western Wall, the western side of the Temple Mount, a religious site like none for them. Israel captured it during the 1967 War and it gave them the East Jerusalem in addition to the West Jerusalem they already had.

East Jerusalem is considered a Palestinian territory under the international law. Among the states which recognise it as Palestinian are 57 nations of Organisation of Islamic Cooperation (OIC), besides biggies such as China, Russia and India of course. Some 61 per cent of its population remain Palestinian Arabs. In 1980, Israel formalized the annexation of East Jerusalem under the Jerusalem Law.

It's East Jerusalem where the Old City is, home to many sacred sites for all three Abrahamic religions—Judaism, Christianity and Islam. It's where the Al-Aqsa is, as there is Temple Mount, Western wall, the Dome of the Rock etc.

Even though the Jewish law forbids Jews from visiting any part of the Al-Aqsa Mosque due to its sacred nature, a place where only Muslims could offer prayers, there have been multiple instances where ultralight Jews flout it with disdain.

In May this year, Israel's far-right national security minister Itamar Ben-Gvir entered the Al-Aqsa Mosque compound, one of his many, where he declared Israel is "in charge here."

Just three days before the Hamas Operation, on October 4, dozens of Israelis forced into the Al-Aqsa Mosque complex, and attempted to perform "Talmudic rituals."

The worst case scenario is if Israel goes to war with Iran. It would help nobody, neither China, Russia, India or the rest of the humanity but only the West. Its control of Middle East and its oil is as important to them as is vassalage of Europe. Middle East in peace and harmony, oil out of bounds, would sink the United States. It won't let that happen. Just won't let that happen.

Reference:

[1] https://edition.cnn.com/middleeast/live-news/al-aqsa-storm-militants-infiltrate-israel-after-gaza-rockets-10-07-intl-hnk/h_5be4066269c8f41eb195a5322b20bfe6

[2] https://www.newsbred.com/do-wonder-what-russia-gains-by-attacking-trailer-and-a-tractor-in-poland/

Link to Article:

https://www.newsbred.com/to-think-hamas-was-but-only-israels-creation/

www.ingramcontent.com/pod-product-compliance
Ingram Content Group UK Ltd.
Pitfield, Milton Keynes, MK11 3LW, UK
UKHW041830200726
13854UKWH00002BA/977

9 798891 863538